The Problem Left

How Leftist policies have destroyed America

B.L. Horak

Disclaimer

This book is a work of political nonfiction and opinion. It reflects the author's interpretations of events, policies, and public figures at the time of writing. While every effort has been made to verify facts, errors or omissions may occur. Readers are encouraged to consult primary sources and make their own judgments.

The views expressed are solely those of the author and do not represent any employer, organization, or affiliate. References to individuals or entities are for commentary and critique; any resemblance to private persons is incidental. Nothing herein constitutes legal, financial, or medical advice.

Strong language and forceful rhetoric are used for emphasis. Reader discretion is advised.

Dedication

Thank you, Charlie. You were the voice, each and every day, that changed me into the man I am today. You were the kindest politics had to offer, and your voice was stolen because of it. I plan to pick up your bloodied mic right where you left it.

Acknowledgment

To my father, RAZ—my fiercest sparring partner and my truest north. You challenged every premise I held, pushed me to earn every conclusion, and proved that love can outlast any argument. A lifelong liberal, you made me a better thinker—and a better son.

To my wife, Stephanie—your steadiness has been my ballast. Through every late night, every draft torn up and rebuilt, you believed. This book stands because you stood beside me.

To my children—Kacey, Austin, Lillian, Sophia, and Olivia. You are the reason I refuse to be vague. Your questions sharpened my convictions; your laughter reminded me what's at stake. You forced me to speak truth, plainly and without apology.

To my team at Western Publishing House—editors, designers, publicists, and the unsung heroes in between—thank you for turning stubborn sentences into a finished book, for insisting on clarity, and for making it all happen on the days I thought it couldn't.

And to the readers who engage, debate, and demand substance: you keep the conversation alive. May this book meet you where conviction and curiosity intersect.

About the Author

Brandon lives at home with his loving family and two dogs. Self-identifying as a political conservative, he has always believed in the right to life, liberty, and the pursuit of happiness. He intends to open a political organization in the near future, as well as start his own podcast based on the premise of this book.

The Problem Left:
An Introduction

There's a moment in every American kitchen when someone opens the fridge, recoils at the smell, and says, "Something's gone bad." The labels say "organic," the packaging looks clean, and yet the funk punches you in the face. That's America under leftism: beautiful labels, rotten center. "Equity." "Climate justice." "Common-sense gun reform." "Defund the police." "Science." "Our democracy."

Suddenly, cities where you can't walk a block without stepping over a used needle are "compassionate," and a border that hemorrhages millions is "humane." The inflation you feel at the grocery aisle is "transitory," while your child's education is "liberated" from math by something called "antiracist pedagogy." The packaging is pristine. The stench is real.

This book is about the smell.

Not the slogans, not the press releases, not the moral preening on prime-time panels, but the consequences. Leftist policies have consequences. Not for the people who write them in glass-walled offices. For the nurse in Tucson who works nights and now double-locks her door. For the small business owner in Minneapolis whose store is looted and told it's just property. For the eighth grader in Baltimore stuck at a reading level below grade school while the district celebrates "equitable outcomes." For the family in Ohio watching their power bill climb to fund a wind farm that can't outproduce an honest natural gas plant on a windless day. For you.

And yes, for me. I didn't wake up as a bomb thrower. I tried to eat my vegetables, read the op-eds, and nod respectfully at the rituals of "dialogue." But reality has a way of ending polite illusions. My red pill wasn't a grand revelation; it was a thousand tiny truths refusing to stay quiet. Broken windows. Broken schools. Broken budgets. Broken promises. And then the left calling the wreckage progress, as if we were the crazy ones for noticing the glass.

I owe a debt to Charlie Kirk, who taught a generation not to bow to the established shrines of nonsense. The first time I heard him on a campus stage, he asked a question so simple it should be boring: "Does it work?" Not, "Does it feel good?" Not, "Does it win you retweets?" Does the policy do what it claims? That question is a wrecking ball to the Problem Left, because nothing they sell survives contact with results.

What the Right Knows

The Right is caricatured as cruel because we reject policies that feel kind but fail. In truth, we stand with reality. Humans aren't clay. Incentives matter. Families matter. Borders matter. Energy drives prosperity. Merit defeats tribalism. Speech keeps us free. Work grants dignity. Faith anchors meaning. These are not partisan tricks; they are civilizational truths. When we honor them, America flourishes. When we mock them, America decays.

2

Charlie Kirk helped me ask, relentlessly: Does it work? Show me the city that got safer under decarceration zealots. Show me the school that taught better after the union took more control. Show me the border that secured itself with slogans. Show me the grid that stabilized on wishful thinking. Show me the company that prospered by pleasing activists rather than customers. Show me the nation that censored its way to wisdom. You can't, because it doesn't exist.

The Road Back

This book isn't just a prosecution. It's a prescription. We will name names and name alternatives.

- **Energy abundance:** fast-track nuclear, unleash natural gas, depoliticize the grid, permit like a serious country.

- **Law and order:** refund and reform policing, restore broken windows enforcement, end cashless bail and rogue prosecutors.

- **Work-first welfare:** time limits, work requirements, marriage incentives, addiction treatment with accountability.

- **Colorblind equality:** ban racial discrimination by any name in government and education, erase DEI bureaucracies, restore merit.

- **Education freedom:** fund students, not systems; expand charters and vouchers; set rigorous standards; teach knowledge, not activism.

- **Sovereign borders:** mandatory E-Verify, physical barriers, Remain-in-Mexico-style adjudication, merit-based legal immigration.

- **Free markets, not ESG cartels:** fiduciary duty restored by law; no coercive scoring schemes in public funds; shareholder primacy over activist capture.

- **The First Amendment restored:** transparency in algorithms, end government-platform collusion, protect lawful speech, robust liability safe harbors for neutral platforms.

- **Pandemic humility:** emergency power limits, school-open policies as default, risk-based guidance rather than universal compulsion.

The road back is not a mystery; it is a spine. We need leaders who can endure the screeching, citizens who can tell the truth to their neighbors, and institutions reformed to serve the public rather than their own guilds. We need to stop apologizing for wanting things that work.

A Word to the Reader

You will be called names for reading this: "Denier." "Extremist." "Bigot." "Threat to democracy." You know the script. Wear it lightly. The people hurling the insults have presided over decline and ask for more time to manage it. The rest of us have work to do: rebuilding a culture that honors competence over credentials, family over ideology, courage over conformity, and results over rituals.

The Left sells a mirage—safety without enforcement, prosperity without production, unity without truth, virtue without sacrifice. We have seen where mirages lead: thirsty people stepping into sand. America deserves water. Real water. Jobs that mean something. Schools that teach. Streets that are safe. Borders that protect. An energy policy that powers the future rather than performs for cameras. A nation that tells your children they are more than the labels hustlers want to pin on them.

I dedicate this to those who never consented to be experiments, who kept showing up—parents at school boards, cops on midnights, nurses on double shifts, pastors, truckers, small business owners, and the kids who learned despite the system. And to Charlie Kirk, who, from campus quads to packed halls, gave many of us the courage to ask simple questions in a culture built on complicated lies.

This is your permission slip to demand outcomes. To reject the browbeating that says failure is justice and success is suspect. To say, without apology, that America is worth saving not as a museum but as a future. The Problem Left is real, and it smells. But rot is not destiny. It's a choice, and so is renewal.

Turn the page. Let us get to work.

Chapter 1:

The Politics of Words

Language doesn't just describe politics; it rigs the game. Since 2015, American progressive institutions have treated a handful of moralized buzzwords—"harm," "safety," "silence is violence," "fascism," "threat to democracy"—like master keys. Why argue when you can sort people into purity or guilt? Why debate when you can narrow the room for disagreement until it becomes a closet? If speech is "violence" and dissent is "harm," then escalation isn't a choice; it's a public service. Convenient, isn't it?

On March 9, 2023, Stanford Law School turned this logic into a live demonstration. A federal judge, Kyle Duncan, tried to talk appellate jurisprudence. Students shouted him down, because nothing says legal education like a chorus of "no." An administrator grabbed the mic not to defend a forum but to sermonize the feelings. "Is the juice worth the squeeze?" Associate Dean for DEI Tirien Steinbach asked, after reciting that some found his presence "harmful" and "denying the humanity of people." Translation: rights are quaint; vibes are policy. That exact line—"Is the juice worth the squeeze?"—is the new measuring cup: not truth, not curiosity, but perceived emotional cost. Two days later, on March 11, 2023, Stanford's president and law dean apologized: "Staff members who should have enforced university policies failed to do so, and instead intervened in inappropriate ways." But by then, the syllabus had been updated: rebrand disagreement as danger, and you can shut it down with a halo.

This diction didn't spring fully formed in 2023. Go back to March 2017, Middlebury College. Charles Murray showed up; a lecture did not. Chants of "Racist, sexist, anti-gay, Charles Murray, go away" made sure of it. When Murray and Allison Stanger tried to leave on March 2, 2017, a crowd surrounded them. Stanger later described how a demonstrator "pulled [her] hair and twisted [her] neck." An alumni letter the day before had already set the thesis: Murray's invitation was "a threat… to every woman, every person of color… their safety, their agency, their humanity and even their very right to exist." See the trick? Call an invitation an existential threat and ordinary hospitality becomes complicity. Who wants to be complicit? Better to be brave by blocking doors.

Summer 2020 pushed the vocabulary into city halls. On June 7, 2020, a majority of the Minneapolis City Council pledged to "defund and dismantle the Minneapolis Police Department." A slogan born as provocation hardened into a loyalty oath within days. Try nuance and you're a traitor to justice. Seattle's mayor, Jenny Durkan, tried euphemism-as-governance on June 11, 2020, when she called an abandoned precinct a "summer of love." How did the romance end? The Capitol Hill Organized Protest delivered shootings and unanswered 911 calls until reality repossessed the metaphor. Austin reallocated police funds under abolition-adjacent rhetoric; response times worsened, the state intervened, and the money boomeranged. Words set priorities, priorities shaped deployments, deployments met public patience—and it turns out patience has a timer.

Media framing didn't just report; it rinsed. In late May and June 2020, "mostly peaceful" floated across chyrons while flames did their own messaging. The intention—to contextualize—collided with the visuals—arson. Audiences believed their eyes, as people tend to do. Meanwhile, activists and academics workshopped "property damage isn't violence." Narrow violence to harm against persons, and voilà: vandalism and arson get moral discounts. If windows aren't people, smash away; think of it as emphatic punctuation.

"Silence is violence" graduated from cardboard to policy. By June 2020, universities and corporations rolled out mandatory pledges and trainings. Emails implied a duty to affirm specific slogans. Ask for viewpoint pluralism? Cue the bias-incident portal. Not because you insulted anyone, of course, but because dissent had been upgraded to harm. A California higher-education resolution in 2023 warned educators not to "weaponiz[e] their right to academic freedom to create educational or work environments hostile to… anti-racism work." An elastic clause: disagreement now maps neatly onto danger. Handy, isn't it?

The accelerants—"fascist," "Nazi," "threat to democracy"— preheated the air. These labels didn't wait for January 6; they sped up after it. In 2016 and 2017, Trump was called a "fascist," and antifa framed opposition as moral emergency. Post-January 6, 2021, the vocabulary calcified: Trump and many supporters weren't merely wrong but an existential "threat to democracy." On August 25, 2022, President Biden dubbed the MAGA philosophy "semi-fascism." Once politics becomes a Weimar cosplay, compromise looks like appeasement. Who negotiates with fascism? Only cowards—or so the script says.

The cascade continued. Campus flyers and petitions called Charlie Kirk a "fascist" or "white supremacist" from 2017 onward; his presence equaled a "safety" risk. Administrators invoked safety to add security fees or cancel venues. Tucker Carlson, from 2018 to 2021, was tagged "white nationalist," "proto-fascist," with advertiser excommunications to match. Ron DeSantis, during pandemic and education fights in 2021–2023, was labeled "fascist" and "authoritarian." Result: statutory disagreements that merited arguments got preempted by apocalypse metaphors. If the house is on fire, who has time for building codes?

Public-health messaging moralized too. In summer 2020, officials discouraged gatherings—unless the gathering hit the moral sweet spot. The virus, apparently, checked protest permits. Parents questioning prolonged school closures were told they endangered teachers and children. Debate? That's hazardous. Please consult your conscience before speaking.

By 2024, campus encampments and building takeovers arrived pre-wrapped in "safety" language. Statements claimed certain speakers or recruiters made communities "unsafe." Administrators must "center safety"; therefore, disruption equals protection. Enforcement, when it finally arrived, was late, uneven, and harsher—because "rules" were replaced with "feelings" until reality reasserted itself. Lesson transmitted: redefine speech as danger and protest evolves from persuasion into coercion. Isn't that efficient?

"Abolish" slogans met the brick wall of operations. "Abolish ICE" went from placards in 2018 to campaign talking points and staff demands by 2019–2020. Offer targeted reforms? Enjoy your complicity badge. Then migrant arrivals surged in 2022–2024, and sanctuary cities discovered limits: shelters, budgets, timelines. Absolutes met spreadsheets; mayors pivoted to capacity. Moral vocabulary narrowed maneuvering room; the check came due.

Consequences landed. Coalitions in blue jurisdictions shrank as working-class, immigrant, and minority voters who wanted both dignity and order felt condescended to. Backlash followed: police funds restored, prosecutors replaced, permitting sped for energy projects, immigration rhetoric inched toward capacity realism. Nationally, treating everything Trump as irredeemable hampered learning from outcomes that worked. Operation Warp Speed validated public-private acceleration; industrial policy and targeted tariffs re-legitimized strategic production; skepticism toward open-ended foreign entanglements broadened. Democrats later adopted pieces—often while maintaining denunciations that made acknowledgment feel like heresy. Why admit he did a thing when you could keep the moral high ground spotless?

To be clear: the right hurls its own grenades, and January 6 was an appalling, criminal rupture. But on the American left between 2015 and 2025, specific words—"harm," "safety," "silence is violence," "fascist," "threat"—moved from slogans to rules. On March 9, 2023, "Is the juice worth the squeeze?" distilled the worldview. On March 2, 2017, "His invitation… is a threat" previewed it. On June 7, 2020, "defund and dismantle" broadcast it. On August 25, 2022, "semi-fascism" nationalized it.

Turn every disagreement into harm, every opponent into an existential enemy, and division isn't a bug; it's the product. The chapters ahead will follow how these words steered choices in schools, streets, city halls, newsrooms, and ballots—and how a different vocabulary, less thermonuclear and more adult, might widen the territory for persuasion, patience, and, yes, peace.

Chapter 2:
Friction and Formation

The morning air in Arlington Heights, Illinois, can feel deceptively gentle: suburban lawns, school bells, the reliable rhythm of Midwestern neighborhoods. For Charlie Kirk, born October 14, 1993, that rhythm set a cadence to push against. He was the kid who liked the argument more than the applause, who preferred the bus ride to Washington over the pep rally at home. The stories that would follow—about influence, provocation, and the collision between youthful ambition and America's culture war—did not arrive all at once. They accreted in meeting rooms, at podiums, on podcasts, and through the friction required to polish a point.

Kirk's early path was not the pedigree type. He attended Wheeling High School and volunteered for political campaigns before most of his peers could vote. In 2010, he interned for then–Illinois Republican U.S. Senate candidate Mark Kirk (no relation), learning retail politics one phone bank at a time. Then, in 2012, a hinge year: Kirk, just 18, penned an essay arguing that college had become an overpriced credential mill for far too many students. The piece, written with the confidence of a freshman and the impatience of a reformer, caught the attention of donors and radio hosts. That spring and summer, he started speaking to youth groups about debt, bureaucracy, and the way institutions forget the people they are meant to serve.

By June 2012, he co-founded Turning Point USA (TPUSA), a student-focused organization advocating for free markets, limited government, and fiscal responsibility. The idea was disarmingly simple: map the ideological terrain of America's campuses and go where conservative messages rarely ventured. He would later recall, "We went where the arguments were lopsided, not because we liked losing, but because we believed the numbers would catch up to the ideas."

The early days were lean: hand-lettered signs, borrowed rental cars, and campus permits negotiated in hallways. In December 2012, TPUSA launched its "Free Markets, Free People" campus tour; by autumn 2013, it published its first "Professor Watchlist"–style materials that, however controversial, succeeded in doing what Kirk intended: forcing a conversation about orthodoxy and dissent inside higher education.

With attention came escalation. Kirk proved unusually adept at modern political entrepreneurship: raising money, building distribution, and refining message. He mastered the talk-radio circuit, sharpened his debating chops at student forums, and used social media as a force multiplier. On March 21, 2016, he told a crowd at the University of Louisville, "You do not lose a debate you refuse to have. That is why we will show up, invite questions, and endure the boos." It sounded combative; it was mostly strategic. If opponents shouted him down, he won on principle. If they engaged, he won on ideas. If they ignored him, he traveled to the next campus.

The 2016 election brought scale. Kirk aligned with populist energy while insisting on a program of deregulation, tax relief, and campus free speech. In December 2016, he met with members of the incoming Trump team about youth outreach. The alignment had costs—critics argued he conflated party with principle—but it also brought a megaphone. On December 22, 2017, when the Tax Cuts and Jobs Act passed, he praised it as "a restoration of the basic American premise that you should keep more of what you earn." To supporters, it was proof that rhetoric could meet policy. To detractors, it was branding.

Success made him a target, and the targeting became part of his biography. Kirk's opponents on the left often tried to collapse his arguments into caricature. At the University of California, Berkeley, on April 26, 2017, a clipped student video circulated that appeared to show him saying, "Diversity is not a strength." The full recording included the rest of the sentence: "Diversity is not a strength if it means lowering standards, but it is a strength when people bring different talents to the same high bar." The truncated version rocketed around social media; the complete thought traveled slower. It was a pattern that repeated—provocation edited into provocation-plus, nuance trimmed to a headline.

Another instance flared during a Q&A at the University of Florida on October 10, 2018. Asked about immigration and national identity, he said, "A nation that does not control its borders is not a nation." Critics framed the line as an attack on immigrants themselves, even though he added minutes later: "Legal immigrants who follow the rules are part of the American story—we should make that process fairer and faster." The second clause rarely made the clips. Kirk's style—short, declarative, and made for virality— made him vulnerable to exactly that: the sentence that stands alone after the paragraph has been amputated.

Yet one cannot chalk up his adversaries' ire to editing alone. Kirk invited conflict. He believed disruption was not the side effect of persuasion but often its precondition. TPUSA's Student Action Summit, launched December 19–22, 2019, in West Palm Beach, became an annual spectacle where he mixed philosophical arguments with tactical training, headlining alongside senators, governors, and media personalities. "We're not just here to win arguments," he said from the stage that year. "We're here to win converts." His critics heard demagoguery. His followers heard confidence.

Still, to treat him as merely a provocateur is to miss the substance of his institutional build. By mid-2020, TPUSA claimed thousands of chapters and tens of thousands of student activists. It ran leadership trainings, voter registration drives, and First Amendment litigation assistance. On September 17, 2020, celebrating Constitution Day, Kirk told a Phoenix audience, "Free speech isn't the permission to be liked; it's the right to be wrong in public without fear of punishment." To students who felt isolated on campus, that line landed like a permission slip to step forward.

The slander question is harder, more intimate. American politics rewards reduction: turn people into symbols and you don't have to reckon with their complexity. In 2020 and 2021, some commentators attributed to Kirk statements that were misquotes or outright fabrications. One viral post claimed he endorsed "ending elections to preserve freedom," a line he never said; the closest antecedent was a June 15, 2021, podcast segment where he asked, "What happens when process overtakes purpose? Do we protect procedures even when they produce chaos?" Critics truncated it into a defense of authoritarianism. The longer exchange was a familiar civics paradox: how to reform systems that are both necessary and fallible. He can be faulted for provocative phrasing; he cannot be fairly accused of the words he did not utter.

He welcomed stakes—and paid them. On February 1, 2022, a TPUSA event at the University of New Mexico ended early amid safety concerns after protesters pulled fire alarms and blocked exits. Kirk later remarked, "For people who claim to defend democracy, they have a curious fear of dialogue." The line was caustic, but the moment was real: campus politics had become a test of wills, and he was content to test them.

Kirk's personal pace never slowed. By 2023, he had built a daily media footprint, published books, and expanded his organization into faith and civics initiatives. He spoke often about gratitude, about his parents and mentors, and about the moral vocabulary he thought America was losing. On July 4, 2023, he told a Nashville audience, "Gratitude turns entitlement into stewardship. When you're thankful for a country, you do the work to keep it." He could be abrasive online and pastoral onstage, a contrast his critics dismissed as calculation and his supporters accepted as range.

There were also notable flashes of bridge-building. On March 5, 2024, he appeared with a progressive campus coalition at Arizona State University in a moderated debate about money in politics. "If we can agree that concentrated power is dangerous," he said, "we can disagree productively about where the concentration is worst." The discussion produced less soundbite heat than usual, and therefore less coverage, but it showcased a different gear, one that rewarded listening as much as sparring.

Through all of it ran a set of convictions that, whether you share them or not, were consistent: that free speech is a prerequisite for pluralism; that markets, though imperfect, best capture human energy; and that citizenship requires obligations as well as rights. The American left's fiercest critics of Kirk often argued that his network platformed demagogues or normalized conspiratorial thinking. He answered that ideas should be refuted, not banned, and that sunlight is a disinfectant, even for views he himself did not hold. That defense is only as strong as the curation he exercised, and reasonable people will disagree about where his line should have been.

But the broader pattern is unmistakable. Kirk's rise mapped directly onto America's algorithmic age: the shorter the clip, the sharper the edge; the sharper the edge, the easier the cut. In such an environment, context becomes collateral damage. "Judge me by the full paragraph," he said in Dallas on November 12, 2024, "not the half-sentence you can fit on a poster." It was a plea to a culture that rewards the poster.

The boy from Arlington Heights turned himself into an institution not because he wanted to be loved but because he wanted to be heard. In a democracy that often confuses volume for truth, that ambition will always be polarizing. Perhaps that is the final irony: the same system that accused him of being too loud also made it nearly impossible to be understood at a normal volume. If his opponents caricatured him, he sometimes helped them sharpen the pencil. If his allies sanctified him, he told them to work the phones. And if the country continues to pull itself into tighter, louder corners, the kind of public square he envisions—a messy one, argumentative and stubborn—may be the only place left where persuasion still has a chance.

The wager that persuasion might still find a foothold met its harshest test on September 10, 2025, in Orem, Utah. Utah Valley University had booked a student forum, a familiar terrain for Kirk, who thrived on the exchange as much as the argument. Organizers called it the first stop of a new tour, a reset toward civics and conversations in rooms where disagreement was expected but not feared.

The hall was packed, the questions already stacked, when a report cracked through the routine. In the startled seconds that followed, panic folded the crowd into the aisles. Kirk, who had made a career of walking into noisy arenas to insist that words beat violence, was rushed from the venue and later pronounced dead.

The language of shock quickly yielded to the language of law. Utah authorities announced an arrest within hours and soon after filed aggravated murder charges. Prosecutors described evidence that included contemporaneous messages and a note, quoting the suspect as having framed the act as retaliation for "spreading too much hate." Officials called it an assassination, a political killing aimed at silencing a voice rather than rebutting it. Kirk's wife, Erika, spoke of a life interrupted and a mission unfinished; his colleagues at Turning Point USA stood before cameras and vowed that the work would continue. "A sleeping giant likely woke up," one of them said, a phrase that tried to alchemize grief into resolve.

In the days after, the country's reflexes—media, social platforms, the partisan chorus—kicked hard. Headlines telescoped the story into a single line. Clips outran context. Old quotes resurfaced, shorn of their paragraphs, offered as exhibits for a moral ledger no one could agree on. Commentators on the left pointed to prior controversies as if Kirk's record were a kind of mitigation. Commentators on the right described a chain of permission, years of "by any means necessary" rhetoric that stigmatized dissenters as beyond the pale, now culminating in a trigger pull. Between the poles, sorrow struggled to compete with certainty.

Kirk had long warned that the logic of deplatforming would not stop at the edge of speech. He liked to say that free expression was the pressure valve of a plural nation, and that if you weld the valve shut, the heat will find another exit. His critics thought that alarmist, a flourish that let him court provocation while claiming innocence about the sparks. Yet here was an act that took the metaphor literally: shut him up, permanently. The argument that ideas should be refuted, not erased, became not just a line in a speech but an autopsy of a moment.

There is a temptation, after political violence, to turn cause and effect into clean arrows: he said, they heard, therefore this. But reality smears. Individuals carry their own demons, their own private accelerants, and no chorus line of tweets can quite substitute for a single human will. Still, culture sets weather. The degradation of opponents into caricatures, the casual conflation of error with evil, and the algorithm's reward for the punchline over the paragraph—all of it makes thunderstorms more likely, even if no one storm can be mapped back to a single forecast. Kirk's life, and the manner of its end, pressed that tension into view: a man who insisted debate was oxygen, felled in a room built for breathing.

In the sanctuaries of grief that followed—church pews, studio sets gone temporarily quiet, a headquarters draped in flowers—his friends reached for the through-lines. Gratitude as an antidote to entitlement. Duty as a more durable glue than outrage. "Judge me by the full paragraph," he had said not a year earlier, a plea that sounded, now, like a last will and testament to a country he believed could still be argued into coherence. The students he had once urged to "show up, invite questions, and endure the boos" showed up again, this time to light candles and to promise, perhaps to themselves more than anyone, that the next microphone would not be ceded to the next shout.

The chapter of his influence will be written, for a while, by those who loved him and those who loathed him. That is how it goes with public lives ended in public ways: the obituary becomes a proxy war. But beneath the edits and the headlines is a harder-to-quote legacy, the stubborn belief that a free people can conduct their fiercest disagreements without treating their opponents as enemies to be erased. If that belief feels more fragile now, it is also more urgent. The country he spent a young life arguing with will decide whether the room where he last stood becomes a relic of what was lost, or a reminder of what must be kept.

Chapter 3:

The First-Term Record:

A Pro-Growth, Pro-Security Reorientation

Donald J. Trump took office in 2017 with a blunt promise: "From this day forward, it's going to be only America first." He governed to that theme: lower taxes and fewer regulations to unleash growth; tougher, leverage-based trade to protect American industry and technology; borders and courts strengthened; energy unshackled; and an unapologetic foreign policy that pursued peace through strength. His methods were unconventional; the results, supporters argue, were concrete: record-low unemployment before the pandemic, a reshaped judiciary, historic Middle East normalization, and vaccines in record time. This chapter recounts the policy through lines, the data that undergird his case, and the media crossfire that accompanied it, with brief acknowledgments of major criticisms where relevant.

The Economy and Tax Reform

Trump's economic project began with the Tax Cuts and Jobs Act of 2017 (Public Law 115-97), the most comprehensive tax overhaul in a generation. Corporate rates fell from 35% to 21%, the standard deduction rose, individual rates ticked down across brackets, full expensing jump-started investment, and a new 20% deduction (Section 199A) supported pass-through businesses that form the backbone of American entrepreneurship. The international system shifted toward territoriality with guardrails such as GILTI and BEAT to curb abusive profit shifting. Paired with Opportunity Zones to draw capital into distressed communities, the package aimed not only to spur headline growth but also to steer it to places that had been left behind.

By late 2019, unemployment hit a 50-year low at 3.5%, while African American and Hispanic jobless rates marked series lows, and prime-age employment climbed near pre-2008 highs (BLS). Wage growth accelerated, especially in the lower quintiles, consistent with a tight labor market drawing people back in. "Wages are rising at the fastest pace in decades," he said in 2019, reflecting data that showed outsized gains for lower-wage workers before COVID-19. The administration argued it had "enacted the biggest tax cuts and reforms in American history," a superlative that depends on measure but conveys the scope of change.

Deficits widened in 2018 and 2019 amid robust growth, a byproduct of rate cuts and bipartisan spending, even as business investment rose. Then came the pandemic: an exogenous shock that collapsed demand and supply almost overnight. Trump's team moved with Congress on the CARES Act, which included direct payments, expanded unemployment insurance, and the Paycheck Protection Program that kept millions on payrolls, and supplemented it with executive actions such as temporary payroll tax deferral. The recession was severe but unusually sharp; the rebound began quickly from the trough.

Citations: Bureau of Labor Statistics; Congressional Budget Office analyses; U.S. Treasury TCJA and Opportunity Zones materials; CARES Act text.

A Regulatory Reset

The administration's deregulatory thrust was as much philosophy as policy. Trump signed E.O. 13771 to impose regulatory budgeting: "two out for every one in." Agencies set cost caps to pare back rules that, in his words, "strangled" small business. Environmental permitting was streamlined, with NEPA timelines shortened to accelerate infrastructure. The "Waters of the United States" replacement rule constrained federal reach to traditional navigable waters, giving farmers and landowners clearer lines. Auto fuel economy and power sector rules were recalibrated, while labor and health rules were revised to reduce compliance burdens.

By the administration's accounting, these actions saved large regulatory costs and sped up project approvals (OIRA annual reports; Federal Register tallies). Trump repeatedly claimed, "We have cut more regulations than any administration in history." The precise counting is debated, but the directional impact—fewer new rules, more rescissions, faster reviews—aligned with his promise to "end the war on American energy" and "let builders build."

Citations: Office of Information and Regulatory Affairs annual reports; Federal Register; agency rule dockets and court decisions.

Trade Rebalanced: China, North America, and Strategic Industry

Trump treated trade as leverage to correct what he called decades of "one-sided" deals. With China, the U.S. deployed Section 301 tariffs to pressure systemic issues such as forced technology transfer, IP theft, subsidies, and market barriers, while tightening export controls and expanding investment reviews under FIRRMA to protect critical technologies. The Phase One agreement secured commitments on purchases, IP, and financial services access, even as broader structural matters remained contested.

In North America, the United States–Mexico–Canada Agreement (USMCA) modernized digital trade and introduced tougher auto rules of origin and labor enforcement mechanisms that addressed offshoring incentives under NAFTA. Steel and aluminum tariffs under Section 232 aimed to safeguard capacity deemed vital for national security. "We rebuilt the U.S. manufacturing base," Trump said. Manufacturing jobs rose pre-pandemic and investment strengthened in select sectors, even if the term "rebuilt" overstates a full return to early-2000s peaks.

Citations: USTR Section 301 reports; USMCA text and summaries; BEA trade, price, and investment data; FIRRMA/CFIUS materials.

Borders, Sovereignty, and the Rule of Law

"If you don't have borders, you don't have a country." That refrain guided a muscular immigration and border policy. The administration constructed new and replacement border barriers across high-traffic sectors, added surveillance technology, and surged personnel. The Migrant Protection Protocols (Remain in Mexico) reduced incentives for fraudulent or non-qualifying asylum claims by requiring certain applicants to await proceedings outside the U.S. The public charge rule and other adjudication changes emphasized self-sufficiency and lawful process. Travel restrictions, after revisions, were upheld by the Supreme Court in *Trump v. Hawaii* as a legitimate exercise of national security authority. Interior enforcement increased, refugee ceilings were reduced, and the pandemic added Title 42 expulsions that reshaped encounter patterns in 2020.

Deportations and removals became a political lightning rod. A simple comparison clarifies rhetoric versus reality. According to DHS, the Obama administration, especially in its first term, oversaw very high numbers of removals; in FY2009–FY2012, annual removals routinely exceeded 350,000 and peaked around 409,000 (FY2012). Activists labeled President Obama the "Deporter in Chief." By contrast, during Trump's term, annual ICE removals were generally lower than Obama's early-term peak years. FY2019 ICE removals were roughly 267,000, and FY2017–FY2020 fluctuated below Obama's peak levels, with FY2020 depressed by pandemic disruptions (DHS/ICE statistics).

Enforcement emphasis under Trump shifted toward rapid border consequences, including MPP and later Title 42 expulsions, and criminal-alien priorities, while Obama's early years combined interior and border removals on a large scale before later reprioritizations. Supporters point to a double standard: mass outrage met Trump's comparatively lower removal totals, while Obama's higher early-term numbers were often muted or rationalized in coverage. The moral fervor, they argue, tracked political branding more than raw enforcement counts. Without dismissing humanitarian debates, facts matter.

Legal disputes around DACA resulted in a Supreme Court ruling that blocked rescission on procedural grounds. A "zero tolerance" prosecution policy at the border led to family separations and was reversed following public outcry. Still, supporters credit clearer rules, credible consequences, and restored control as necessary to protect migrants from dangerous journeys, disrupt smuggling, and uphold sovereignty.

Citations: DHS *Yearbook of Immigration Statistics*; ICE Enforcement and Removal Operations annual reports (FY2009–FY2020); Supreme Court opinions (*Trump v. Hawaii*; *DHS v. Regents of the University of California*); CBP data; Federal Register notices.

Courts and Criminal Justice: A Generational Imprint

Trump's judicial legacy is unmistakable. With Senate partnership, he appointed three Supreme Court justices: Neil Gorsuch, Brett Kavanaugh, and Amy Coney Barrett, cementing a 6–3 conservative majority centered on textualism and originalism. More than 200 Article III judges were confirmed across appellate and district courts, rebalancing circuits that shape national law for decades. "We will appoint judges who interpret the Constitution as written," he promised; in office, he delivered.

In criminal justice, he signed the bipartisan First Step Act (2018), a landmark reform that recalibrated certain mandatory minimums, expanded earned-time credits, and improved prison programs to reduce recidivism. The law's cross-partisan coalition underscored a pragmatic streak: tough on violent crime, supportive of law enforcement, yet open to data-driven rehabilitation that gives returning citizens a better second chance.

Citations: Senate Judiciary records; Administrative Office of the U.S. Courts; First Step Act text; DOJ/BOP implementation updates.

Peace Through Strength: The Middle East and Beyond

Abroad, Trump favored direct leverage and clear lines. He pressed NATO allies to move toward the 2% of GDP defense target, and allied defense outlays rose during his tenure. In the Middle East, the Abraham Accords normalized relations between Israel and the UAE, Bahrain, Sudan, and Morocco, a diplomatic breakthrough that rewired regional alignments from confrontation toward commerce and tourism. The U.S. recognized Jerusalem as Israel's capital and moved its embassy, a long-promised step prior administrations declined to take.

Against ISIS, the coalition completed the territorial defeat of the caliphate, culminating in the 2019 raid that killed Abu Bakr al-Baghdadi. Trump withdrew from the JCPOA, pursuing a "maximum pressure" campaign on Iran. He engaged North Korea in leader-level summitry that paused some testing cycles even without a final denuclearization deal. In Afghanistan, his administration negotiated a conditions-based framework that initiated the drawdown toward ending America's longest war. The through line was succinctly captured in a phrase he often used: "Peace through strength."

Citations: White House and State Department Abraham Accords documentation; DOD reports on ISIS; NATO burden-sharing data; presidential statements.

Energy Abundance and Environmental Policy

"Energy dominance" became both slogan and policy. By clearing permitting backlogs, revising methane and power sector rules, opening additional leasing on federal lands and waters, and approving pipelines, the administration aimed to keep energy prices low for families and industry while expanding jobs in oil, gas, and related supply chains. The U.S. led the world in oil and natural gas production during these years, with consumers benefiting from affordable gasoline and electricity in the pre-pandemic period (EIA). The United States formally notified its intent to withdraw from the Paris Agreement, underscoring a view that climate policy must align with growth and sovereignty.

Citations: Energy Information Administration production, price, and export series; EPA rulemakings; presidential communications on Paris.

The Pandemic Trial: Mobilization and Warp Speed

Nothing tested the administration like COVID-19. The White House restricted travel from China in January 2020 and later from Europe, declared a national emergency, invoked the Defense Production Act to expand PPE and ventilator output, and stood up public-private supply chains under FEMA and HHS. The economic response—CARES Act checks, expanded UI, and PPP—put a floor under freefall.

Operation Warp Speed (OWS) was the crown jewel. Through at-risk manufacturing, portfolio hedging across platforms, and aggressive contracting, OWS enabled two mRNA vaccines and one adenovirus-vectored vaccine to receive FDA emergency use authorizations in late 2020, less than a year after the virus emerged. "We are marshaling the full power of the federal government and the private sector," Trump said in March. Supporters call OWS one of the most consequential biomedical efforts in American history.

Citations: HHS/BARDA OWS documents; FDA EUAs; CDC timelines; CARES Act text.

Law, Order, and Community Safety

Alongside the First Step Act's reforms, the administration championed a robust law-and-order posture. After high-profile unrest in 2020, DOJ initiatives like Operation Legend bolstered local police departments with federal resources targeting violent offenders. Trump signed an executive order encouraging best practices and certification for safe policing while emphasizing support for officers. "We support the men and women of law enforcement 100%," he said.

Citations: Department of Justice reports; FBI UCR releases; White House executive orders and fact sheets.

Media Crossfire: Labels, Narratives, and the Direct Presidency

Trump's media relationship was open combat, and often quotable on both sides. He used Twitter as a presidential loudhailer, labeling hostile coverage "fake news" and sometimes "the enemy of the people." "The Fake News Media is the enemy of the American people," he tweeted in 2017, later clarifying he meant certain outlets he viewed as dishonest. At rallies and briefings he said, "I have a running war with the media," framing his approach as bypassing gatekeepers to speak directly to voters.

Major outlets responded in kind. A New York Times editorial headline declared, "Donald Trump Is a Racist." An MSNBC chyron during one segment described him as "a dictator loving tyrant."

CNN's on-air commentary referred to him as "authoritarian," and an opinion column called him "a xenophobe." On primetime, he was labeled "Putin's puppet." These were not stray social posts but language that migrated into mainstream discourse and sometimes onto cable chyrons.

Trump reciprocated with epithets for opponents and media figures: "Crooked," "Sleepy," "Shifty," and "Pencil-Neck," and broadened the critique: "They are truly the enemy of the people." The effect was a feedback loop: sharper scrutiny and name-calling from media, matched by a president who relished rhetorical counterpunching. Supporters saw candor; detractors saw norm-breaking. Either way, the direct-to-voter presidency became a defining feature of the era.

Citations: Presidential tweets and transcripts; newspaper archives and editorials; cable news transcripts.

False Claims: His and About Him

The Trump years unfolded amid a fog of claims and counterclaims, but nowhere was the asymmetry more evident than in the myths that calcified about him. He could be hyperbolic, sometimes spectacularly so, but the volume of falsehoods about Trump himself created a parallel narrative often unmoored from the record. What follows is a concise, narrative account: first, emblematic statements from Trump that overshot the facts, and then a broader catalog of widely circulated falsehoods about him, with direct quotes and dates, whose repetition shaped public perception far more than the underlying evidence warranted.

Trump's emphatic style produced some claims that did not hold up. On January 21, 2017, at CIA Headquarters, he said, "We had the largest audience to ever witness an inauguration, period," a flourish contradicted by photos and transit data. He insisted on November 27, 2016, and again afterward, "I won the popular vote if you deduct the millions of people who voted illegally," a contention never substantiated. He liked superlatives: "We've achieved the biggest tax cuts and reforms in American history" (State of the Union, Jan. 30, 2018), a major tax cut, but not the biggest by share of GDP. In the first months of COVID, optimism sometimes outran reality: "We have it totally under control" (CNBC, Jan. 22, 2020); "Anybody who wants a test can get a test" (Mar. 6, 2020); "We're rounding the corner" (fall 2020). And after Election Day, he tweeted, "I won this election, by a lot" (Nov. 7, 2020), even as courts and certifications moved the other way.

Yet those missteps do not excuse, and certainly do not justify, the cascade of false or misleading claims aimed at him—many delivered with the authority of headlines, chyrons, and viral posts. These were not stray exaggerations in rally mode; they were assertions that hardened into public "truths," despite contrary records.

False or misleading claims about Trump (selected, with quotes and dates):

- "Trump called neo-Nazis 'very fine people.'" — August 2017 shorthand repeated for years. The full August 15, 2017 transcript shows he said there were "very fine people on both sides" of the statue debate and added, "I'm not talking about the neo-Nazis and the white nationalists... they should be condemned totally."

- "Trump mocked a reporter's disability because he's disabled." — November–December 2015 claim revived throughout his presidency. The gesture he used, an exaggerated flailing, was a stock bit he had used about various non-disabled figures; the target was a reporter's changing story. The interpretation as a disability taunt became canonical, but context complicates it.

- "He called all immigrants 'animals.'" — May 16, 2018. In a California roundtable, Trump said, "They're not people. These are animals," in response to a reference to MS-13. Context limited the remark to gang members; wide circulation stripped that context.

- "Trump ordered a 'Muslim ban.'" — January–February 2017. His travel orders targeted specific countries identified in statute and prior policy for security vetting; after revisions, the Supreme Court upheld the policy (*Trump v. Hawaii*, 2018). The shorthand suggested a global religion test that never existed.

- "He tear-gassed peaceful protesters for a photo-op." — June 1, 2020, Lafayette Square. Early coverage framed it that way; later reviews and watchdog findings documented that the clearing predated the President's walk and involved multiple agencies and irritants, with no evidence of a direct presidential order to use tear gas "for a photo."

- "Trump banned masks nationwide." — Spring–Summer 2020 rumor. No national mask ban was proposed or issued; policies varied by state and locality.

"He refused all ventilator purchases.": March–April 2020 narratives. The administration invoked the Defense Production Act and contracted for ventilators in spring 2020; by summer, supply exceeded demand.

"He dismantled the pandemic team, leaving no one on duty.": 2018/2020. NSC directorates were reorganized; functions continued across NSC, HHS, and CDC. The claim of "no team" overstated what was a restructuring.

"He told people to inject bleach.": April 23, 2020. He mused about disinfectants and light as potential treatments in a garbled briefing exchange; he did not instruct injections. The "inject bleach" line became a meme detached from the transcript.

"He called fallen soldiers 'suckers' and 'losers.'": September 3, 2020, anonymously sourced report echoed widely. Multiple on-the-record witnesses who were present denied the remarks, and no corroborating documents surfaced.

"He praised Putin as his boss and worked for Russia.": 2017–2019 cable shorthand. After lengthy investigation, no conspiracy or coordination was established; policy actions, including sanctions, expulsions, and arming Ukraine, ran counter to the "puppet" narrative.

"He told Georgia officials to 'find' fake votes.": January 2, 2021 call. The quote "I just want to find 11,780 votes" appeared; the longer transcript shows he claimed lawful votes were wrongly excluded and pressed for investigation. Still improper pressure, but not the cartoonish order to manufacture ballots that headlines implied.

"He banned Muslims from serving in the military.": 2017 social media claim. No such policy existed.

"He banned the CDC from saying 'climate change.'": 2017–2018 rumor. CDC issued guidance on budget language; there was no formal ban on the phrase.

"He ordered USPS to destroy mail-in ballots.": Summer 2020 conspiracy meme. No evidence; DOJ and states found isolated fraud cases, not a federal ballot-destruction plot.

"He never condemned white supremacists.": Repeated across 2017–2020. He publicly said, "I totally disavow the KKK" (Mar. 3, 2016) and "white supremacists… should be condemned totally" (Aug. 15, 2017), among other statements. Critics found his responses insufficient or delayed, but "never" is false.

"He cancelled all refugee admissions permanently.": 2017 claim. Caps were reduced substantially, not eliminated; admissions continued at lower levels.

The difference matters. Trump's showman's rhetoric could color outside the lines; the record shows it, and history should note it. But the mythology about Trump, flattened context, attributed quotes, and sweeping claims of motives and orders never given, also deserves correction. In the end, facts are stubborn things: the transcript that includes the condemnation as well as the clumsy "both sides," the procurement contracts that actually delivered ventilators, the NSC memos that show reorganization rather than abolition, and the court opinions that upheld a security-based policy rather than a religious test. Peel back the caricature, and the picture is more complicated, and fairer, than the loudest chyrons ever allowed.

How Supporters Argue It Made America Better

Supporters stitch these threads into a coherent thesis. The pre-COVID economy delivered opportunity broadly, pulling sidelined Americans back into the workforce with rising pay at the bottom. Tax reform and deregulation rekindled investment and entrepreneurship; energy abundance lowered costs for families and made industry more competitive. Trade policy reset expectations with China and modernized North American commerce through USMCA. Judicial appointments restored a constitutionalist approach that, in their view, enhances predictability and liberty. Abroad, the Abraham Accords opened a new chapter of Arab-Israeli relations, and the ISIS caliphate's defeat removed a brutal threat. In crisis, Operation Warp Speed mobilized science and manufacturing at a scale and speed few thought possible.

Chapter 4:
Sex, Gender, and the Politics of Truth

What is a woman? Not a vibe, not a playlist, not a password you tell HR. A woman is an adult human female: a member of the reproductive class oriented toward producing large gametes, eggs, with ovaries, a uterus ordered toward gestation, and an endocrine ecology dominated by estrogen and progesterone. That's biology, not bigotry. Law recognized it, medicine relied on it, and culture built sane guardrails, sports categories and privacy norms, around it.

Only recently did a new orthodoxy insist that sex is "assigned," that declarations override chromosomes, and that institutions must compel your speech to keep the fiction afloat. Is compassion now defined as pretending gravity doesn't pull? Or is it telling the truth kindly, even when truth is unfashionable?

The modern story of transgender medicine begins with clinicians like Harry Benjamin, who in the mid-20th century described patients in deep distress over their sexed bodies. Diagnostic manuals mirrored that reality. DSM-III (1980) used "transsexualism." DSM-IV (1994) moved to "Gender Identity Disorder," a clinically significant conflict between experienced gender and sex. Then came DSM-5 (2013), which reframed the diagnosis as "Gender Dysphoria," locating the disorder in the distress rather than the identity (American Psychiatric Association, 2013). The World Health Organization went further with ICD-11, relocating "gender incongruence" from mental disorders to conditions of sexual health (World Health Organization, 2019). Humane? Perhaps. Convenient for activists eager to collapse clinical description into a civil rights mandate? Absolutely. Notice the sleight of hand: a category shift in a codebook becomes a cudgel to declare debate settled, science silenced, and policy rewritten.

Meanwhile, WPATH, the advocacy group that writes "Standards of Care," marched from caution to rubber stamp. Early editions demanded thorough psychological evaluations and "real-life experience" before irreversible steps. By SOC-8 (2022), gatekeeping gave way to "informed consent" formalities and soft age thresholds that read like aspirations rather than rules (World Professional Association for Transgender Health, 2022). Since when does medicine drop the demand for high-quality evidence just as it ramps up irreversible interventions? Since activists captured the language. Federal agencies in the U.S. followed suit, reading "sex" to include "gender identity" and letting bureaucratic memos accomplish what Congress never voted on. Corporate HR adopted pronoun rituals like a new sacrament. Dissent? That's "harm." Skepticism? "Violence." What's next, mandating belief in transubstantiation of the body?

Let's re-anchor to reality. Sex is not assigned; it's observed because it's there. The human species is sexually dimorphic, divided into two reproductive classes: male (small gametes, sperm) and female (large gametes, ova). Disorders of sexual development are rare deviations in development, not new sexes. Chromosomes, XX and XY, launch developmental cascades through genes such as SRY, SOX9, and FOXL2, with endocrine milieus sculpting bodies for distinct reproductive strategies. Male puberty confers durable advantages in strength, speed, and cardiorespiratory capacity. Female physiology orders itself around ovulation and gestation with different disease profiles and pharmacokinetics. These facts aren't insults; they're instructions life follows. You can wish away the scoreboard, but the score remains.

What about "gender identity," the inner sense some people have of being the other sex? Neuroscience offers no diagnostic litmus test, no scan that reads "boy brain/girl brain." Studies show modest average sex-linked brain differences, but findings are mixed and confounded by hormones, sample bias, and neuroplasticity. Identity sits in the mind, not in a detectable organ signature. The stable thing is sex; the subjective thing is identity. Both deserve respect; only one should anchor medicine and law where bodies, risks, and outcomes are on the line. Isn't that the adult way to run a country?

Now, the evidence on medical transition. For adults, observational studies frequently report short-term relief of dysphoria after cross-sex hormones and surgeries. Good—people in pain deserve relief. But the literature is mostly low to moderate quality: small cohorts, no randomized trials, high loss to follow-up, and heavy psychiatric comorbidity muddy the waters. Sweden's population study found persistently elevated all-cause mortality and psychiatric morbidity in surgically treated patients compared to controls, even after adjustments (Dhejne et al., 2011). You can argue over causation, but you can't wish away the signal: vulnerability remains. If a therapy leaves long-term outcomes this fragile, should the mantra be "affirm faster" or "slow down and be honest"?

With minors, the stakes rise and the evidence thins. The Dutch protocol—tight screening, early childhood-onset dysphoria persisting into puberty, careful progression from blockers to hormones—reported improved outcomes for a narrow, highly selected cohort (de Vries et al., 2014). That protocol became a brand slapped onto American clinics serving a very different population: predominantly adolescent girls with rapid-onset dysphoria, anxiety, depression, trauma histories, and autism traits. That is not the same clinical question. No wonder Europe, which led on affirmation, is now tapping the brakes. Sweden's National Board of Health and Welfare (2022) concluded the evidence for pediatric medical transition is uncertain and restricted hormones to exceptional cases, preferably within research (Sweden NBHW, 2022). Finland prioritized psychotherapy in 2020 and constrained medicalization for minors to narrow circumstances (PALKO/COHERE, 2020). The UK's Cass Review (2024) called the evidence "remarkably weak," triggering an NHS pause on puberty blockers outside trials and a redesign of services (Cass, 2024). Norway and France issued cautionary guidance. Are Sweden, Finland, and the NHS all suddenly in league with Bible Belt fanatics, or did they read the studies?

Consider the slogans. "Puberty blockers are fully reversible." Based on what? Blockers used to delay abnormally early puberty aren't the same as halting normal puberty in a healthy adolescent. Evidence flags risks to bone density, sexual development, and unknown neurocognitive effects. And the majority of teens who start blockers proceed to cross-sex hormones—so much for a "pause." Cross-sex hormones can permanently impair fertility and carry cardiovascular and thromboembolic risks. Surgeries add irreversibility to uncertainty. Does any of this sound like "settled science" to you, or like a field sprinting ahead of its headlights?

So why the intolerance for skepticism? Because the win was rhetorical, not empirical. The activist sequence goes like this: redefine sex as gender; redefine gender as inner truth; criminalize dissent as "harm." Then bolt it all into policy via HR mandates and agency "guidance." Suddenly, your job depends on declaring that words can change bodies. Ask a basic question—What is a woman?—and you're told to sit down and recite the creed. Since when did free citizens in a liberal republic owe metaphysical allegiance to anyone's inner feelings?

The human costs of this coercion are visible. Maya Forstater lost her job in the UK for saying sex is immutable; only after a grinding legal process did a tribunal affirm her belief as a protected philosophical position (Forstater v. CGD Europe, 2021–2022).

Kathleen Stock, a philosopher at Sussex, was hounded until she resigned for defending sex-based rights (Stock, 2021). In Virginia, teacher Peter Vlaming was fired for declining to use male pronouns for a female student. His suit advanced on free speech and free exercise grounds, and the district settled (Vlaming v. West Point School Board, 2023–2024). Nicholas Meriwether, disciplined over pronouns, won at the Sixth Circuit and settled with his university (Meriwether v. Hartop, 2021). These are the names we know because they fought back. How many others got the message and kept quiet to keep a paycheck?

The conservative position isn't cruelty; it's competence plus courage. Medicine's first duties are to do no harm, tell the truth, and secure informed consent. That means saying plainly: for minors, evidence is low quality and long-term outcomes uncertain; blockers are not a magic eraser; cross-sex hormones often foreclose fertility; surgeries are irreversible and may not resolve underlying distress (Cass, 2024; Sweden NBHW, 2022; PALKO/COHERE, 2020; Levine et al., 2022). It also means clinicians must be free to recommend psychotherapeutic exploration first, especially when adolescents present with heavy comorbidities, without being branded bigots. Isn't it odd that in every other domain we treat major, body-altering interventions on minors with extreme caution, yet here the accelerator is welded to the floor?

For adults, liberty matters. After serious assessment and full disclosure of risks, adults may choose medical pathways to relieve persistent dysphoria. But public policy must still track biology where biology governs outcomes. Sports are physiology, not poetry; male puberty confers advantages that suppression cannot fully unwind (Hilton & Lundberg, 2021). Female athletes deserve fairness and safety. Prisons and shelters exist to protect the vulnerable; admitting male-bodied offenders to women's facilities by self-identification has produced harms that anyone with a newspaper subscription could have predicted. Medicine itself—drug dosing, disease risk, diagnostics—relies on sexed baselines. Blurring sex in records to appease ideology isn't compassion; it's malpractice.

Internationally, the map is pointing one way. Sweden, Finland, and the UK—hardly outposts of social conservatism—have raised the drawbridge on pediatric medicalization, moved psychotherapy to the front of the line, and demanded research-grade evidence before reopening the gates (Sweden NBHW, 2022; PALKO/COHERE, 2020; Cass, 2024; Norway HTA, 2023–2024; French advisories, various). Are we really going to pretend America is too enlightened to learn from Scandinavia?

So, what is a woman? An adult human female. Membership in the female reproductive class isn't revoked by hysterectomy, menopause, or atypical development, because sex is about the body's organization toward reproduction, not about stereotypes. Gender expression—tomboy chic or lipstick glam—is personality and culture. The law's job is to honor reality while preventing unjust discrimination: keep sex-based categories where safety, fairness, and medical accuracy require them; offer reasonable accommodations to those who identify differently; and stop compelling citizens to declare things they do not believe. If we can't preserve truthful speech in medicine and education, where exactly do we think truth will survive?

Compassion isn't capitulation. It is patient truth-telling, the courage to explore comorbidities, the humility to say "we don't know" when the data are weak, and the backbone to protect kids from irreversible decisions before they can legally buy a tattoo. It honors the dignity of people with gender dysphoria without demanding that everyone else abandon reality. You don't rescue a drowning man by throwing him a stone labeled "identity." You throw him a rope called "truth," and you pull.

Here is a saner settlement. For minors: restrict medical transition to rare, rigorously screened cases within research frameworks; fund robust mental-health services; protect parental rights (Cass, 2024; Sweden NBHW, 2022; PALKO/COHERE, 2020). For adults: safeguard free speech and conscience; require transparent, risk-forward informed consent; protect sex-based spaces with reasonable accommodations; collect sex-accurate medical data (Meriwether v. Hartop, 2021; Hilton & Lundberg, 2021). For institutions: separate advocacy from guideline writing; grade evidence honestly; end ideological loyalty oaths as hiring criteria (Levine et al., 2022). For culture: teach children respect for persons and reality for bodies; stop outsourcing courage to HR.

We can remember what a woman is. We can rebuild medicine on evidence, not edict. And we can force politics to kneel, briefly, before truth. Our daughters and our sons deserve nothing less.

Inline Citations:

• American Psychiatric Association (2013), *DSM-5*

• World Health Organization (2019), *ICD-11*

• World Professional Association for Transgender Health (2022), *Standards of Care, Version 8*

• Sweden National Board of Health and Welfare (2022), pediatric guidance

• Council for Choices in Health Care in Finland— PALKO/COHERE (2020), guidance

• Cass Review (2024), NHS England

• Norway Health Technology Assessments (2023–2024); French advisories (various)

• de Vries et al. (2014), *Pediatrics*

• Dhejne et al. (2011), *PLoS ONE*

• Levine, Abbruzzese, et al. (2022), *Journal of Sex & Marital Therapy*

• Hilton & Lundberg (2021), *Sports Medicine*

• Forstater v. CGD Europe (2021–2022); Meriwether v. Hartop (2021); Vlaming v. West Point School Board (2023–2024); public statements and reporting on Kathleen Stock (2021)

Chapter 5:
The First Light

The first time I held an ultrasound wand in my palm, the gel was cold and the room was quiet. There was no grand music, no moral argument written on the wall, only the low hum of a machine and a small, determined flicker on the screen. It was six weeks into a pregnancy, the embryo no larger than a lentil.

"There," the technician whispered. "That's the heartbeat."

A cluster of cells? A bean? No. It was a pulse staking a claim in the darkness, the earliest drum of a human life that did not ask my permission to exist. It simply was. And in that moment, the black-and-white quiver, the sound like boots on a far-off road, the gravity of the question announced itself with unstoppable clarity: When does a human being begin? Because if we get that wrong, everything else we get wrong follows.

We live in an age that prizes mastery of language, spin, and slogans, an age that turns terms into tools of power. But biology is not a slogan, and the moral law, like gravity, does not yield to the loudest voice. The abortion debate is too often dressed in euphemism: "choice," "healthcare," "products of conception," "tissue," "terminating a pregnancy," as if ending the pregnancy did not end someone. Yet the conscience resists the softening of truth.

If the object of abortion were merely tissue, why does silence follow the procedure like a long shadow? Why do we speak softly, why do some women pause in doorways, why does the clouded gaze of a culture reveal it knows what it claims it does not? Human beings have always had a tell when they are nearing a sacred boundary. Their language frays.

What follows is not a sermon from a pedestal; it is a case—scientific, moral, philosophical, legal, and humane—for why personhood begins at conception, why abortion is wrong, and why a civilization that forgets this will misremember itself into ruin. It is also a plea to see, to think beyond slogans, to straighten what has been twisted, and to honor the first light that appears in the darkness.

1. Opening Narrative: The Unignorable Pulse

Imagine a field before sunrise. It appears empty, a flat silhouette. But bend low and you will find dew, woven webs, the tiny labor of ants, a world beginning before the sun. So it is with early human life: the eye untrained calls it "nothing," and the heart untrained permits what the eye misses. But within hours of fertilization, a new human organism begins—a unique genomic signature, an unfolding developmental program, a living being whose arc is not the mother's, not the father's, but his or her own. The field was never empty; the sun had not yet risen.

A friend of mine, the father of four, keeps the ultrasound of his fifth child in his wallet. It's a smudge to anyone else, but he sees a son who did not arrive. He can tell you the month, the clinic, the namelessness of waiting rooms, the advertisement on the wall: "You have options."

Options are good when choosing cereal and bad when choosing whom we can kill. He shakes his head. "I'd give anything to reverse a Tuesday." It is easier to crush a seed than a tree. But the moral question is not how easy the act is. The moral question is what the act is.

2. The Science of Early Human Life

Start with the uncontroversial: at fertilization, a new organism begins. The embryo is alive (metabolizing, growing), human (species-specific DNA), and an organism (a whole, self-directed entity with a developmental trajectory). It is not a part of the mother the way a kidney is a part. The embryo organizes itself; it is not assembled from the outside. The zygote is the first cell of a new human organism, not a mere "blob" without identity. It inherits a sex—male or female—at conception, not at birth. It is genetically distinct from every other human ever to live.

Modern embryology does not speak in poetry; it speaks in exactness. From conception:

• **Day 1:** Complete human genome, syngamy, the first cell division begins.

• **Days 3–5:** Cleavage, compaction, blastocyst formation; differentiation of inner cell mass from trophoblast.

- **Days 6–9:** Implantation; the embryo "decides" its home, signaling biochemically with the uterine lining for acceptance.

- **Weeks 3–4:** Primitive streak, gastrulation; the body plan, the axial orientation, emerges.

- **Weeks 5–6:** Cardiac activity detectable; neural tube closure; limb buds.

- **Weeks 7–8:** Organ primordia; reflexes begin to flicker; hands that will hold, feet that will run.

- **End of first trimester:** All major organ systems present; the rest is growth and maturation.

None of this is in dispute among embryologists. What is in dispute is whether this living, human organism is also a person with an inalienable right to life. But before we address that question, note what the science forbids us to say:

- We cannot say the embryo is "potential life." It is life with potential. A seed is not a potential acorn; it is an acorn at a stage that precedes oakhood. The human embryo is a human at an early stage.

- We cannot say it is "just the mother's body." The embryo has different DNA, may have a different sex, and exerts signals on the mother's body (immunological tolerance, hormonal shifts) as a distinct agent.

- We cannot say the embryo is a mere part lacking organization. It is a self-organizing whole with a built-in telos, to mature into later stages of the same entity.

If biology were the only vote, the verdict would be short. But modern politics has learned to step around biology as around a puddle. So we must follow the argument into philosophy.

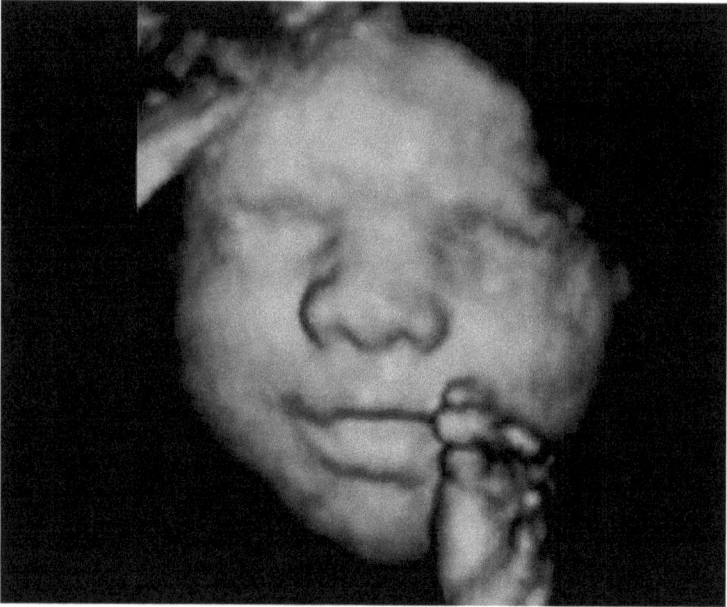

3. **Personhood From Conception**

The decisive question: When does a human being become a person? There are only a few options.

Option A: Personhood begins sometime after conception, when we can detect certain abilities (consciousness, sentience, viability, self-awareness).

Option B: Personhood begins at conception, when the human organism begins.

Option A is popular in the academy and on the American left because it appears to allow abortion while preserving moral language. But it collapses under pressure.

Thought Experiment 1: The Coma Traveler

A woman is in a temporary coma for three weeks after a car accident. She has no current consciousness or sentience. Do we say she is no longer a person and may be killed? No. We ground her dignity not in current functions but in the kind of being she is: a rational animal whose capacities are present in root, even if not currently exercised. If personhood depends on present functions, the comatose, the sleeping, the anesthetized, and the infant born at 28 weeks must all be teetering on the edge of non-personhood. Our moral intuitions recoil for good reason.

Thought Experiment 2: The Space Voyager

Suppose we discover a being on Mars with a genome, metabolism, self-directed development, and, given time, the maturation of rational capacities. It cannot survive without a Martian life-support system (nonviable outside its environment). Do we say it is not a person until viability elsewhere? No. Viability is not a property of the organism but of the environment and technology around it. A newborn in 1500 would not be viable in 2025's NICU sense. Did personhood change with time? Absurd. Viability is a moving target; rights cannot rest on the speed of our machines.

Thought Experiment 3: The Gradualist's Trap

If personhood arrives gradually, where is the line? Four weeks, when the heart beats? Fifteen, when pain might be felt? Twenty-four, when survival odds cross a threshold? Any line post-conception is arbitrary in the sense that it is not about what the being is, but about when it becomes convenient to call it someone. Law sometimes needs bright lines, but morality needs true ones. Conception is the only non-arbitrary line because it is the only point at which a new human being begins. Anything later imports an extrinsic quality (ability, location, dependence) as if that defined who counts as us.

Thought Experiment 4: The Equal Rescue

Two buildings are burning. In one, there is a conscious adult trapped on the third floor. In another, a CryoBank contains one hundred frozen embryos. You can save only one building. Most people save the adult, and some take this to mean embryos do not matter. But triage is not identity. We routinely save one rather than many for reasons unrelated to the value of the persons involved (accessibility, probability of success). This thought experiment shows not that embryos are not persons, but that our moral intuitions about rescue logistics are complex. It does not validate killing; it speaks to prioritization under duress, not to the permissibility of intentional destruction.

The common thread: capacities-based personhood fails because it makes human rights contingent on what we can do rather than on what we are. The conservative view, personhood from conception, preserves equality at its roots. If human worth depends on accidental properties, then the strong write the definition. If human worth depends on human nature, the definition is given, not granted.

4. Moral Reasoning and Human Rights

The moral law: Do not intentionally kill innocent human beings. The embryo is an innocent human being. Therefore, do not intentionally kill the embryo. That syllogism is simple, and its power lies in its clarity. The main attempts to avoid it shift the terms: "not a person," "not innocent," "not killing," "not human." All fail.

The American left often appeals to autonomy: a woman's body, a woman's choice. Autonomy is good; it protects the dignity of the person against domination. But autonomy has a boundary where another person begins. Property rights end at your neighbor's fence. Liberty ends at the other's life. When a pregnant woman carries another living human within her, the old categories of self and other become complex, but they do not collapse. There is an "I" and a "thou" under one skin. The rights of the small do not evaporate because they are out of sight.

Consider the ethics of dependency. A newborn cannot survive without constant care. We do not say, "Because you depend on me, I may kill you." Dependence imposes duties; it does not erase rights.

The embryo is the most dependent among us. That amplifies our responsibility; it does not diminish the embryo's claim.

Some argue from hard cases: rape, incest, severe fetal anomaly. Heart-wrenching cases can tempt us to alter the principle. But principles exist precisely to guide us when the heart breaks. The horror of rape reveals the evil of violating personhood; it does not justify a second violation. The child is not the crime. The presence of disability does not place one outside the human family; on the contrary, it tests whether our claim to inclusion is genuine. The humane response to suffering is support, care, and protection, not killing the one who is weakest because we cannot bear the weight.

Human rights charters speak in universal terms: "everyone," "every human being," "without distinction," "inherent dignity." If "human rights" do not begin when a human begins, they are merely "person rights" bestowed by the powerful. The conservative insistence on conception is not theological fussiness; it is democratic necessity. The first role of the state is to protect those who would otherwise be harmed. If the state can declare a class of humans "non-persons," the spell can be recast whenever convenient. History keeps the receipts.

5. The American Left's Case—and Rebuttals

A) "My body, my choice."

Rebuttal: Two bodies, two choices, two rights. The embryo is genetically distinct, with a separate heartbeat and developmental trajectory. The "my body" claim assumes the very point in dispute: that there is not another person present. If a woman carries a unique organism whose life will continue unless actively ended, the language of bodily autonomy must be balanced by the obligations that autonomy entails when it intersects with another's life.

B) "A fetus isn't a person; it lacks consciousness or sentience."

Rebuttal: We do not withdraw personhood from the unconscious or those without current sentience. We protect them precisely because their personhood does not rest on functions. Consciousness arises gradually from the developmental program present from conception. The right not to be killed cannot depend on having already developed the very capacities whose development we are deciding to interrupt.

C) "Viability determines personhood."

Rebuttal: Viability is a technological measure, not a moral one. A 22-week infant might be viable in one hospital and not in another. Rights cannot be pegged to the zip code of a NICU. Moreover, all infants are nonviable without adult care; dependence is a human constant.

D) "Abortion is healthcare."

Rebuttal: Healthcare aims at the healing of bodies and the flourishing of human life. Abortion, by design, ends a human life. Calling it healthcare equivocates. There are rare cases of medical emergency where early delivery may be needed to save the mother (ectopic pregnancy, sepsis). But intention matters. In a life-threatening ectopic pregnancy, the embryo tragically cannot survive in the fallopian tube. Removing the pathological condition is distinct from intentionally dismembering or poisoning a fetus who could live if carried to term. Moral analysis hinges on what we intend, not only on physical outcomes.

E) "Criminalizing abortion harms women; they will seek dangerous alternatives."

Rebuttal: Law is a teacher; it shapes norms. We do not legalize theft to make stealing safer. Instead, we strengthen support systems, provide life-affirming healthcare, and discourage violent practices. Where protective laws exist alongside robust social support—perinatal hospice, prenatal care, housing, and child support enforcement—both maternal health and the birth rate of vulnerable populations improve. The solution to a predicted harm is not to enshrine the harm, but to remove its causes and offer better paths.

F) "Men shouldn't control women's bodies."

Rebuttal: The argument from identity is a diversion. The truth of a moral claim does not depend on the chromosomes or politics of the one who states it. To say the child has a right to life is not to seize a woman's body; it is to deny anyone the right to destroy someone else.

G) "Women need abortion to thrive in education and the workforce."

Rebuttal: If a society's path to female equality requires the destruction of children, that society has indicted itself. True equality innovates to support motherhood and work—paid leave, flexible schedules, campus housing for mothers, and childcare vouchers— rather than demand that women mimic the male reproductive pattern. The fact that abortion is framed as an "equalizer" is evidence that our structures are unjust. The remedy is to humanize the structures, not to humanize killing.

6. Women's Health, Coercion, and Informed Consent

A quiet truth seldom told: many abortions are not free choices. Behind clinic doors, there are boyfriends threatening to leave, parents threatening to disown, employers threatening to fire, and landlords threatening eviction. The rhetoric of autonomy conceals a traffic in coercion. When researchers have asked post-abortive women the reasons for their decision, a significant portion cite pressure, fear of losing relationships or economic survival, and lack of support. Consent in a context of abandonment becomes a performance, not a choice.

Informed consent must be fully informed. Many women are not made aware of fetal development—the heartbeat by six weeks, the neural activity, the pain debate—or of alternatives such as adoption or perinatal hospice for lethal fetal diagnoses. They are often not told of potential psychological aftereffects. While the literature is contested and politicized, it is not controversial that significant grief, guilt, and depression can follow abortions, particularly those later in gestation or chosen under pressure. A humane culture would slow down the conveyor belt and open doors to support, counseling, and community.

Medical science also complicates the "simple procedure" narrative. Second-trimester abortions (dilation and evacuation) involve dismemberment of a fetus with formed limbs and organs. Late-term abortions, though a small percentage, are brutal by any ordinary language. Chemical abortions, now a majority, often involve cramping, bleeding, and the passage of a recognizable child at home, sometimes into toilets. The reality is visceral; we sanitize language because we cannot sanitize what is done.

Some will say that speaking this way shames women. No. It seeks to tell the truth so that fewer women are brought to such a door by a culture that abandoned them and a politics that told them this was power. Mercy and truth are not enemies. A pro-life ethic must be pro-woman in practice: crisis pregnancy centers with licensed medical staff, insurance coverage for prenatal and birth expenses, fatherhood support programs, domestic violence shelters, enhanced child support enforcement, adoption streamlining, and postpartum care through the first year.

7. Law and Comparative Perspectives

Across the world, democracies wrestle with abortion. Some protect earlier, some later, and some—too many—treat it as a right without horizons. But law, to be just, must align with what is true: that the unborn is a member of the human family.

Consider several strands of legal insight:

• The principle of double effect, rooted in classical moral philosophy and echoed in medical ethics, distinguishes between foreseen but unintended harm and directly intended killing. This undergirds how ethical physicians manage life-threatening pregnancies. They aim to save both, and where that is impossible, they treat pathology with grief, not precision killing.

• Wrongful death statutes in numerous jurisdictions recognize the unborn child as a victim when killed by criminal acts or negligence. If a drunk driver strikes a pregnant woman and kills the fetus at, say, 20 weeks, the law often charges homicide. The moral schizophrenia is apparent: the same being killed in a clinic is declared a non-person, while the same being killed on a highway is declared a victim.

• In perinatal hospice programs around the world, parents carry to term children diagnosed as terminal, accompanied by doctors and nurses who do not pretend death is not coming but who refuse to schedule it. The testimonies from these programs are luminous.

They reveal that our capacity to love is not contingent on the length of life but on the fact of it.

• Nations vary, but note this: many European countries set limits earlier in pregnancy than the United States has tolerated for decades. If the "global norm" is the left's appeal, they should be reminded that the norm is tighter protection for the unborn than American abortion politics have delivered.

8. Policy Pathways: Culture With Teeth

The conservative pro-life vision must be more than a negative. It must be a "yes" with architecture. If we believe personhood begins at conception, our policies must honor both mother and child.

• **Prenatal and birth care:** universal coverage for prenatal visits, childbirth, and postpartum care, including mental health support. No mother should abort for fear of medical bills. (This could easily be done by reallocating funds already given to abortion clinics. We would not be spending money we are not already spending. Instead, we would no longer be spending it on death.)

• **Paid family leave:** at least twelve weeks post-birth, with wage replacement that does not punish small businesses. Encourage pooled risk and tax credits.

• **Childcare support:** vouchers for working families; deregulate in ways that maintain safety while lowering costs; expand faith-based providers.

- **Fatherhood enforcement and support:** robust child-support laws, job training for noncustodial fathers, and legal reforms that make it easier for men to fulfill responsibilities without bureaucratic traps.

- **Adoption reform:** streamline interstate adoption, reduce costs with tax credits and grants, expand safe haven laws, and improve foster-to-adopt pathways.

- **Campus and workplace accommodations:** Title IX–style protections for pregnant and parenting students and employees, with housing, lactation spaces, and flexibility.

- **Data transparency:** require abortion providers to report detailed outcomes, complications, gestational ages, and reasons so policy is reality-based, not rhetoric-based.

- **Crisis pregnancy centers:** fund legitimate medical services and counseling. Ensure quality control so the left's caricature cannot stick, and pair with public assistance pathways.

Justice is not merely punitive. It is formative. Pro-life laws should prohibit intentional killing while building a culture where saying yes to life is the easiest and most supported choice a woman can make.

9 The Metaphysics We Cannot Escape

Every culture answers, even if by silence, two questions: Who counts as one of us? What may we do to them? The conservative answer is simple: all of us, and we may not kill the innocent. This is not a sectarian claim. It is a civilizational hinge. If we may kill some humans because they are small, unseen, dependent, or inconvenient, then human rights are a costume we wear until the feast is over.

The American left often speaks as if compassion were on its side. But true compassion requires seeing the one who cannot speak. It requires bracketing our convenience. Compassion without truth is sentimentality. Truth without compassion is cruelty. The pro-life position marries both: it names the child and embraces the mother.

The vocabulary of the left—choice, autonomy, liberation—has noble roots. But when those words are stretched to cover the intentional killing of a child, they splinter. Choice is sacred when it concerns the good; it is counterfeit when it licenses harm. Autonomy is a virtue when it respects boundaries; it is a vice when it refuses to see another's face. Liberation is light when it frees the oppressed; it is darkness when it declares the smallest among us expendable.

10 The Human Face

Let us return to the ultrasound room. The heartbeat appears as a scatter of pixels. The machine translates electricity into sound, the sound into a thrum. There is no manifesto there, no protest sign, no Supreme Court opinion. But there is a claim older than law: *I am.* Not *I will be.* Not *I might be. I am.*

The role of adults in a just society is to hear that claim and answer: *You belong. We will not pretend you are not here. We will not break you so that we may proceed unencumbered. We will change ourselves before we declare you changeable.*

I have heard objections dressed in strong cloth. I have listened to the careful philosophers. I have read the case law that twists itself into shapes to permit what it dare not name. But I have also held the hands of women who wept in parking lots and in church pews, and men who learned too late what they had agreed to, and nurses who could not look anymore at what their hands had done. Those stories do not replace arguments, but they prove an old point: the heart knows.

The unborn child is not a metaphor. He is a son playing with his toes at twelve weeks, a daughter with hiccups at twenty, a citizen in the waiting room of our common life. He does not become one of us when we say so. He is one of us from the first moment his being begins. Conception is not a slogan. It is the threshold where a new human being crosses into existence. We cross our own moral threshold when we decide what we will do about it.

11 Final Thought Experiments: The Mirror and the Ledger

The Mirror

Imagine a mirror that shows not your face, but your beginning. You look into it and you see a single cell, a tiny spark with your entire story packed inside. You do not see your diplomas, your humor, your triumphs—only the seed of all that. Would you judge that seed unworthy of protection because it cannot recite your name?

Or would you feel a chill of gratitude? The embryo you were asks for nothing you would not have wanted: time, nourishment, shelter.

The Ledger

Suppose a future historian compiles a ledger of our century's contradictions. On one page: environmental campaigns to protect polar bear cubs and turtle eggs, the urgent language of fragility, interdependence, and stewardship. On the opposite page: clinical brochures treating human embryos as disposable. The historian will not need to editorialize. The ledger will suffice. A culture that cradles animal young while discarding its own is not compassionate. It is confused.

12 A Conservative Argument Without Apology

To be conservative is to conserve what is worth saving: the family, the rule of law, the dignity of the person, the language that keeps faith with reality. On abortion, conservatism says: human life begins at conception; personhood is not a prize for the mighty to bestow; the innocent may not be intentionally killed; the law must reflect these truths; compassion requires provision; responsibility requires restraint.

No topic is off-limits, and so I will name what must be named. Abortion industries profit from shortcuts in human loyalties. Media power launders the language. Politics sells exemptions to the moral law. Men often abdicate, and women are too often left alone with decisions no one should shoulder alone.

If there is guilt, there is also forgiveness. If there is loss, there is also healing. The path forward is not silence or scorn, but a fierce tenderness that binds the wound and shields the next child from harm.

We are told the debate is over. It is not. Debates about first principles never end because new generations must learn them anew. The first principle here is not complicated: the life you cannot see is still a life. It is wrong to kill an innocent person. The unborn is an innocent person. From that simplicity flows the architecture of a just society.

13 Closing Vignette: The First Light

A mother stands at a window at dawn, her hand over a small swell that has begun to show. She is not a political theory. She is not a statistic. She is someone who has been told she is alone. But she is not alone.

Along the curve of her abdomen, another hand would fit—the hand of a child who now moves in silent dances. Inside, a heart beats. The first light breaks over the neighborhood, over old trees and roofs and sidewalks chalked by last night's games. Somewhere a dog barks. Somewhere a newspaper lands with a thud. Somewhere a clinic opens its doors and turns on the lights. And somewhere a crisis pregnancy center opens theirs too, and a volunteer turns the sign to *Welcome.*

What we decide in the next decades will determine which doors define us. The question is not whether we will be a compassionate people. We will. The question is whether our compassion will include the one we cannot see. It must. To see the unseen is the oldest test of justice. To protect the smallest is the first duty of strength. To say yes to the first light is to honor all the lights that follow.

We owe them nothing less. And we owe ourselves the truth. Personhood begins at conception. On that rock, a culture can stand.

Chapter 6:

Moral Clarity in a World of Fog — Israel, Gaza, and the American Conservative Case

The modern Middle East is a study in contrasts: between a small, embattled democracy and a chorus of regimes and militias that have treated terror as policy; between a rules-based order born from the ashes of World War II and those who would weaponize its language to undo its principles.

To see the Israel–Gaza conflict clearly is to trace the line from statehood and siege to law and legitimacy, from sanctioning terrorism to pursuing peace, and from the rhetoric of "resistance" to the reality of rockets. It is also to maintain respect—a discipline of mind that distinguishes judgment from contempt.

The American conservative case for Israel begins not with sentiment but with first principles: national self-determination, the right of self-defense, the sanctity of treaty and law, and the belief that free societies, though fallible, are worth defending.

The Partition and the Principle of Legitimacy

Start at the beginning, because beginnings matter. In 1947, the United Nations Special Committee on Palestine recommended partition—two states for two peoples. The UN General Assembly adopted Resolution 181 on November 29, 1947, proposing an Arab state and a Jewish state, with economic union and special international status for Jerusalem (UNGA 181 [II], 1947) [1].

Jewish leaders, despite grievous concessions, accepted the plan (UNGA 181, 1947) [1]. Arab leaders rejected it, seeking, in the words of contemporaneous records, "the violent prevention of the establishment of a Jewish state" (Arab Higher Committee/Arab League statements, 1947–48) [2]. That choice—acceptance of compromise versus commitment to eradication—was not some footnote; it was the thesis statement of the conflict.

When Israel declared independence on May 14, 1948, five Arab states invaded. Israel survived, barely, while absorbing hundreds of thousands of Jewish refugees expelled or fleeing from Arab lands. Palestinian Arabs, meanwhile, suffered their own catastrophe (1948–49 Armistice context) [2]. Sovereignty was earned under fire. As Abba Eban quipped with brutal accuracy, "The Arabs never miss an opportunity to miss an opportunity" (Eban remarks) [3].

Is that glib? Or is it a lament dressed as wit—because the opportunities were real, and they were missed repeatedly.

The 1949 Armistice Agreements froze lines; they did not create peace. Jordan occupied the West Bank and East Jerusalem, and Egypt administered Gaza (Armistice Agreements, 1949) [2]. In those 18 years, from 1949 to 1967, not a single Arab regime created a Palestinian state in those territories.

Why not? If the grievance was occupation per se, why the silence when the occupiers were Arab? The inconvenient answer is that the conflict has never been primarily about borders; it has been about Israel's existence.

The Defensive War of 1967 and the Framework of Land-for-Peace

By June 1967, Egypt expelled UN peacekeepers, massed troops in Sinai, and closed the Straits of Tiran—*casus belli* under any sane reading of maritime law and state practice. Israel launched a preemptive strike and, in six days, took Sinai, Gaza, the West Bank, East Jerusalem, and the Golan Heights (June 1967) [4].

The Security Council answered with Resolution 242: withdrawal "from territories occupied in the recent conflict" in exchange for "termination of all claims or states of belligerency" and "secure and recognized boundaries" for every state (UNSC 242, 1967) [4].

Note the phrasing: "from territories," not "from the territories." That omission was deliberate—land for peace, yes; suicide for slogans, no (UNSC 242 negotiating history) [4].

This is the conservative template: security for recognition, not appeasement for applause. Israel proved the concept. It returned Sinai for a real peace with Egypt (1979 treaty) [5]. It normalized and secured its frontier with Jordan (1994 treaty) [6]. Where there is a credible partner, land can buy peace. Where there isn't, land buys only a new launchpad for rockets.

From Oslo's Promise to Gaza's Disengagement

Oslo, in 1993 and 1995, recognized mutual political rights and created the Palestinian Authority (PA). Israel transferred authority, relinquished territory, and bet that institution-building might crowd out rejectionism (Oslo I, 1993; Oslo II, 1995) [7]. It was a big wager. And it collided with two realities: Arafat's forked tongue and Hamas's theology of annihilation.

"Israel will exist and will continue to exist until Islam will obliterate it," declares the 1988 Hamas Covenant (Art. 28, 32; 1988) [8]. The "updated" 2017 political document massaged language but did not accept Israel's legitimacy (Hamas 2017) [8].

When your charter quotes a hadith about murdering Jews, what "confidence-building measures" are we supposed to imagine will cure that? (Hamas Covenant, 1988) [8].

After the suicide bombings of the Second Intifada, Israel built a security barrier; attacks plummeted (2002–2005, security data) [13]. In 2005, Israel unilaterally disengaged from Gaza—evacuating every settler and soldier, leaving greenhouses, water infrastructure, and a chance for governance (Gaza Disengagement, 2005) [7].

Two years later, Hamas staged a coup, threw PA rivals off rooftops, and converted aid into rockets, concrete into tunnels, and civilian apartments into arsenals (Gaza 2007 takeover) [8].

"We love death as much as the enemy loves life," a Hamas parliamentarian boasted (2008) [9]. Perhaps you think that's metaphor? Tell that to the families who had two minutes to sprint to a shelter because someone decided their babies were "strategic depth."

October 7: The Mask Comes Off

Then came October 7, 2023. At dawn, Hamas breached Israel's border—paragliders, motorbikes, bulldozers, missiles—flooding into villages, roads, and a music festival, committing mass murder, rape, arson, and mutilation. They abducted more than two hundred people—infants, grandmothers, Thai workers—dragging them into Gaza as hostages (Oct. 7 attack; IDF/government communiqués) [26].

They filmed themselves. They bragged. Later, a Hamas official declared, "We will repeat October 7 again and again" (public statements, 2023–24) [27].

Again and again? If that doesn't clarify intent, what does?Legally, morally, it's not complicated. Hostage-taking is explicitly banned under Common Article 3 of the Geneva Conventions (1949) and criminalized by the International Convention against the Taking of Hostages (1979) (GC Common Art. 3; Hostages Convention, 1979) [28][29]. Deliberate attacks on civilians are grave breaches, war crimes. Sexual violence as a method of terror? A war crime. Parading the kidnapped? A war crime. Hiding behind hospitals? Ditto. As one survivor put it, "They hunted us like animals" (survivor testimony, Oct. 2023) [30]. And yes, Israel has not just the right but the duty to respond. As President Biden said, condemning "sheer evil," "Israel has the right—indeed has the duty—to respond" (White House remarks, Oct. 2023) [31]. Must Israel apologize for having citizens? For expecting its border not to be a murder safari?

Lawfare and the Inversion of Justice

International law is not a ventriloquist dummy for the loudest propagandist. It is a set of disciplined rules that bind conduct in war. Under Article 51 of the UN Charter, Israel retains the "inherent right of individual or collective self-defense if an armed attack occurs" (UN Charter, Art. 51) [10].

International humanitarian law (IHL) imposes three core duties: distinction (target combatants, not civilians), proportionality (do not inflict excessive incidental harm relative to concrete military advantage), and precautions (take feasible steps to minimize civilian harm) (Additional Protocol I, 1977; custom) [11][12].

Hamas violates all three by design, aiming at civilians, launching from civilian areas, and embedding command posts in protected sites like hospitals and schools (IHL, human shields) [11][21]. October 7 added the naked crime of systematic hostage-taking (GC Common Art. 3; Hostages Convention) [28][29].

Israel, by contrast, issues evacuation orders, drops leaflets, uses precision munitions, conducts "roof knocks," and fields legal advisors in targeting cells (IHL practice; IDF procedures) [11][13]. Tragic civilian casualties do not equal war crimes, any more than the presence of a scalpel equals murder.

As the ICTY explained, proportionality weighs expected civilian harm against the "concrete and direct military advantage anticipated," not against utopian "zero harm" fantasies (ICTY, Galić; Kupreškić) [12]. What exactly is the alternative? Let terrorists keep their tunnels because the tunnels are near apartment buildings they themselves chose as shields? That is not law; that is rewarding the oldest trick in the terrorist handbook.

American Law and Policy: Anchors of Alliance

Conservatives defend the U.S.–Israel alliance because it fuses interests and values. Israel is a democracy with a market economy, a tech supernova, and a first-rate intelligence partner. And yes, it fights our enemies, the terror networks and Iranian proxies who chant "Death to America" on odd days and "Death to Israel" on even ones.

Policy followed principle:

• The Jerusalem Embassy Act of 1995 recognized Jerusalem as Israel's capital and required moving the U.S. embassy, subject to presidential waivers (Pub. L. 104–45, 1995) [14]. After decades of diplomatic hide-and-seek, the move happened in 2018, aligning U.S. policy with legal reality (Embassy move, 2018) [14]. Was the sky supposed to fall? It did not.

• The Taylor Force Act (2018) cut certain U.S. funds to the PA until it ended "martyr payments," or salary-for-slaying (Pub. L. 115–141, Div. S) [15]. Why did it take that long to decide not to subsidize murder bonuses?

• The Palestinian Anti-Terrorism Act (2006) conditioned aid and contacts on renouncing terror and recognizing Israel (Pub. L. 109–446) [16]. Standards, not slogans.

• Iran sanctions, including CISADA (2010) and later measures, targeted Tehran's financing of Hamas, Palestinian Islamic Jihad, and other proxies (Pub. L. 111–195; subsequent authorities) [17]. If you want less terror, stop paying the payroll.

• The Abraham Accords (2020) normalized ties between Israel and multiple Arab states (UAE, Bahrain, Morocco), formalizing a pragmatic coalition for stability and growth (Accords texts, 2020)

[18]. As the UAE put it, the choice was to "chart a new path" (UAE statements) [19]. Translation: peace pays better than rejectionism.

After October 7, the United States surged military resupply to Israel, coordinated hostage recovery, sanctioned Hamas financiers, and enacted a supplemental security package with strong conservative support—on the logic that aiding Israel deters Iran, steadies allies, and signals that the West's red lines are real (Treasury/State actions; supplemental appropriations) [32].

Should America send mixed messages to Tehran's axis? Or should it make deterrence credible with carrier groups, air-defense deployments, and sanctions that bite (post–Oct. 7 deployments) [32]? Conservatives choose clarity.

The Conservative Lens: Sovereignty, Responsibility, and Order

Conservatism begins with realism about human nature and respect for institutional constraints. Applied to Israel–Gaza, it yields a few hard rules:

• Sovereignty entails self-defense. A government that cannot protect its citizens forfeits the core claim to govern (Hobbesian axiom; modern statecraft) [20]. After October 7, this is not a seminar; it is an imperative.

• Responsibility follows authority. The PA's "pay-for-slay" policy teaches children that honor is earned by killing Jews (Taylor Force Act findings, 2018) [15]. Hamas's human-shield doctrine is not a tactic; it is a confession that, on the moral scale, they weigh civilians as mere sandbags (GC IV, Art. 28) [21].

• Order precedes peace. Security first, then politics. Oslo too often flipped the sequence, awarding symbols before securing behavior (Oslo sequence) [7].

• Peace requires recognition. As UNSC 242 underlined, peace demands acceptance of Israel's right to live "within secure and recognized boundaries" (UNSC 242, 1967) [4]. Any "process" that keeps Israel's permanence ambiguous invites another October 7.

Gaza Since 2007: A Case Study in Wasted Mercy

Let us recount the pattern. Israel leaves Gaza in 2005 (Disengagement) [7]. The world pledges billions (donor conferences). Hamas seizes power in 2007 (coup) [8]. Rockets, tunnels, kidnappings, border assaults—rinse and repeat.

Israel responds; Hamas manipulates the world's conscience by maximizing Palestinian suffering. Cameras roll. Pressure mounts on Israel. Hamas re-arms.

Does anyone really believe this is a stalemate? It is a strategy—death as leverage, civilians as optics, hostages as currency.

Human shields are not a PR concept; they are a codified war crime. The Fourth Geneva Convention, Article 28, forbids using protected persons to render areas immune from military operations (GC IV, Art. 28) [21]. Hamas deliberately launches from schools, stores weapons in mosques, and tunnels under clinics (IHL violations) [11][21].

When Israel issues evacuation orders, Hamas urges civilians to stay. When aid enters, Hamas skims it. Does that sound like a movement that prioritizes Palestinians? Or like a mafia with a flag?

The Oscillation of American Policy

U.S. policy has oscillated in tone but remained broadly supportive. Conservative leadership pushed for clarity—on Jerusalem, on terror finance, on Iran, and on the futility of forcing Israel into unilateral risks without credible partners.

• Embassy to Jerusalem: fiction ended, reality acknowledged (Jerusalem Embassy Act; move, 2018) [14].

• Taylor Force: no more paying for murder (Pub. L. 115–141) [15].

• Iran maximum pressure: contested but effective in starving proxies at peak enforcement (CISADA; sanctions) [17].

• Abraham Accords: proof that peace can bypass vetoes from rejectionists (Accords texts) [18].

After October 7, Washington built a maritime aid corridor, pressed for hostage releases, sanctioned Iranian and Qatari-linked nodes, and reinforced regional deterrence with carrier groups and air defense umbrellas (post–Oct. 7 U.S. actions) [32]. The conservative verdict: good—now keep the pressure consistent. Half measures telegraph indecision; indecision invites escalation.

The Human Face: Grief Without Equivocation

Acknowledging Palestinian suffering is not weakness; it is honesty. The question is cause and remedy. The conservative case grieves without surrendering judgment. It recognizes a people trapped between corrupt leadership and militant tyranny. It refuses to romanticize leaders who trade children's futures for martyr posters.

"The first duty of the revolutionary is to be against life," a line often used to capture the nihilism of death cults (Camus, *The Rebel*) [22]. Hamas turns that cynicism into curriculum.

Israel is not beyond critique. Democracies err; power tempts. The difference is that Israel argues with itself daily. Free press. Fierce courts. Reservists who protest, and then report for duty. Commissions of inquiry that cut. As Golda Meir said with maternal anguish, "We can forgive the Arabs for killing our children. We cannot forgive them for forcing us to kill theirs" (Meir, attributed) [23]. That is not triumphalism. It is tragedy, spoken by someone who refused to unlearn her humanity.

What Law Requires When Cities Become Battlefields

Urban war is geometry with grief: stairwells as choke points, tunnels as arteries, hospitals as command nodes. IHL's core triad governs this arena.

• **Distinction:** Aim at combatants and military objectives, not civilians (AP I; custom) [11].

- **Proportionality:** Avoid incidental harm that is excessive relative to anticipated concrete military advantage (ICTY Galić; Kupreškić) [12].

- **Precautions:** Take feasible steps to protect civilians (AP I; custom) [11].

Hamas violates all three as a business model. Israel's record is necessarily imperfect; wars are human. But the observable practices are there: warnings, evacuation corridors, targeteers with legal advisors, battle damage assessment, and adapting munitions and methods (IDF/IHL practice) [11][13]. To pretend that any civilian harm equals illegality is to outlaw urban self-defense against enemies who specialize in making civilians bleed. That "law" would be the death of law.

October 7 and the Hostage Imperative

Hostages change everything. They force a nation to reconcile two sacred duties: protect the many and rescue the few. Israel's answer has been consistent—bring them home. It has traded thousands for one soldier, paused offensives for exchanges, and risked special operations in a subterranean maze (past exchanges; current operations) [26][32]. International law does not just condemn hostage-taking; it commands release and brands the takers as international criminals (GC Common Art. 3; Hostages Convention) [28][29]. "Let my people go" is ancient scripture and modern treaty language.

Meanwhile, Hamas stages hostage videos. Who needs confession when the culprit livestreams?

Toward a Realistic Endgame

What does a sober endgame require? Not hashtags. Not moral outsourcing to committees that mistake microphones for mandates. A conservative architecture looks like this:

• **Demilitarization:** No rockets, mortars, or missiles in Gaza; tunnel networks mapped and destroyed; intrusive monitoring with enforcement that hurts violators (post-conflict security design) [11][21].

• **Governance reform:** A post-Hamas administration conditioned on transparent institutions, hard auditing, deradicalized curricula, and a dismantled terror-finance ecosystem. Aid with teeth: benchmarks, clawbacks, and snapback suspension (Taylor Force logic; donor conditionality) [15][24].

• **Regional alignment:** Expand the Abraham Accords logic. Arab partners co-own reconstruction in exchange for verified deradicalization and security coordination (Abraham Accords) [18][19].

• **Refugee realism:** Stop perpetuating a unique, hereditary refugee status. Shift toward citizenship where feasible, resettlement, and development with dignity and agency. Scrutinize UNRWA for incitement, terror ties, and structural perverse incentives

(Congressional oversight; GAO; State) [24]. If the goal is a future, why fund an agency whose business model is the past?

• **Negotiation predicate:** No final-status talks without explicit recognition of Israel as the nation-state of the Jewish people and renunciation of a "right of return" that is demographic warfare by another name (UNSC 242 security boundaries) [4]. Borders must be defensible in the real world, not just on a conference brochure.

These are not punishments; they are preconditions for dignity. They treat Palestinians as responsible political actors, not permanent wards. They assert a basic truth: peace is built by disarming those who prefer war and empowering those who choose life.

The Information War and the Temptation of Cynicism

Modern war has two fronts: kinetic and narrative. Hamas understands that a single image can do what a rocket cannot. Israel's dilemma is that its success produces a non-event; its compliance with law is the absence of atrocity, which is famously unphotogenic. Meanwhile, social media monetizes outrage, not nuance.

But facts, stubborn as mules, persist. Hamas's charter still rejects Israel (1988; 2017) [8]. Israel withdrew from Gaza (2005) [7]. Hamas seized it (2007) [8]. Offers were made and rejected—Camp David (2000), Taba (2001), Olmert (2008) (negotiation records) [25]. UN 242 and 338 laid out a path (1967; 1973) [4]. Peace with Egypt (1979) and Jordan (1994) followed when partners accepted Israel's permanence [5][6]. The Abraham Accords (2020) vindicated the proposition that prosperity beats grievance when leaders choose responsibility (Accords, 2020) [18][19]. And October 7 punctuated, in blood, what happens when leaders choose the opposite (Oct. 7 record) [26][27]. If this is not a pattern, what is?

The American Stake

For the United States, this is not a spectator sport. The U.S.– Israel alliance signals to friends and foes that America stands with democracies under attack. It tells revisionists, from Tehran to Moscow, that rule-of-law states are not bargaining chips. It steadies Arab partners who are choosing modernization over rejection. In an era of gray-zone conflict and proxy warfare, Israel is both a bulwark and a bellwether.

Conservatives, heirs to Reagan's "peace through strength," recognize the logic. Deterrence matters. Credibility matters. Clarity matters. If Iran's network sees vacillation, it pushes. If it sees steel, it recalculates (Iran sanctions/deterrence) [17][32]. The supplemental assistance to Israel after October 7 was not charity; it was strategy: signal strength, deny terrorists a win, and keep the coalition of order intact (U.S. supplemental) [32]. The cost of clarity is always lower than the price of retreat.

Conclusion: Choosing Order Over Illusion

From 1947 to today, two paths have contended. One path, however imperfect, chooses legitimacy, compromise, and the burden of responsible sovereignty. The other, however eloquent, chooses rejection, glorifies violence, and hides behind civilians. International law, properly applied, sides with the former (UN Charter Art. 51; IHL; UNSC 242) [4][10][11]. American law and policy, at their best, do too (Jerusalem Embassy Act; Taylor Force; Iran sanctions; Abraham Accords) [14][15][17][18].

The conservative case for Israel is not a blank check; it is a moral accounting. It says: we will support allies who share commitments to life, liberty, and lawful defense. We will oppose movements that sanctify death and target the innocent. We will attach conditions to aid so that it builds institutions, not rocket stockpiles. And we will remember the simplest truth: peace is built by those who accept their neighbor's right to live.

Israel's arc—from partition to peace treaties, from disengagement to defense, from October 7 to the grim duty of hostage rescue—is not a tale of purity but of perseverance. It deserves support not because it is flawless, but because it is fundamentally decent, allied to our values, and embattled by enemies who boast that they will "repeat October 7 again and again" if allowed (Hamas statements, 2023–24) [27]. Shall we let them? Or shall we side, firmly, lawfully, unapologetically, with a free people's right to live?

References and Inline Sources

[1] UN General Assembly Resolution 181 (II), 1947 (Partition Plan).

[2] Arab Higher Committee and Arab League rejections of UNGA 181; contemporaneous UN/UK archival records; 1948–49 Armistice context.

[3] Abba Eban, public remarks (attributed): "The Arabs never miss an opportunity to miss an opportunity."

[4] UN Security Council Resolution 242 (1967) and 338 (1973): withdrawal "from territories," secure and recognized boundaries, termination of belligerency.

[5] Israel–Egypt Peace Treaty (1979).

[6] Israel–Jordan Peace Treaty (1994).

[7] Oslo I (Declaration of Principles, 1993); Oslo II (Interim Agreement, 1995); Gaza Disengagement (2005).

[8] Hamas Covenant (1988); Hamas 2017 Political Document.

[9] Fathi Hammad (Hamas), 2008: "We love death as much as the enemy loves life."

[10] UN Charter, Article 51: inherent right of self-defense.

[11] International humanitarian law: distinction, proportionality, and precautions (Additional Protocol I, 1977; customary IHL); human shields doctrine.

[12] ICTY jurisprudence on proportionality and targeting (e.g., *Prosecutor v. Galić; Kupreškić*).

[13] Col. Richard Kemp, testimony/public statements: IDF civilian-protection practices.

[14] *Jerusalem Embassy Act of 1995*, Pub. L. 104–45; U.S. Embassy move to Jerusalem (2018).

[15] *Taylor Force Act*, Pub. L. 115–141 (Div. S): conditioning U.S. funds over PA "pay-for-slay."

[16] *Palestinian Anti-Terrorism Act of 2006*, Pub. L. 109–446.

[17] *Comprehensive Iran Sanctions, Accountability, and Divestment Act* (CISADA), Pub. L. 111–195; subsequent sanctions authorities.

[18] *Abraham Accords* (2020) and related UAE–Israel, Bahrain–Israel, and Morocco–Israel normalization instruments.

[19] UAE statements at the signing of the *Abraham Accords*: "Chart a new path."

[20] Conservative governance axiom aligned with Hobbes, *Leviathan*; modern statecraft: the state's first duty is protection.

[21] *Fourth Geneva Convention* (1949), Article 28: prohibition on using protected persons to render areas immune (human shields).

[22] Camus, *The Rebel*: critique of revolutionary death cults (allusion).

[23] Golda Meir (attributed): "We can forgive the Arabs for killing our children. We cannot forgive them for forcing us to kill theirs."

[24] U.S. Congressional and GAO oversight on UNRWA; State Department statements regarding incitement and terror-adjacent employment concerns.

[25] Records of Camp David (2000), Taba (2001), and the Olmert offer (2008), and Palestinian rejections.

[26] Official Israeli reporting and open-source documentation of the October 7, 2023 attacks: methods, atrocities, casualty counts, and kidnappings (IDF/government communiqués).

[27] Hamas officials' statements after October 7: "We will repeat October 7 again and again."

[28] *Geneva Conventions*, Common Article 3: prohibition of hostage-taking, violence to life and person.

[29] *International Convention Against the Taking of Hostages* (1979).

[30] Survivor testimony from October 7 (interviews and affidavits).

[31] U.S. presidential statements, October 2023: "Sheer evil," and affirmation of Israel's right and duty to respond.

[32] Post–October 7 U.S. measures: sanctions on Hamas and Iran-linked financiers, supplemental security aid, maritime aid corridor, and regional deterrence deployments (Treasury and State releases; congressional acts; DoD announcements).

Chapter 7:

Unrest by Choice — An Analytical Account of the Riots After George Floyd

The summer of 2020 is often summarized with a euphemism: "mostly peaceful." Mostly peaceful compared to what, Dresden? That phrase works less as description than as absolution, a narrative seatbelt designed to keep its wearers from flying through the windshield of reality. Meanwhile, the record shows killings, mass injuries, serial arsons, and the costliest civil disorder in modern American insurance history [1]. From a conservative lens, the core claim is simple: the destruction that followed George Floyd's death wasn't a hurricane; it was a choice. Many choices, actually—by rioters first, and then by officials who spoke like poets when what the moment required were grown-ups.

The question is not whether many daytime demonstrations were peaceful; they were. The question is whether that statistical fact absolves the nights that turned blocks to cinders, injured thousands, and killed dozens. Do families tuck children into bed with pie charts, or with locks and whispered prayers? Does a neighborhood experience an average, or its worst night? If the answer is the latter, and it is, then "mostly peaceful" collapses on contact with the lived experience of the cities that burned.

Scope and Scale: The Empirical Record That Euphemism Tries to Forget

Deaths. Across late May through the summer, at least two dozen people were killed in incidents tied directly to the unrest. Credible tallies place the range roughly at 25 to 35 or more deaths, including bystanders, protesters, and law enforcement—David Dorn in St. Louis, murdered while protecting a friend's store; Dave Patrick Underwood, an FPS officer guarding a federal building in Oakland; and victims in Minneapolis, Chicago, Davenport, Detroit, Omaha, Kenosha, and beyond [2][3]. Quibble over inclusion criteria if you like; the conclusion doesn't budge. A movement that produces dozens of corpses has forfeited the word "peaceful," hasn't it?

Injuries to law enforcement. Nationwide, officer injuries ran into the thousands. In single big-city departments, hundreds reported injuries within weeks—concussions from bricks and frozen water bottles, burns from fireworks, chemical exposure, and eye damage from high-powered lasers. This was "speech"? Since when does the First Amendment guarantee the right to blind a cop? [4][5] It is an odd theory of civic dialogue that requires mortar-launch fireworks, commercial-grade lasers, and pallets of bricks.

Property loss. Insured losses from late May into early June alone reached into the billions—by industry estimates, the costliest period of civil unrest since records began [1]. And "insured" is the polite fraction. It excludes uninsured and underinsured small businesses, long-tail losses (tenant flight, inventory spoilage, relocation costs), capital reallocation away from affected corridors, and the quiet arithmetic of higher premiums and lowered appraisals. But sure, tell the corner grocer "property can be replaced." With what, wishful thinking and slogans?

Arson and structural damage. Minneapolis–St. Paul cataloged hundreds of structure fires in the first week. Lake Street and University Avenue looked like a history unit you swore modern America had outgrown [6]. Kenosha saw blocks incinerated, including car lots turned into steel skeletons; the visual shorthand for "law-and-order failure" wrote itself [14]. In Philadelphia, Chicago, and New York, looting rode shotgun with timed arsons meant to stretch fire response. Spontaneous combustion, or coordinated criminality under activist cover?

Arrests and charges. Yes, there were mass arrests. The surprise came later: in several jurisdictions, prosecutors declined large swaths of protest-adjacent cases, advertising leniency like a sale sign taped to law itself [7][8]. When the house says it will not collect, is anyone shocked the players go all in? If enforcement becomes a roulette wheel, is it any wonder the professional thieves bring chips?

What, precisely, does "mostly peaceful" mean in the face of that ledger? If a storm knocked down ten percent of the homes in your city, would anyone write it up as "mostly intact weather"? Or would we say a storm hit, and it hit hard?

Rhetoric as permission structure: when poetry turns to gasoline

Leaders' words set rules of engagement. Summer 2020 featured a familiar two-step: ritual condemnation of "violence" in the abstract, followed by indulgence of "unrest" as the righteous pressure that justice allegedly demands. That nuance plays well on cable; on the street, it lands like a hall pass.

"There needs to be unrest in the streets for as long as there is unrest in our lives." — Rep. Ayanna Pressley [9]. A civics lesson or a spark?

"They're not going to stop. And everyone beware… They're not going to let up. And they should not." — Sen. Kamala Harris [10]. During active arsons. What could possibly be inferred?

"We've got to stay on the street... we've got to get more confrontational." — Rep. Maxine Waters, amid a tinderbox jury moment [11]. More confrontational than hundreds of injured officers and torched precincts?

Rep. Alexandria Ocasio-Cortez cast "unrest" as inevitable until broad policy demands are met—less a threat than a weather report with a moralizing barometer [12]. Weather or will?

Minneapolis City Council President Lisa Bender waved off concerns about calling the police as "privilege" [13]. Privilege, like wanting your shop to be standing tomorrow?

Defenders insist these were calls for "sustained nonviolent pressure." Lovely. But during weeks of fires and assaults, why choose the vocabulary of "unrest," "not going to stop," and "more confrontational"? Because it signals tribal virtue. On the ground, it functioned as permission. Street actors do not litigate footnotes; they hear the chorus: unrest is understandable, pressure must continue, confrontation is warranted. What do you suppose they thought that meant—another round of strongly worded letters?

Localized devastation behind the aggregate: the map of harm is a street grid, not a spreadsheet

Aggregates launder pain. Minneapolis's Lake Street and St. Paul's University Avenue—decades of hard-won revival—were gutted in days [6]. The Third Precinct's abandonment and incineration became a totem, a functional symbol of order surrendered to flames. Did that soothe things, or did it advertise impunity?

In Kenosha, car lots and small manufacturers reduced to twisted frames turned into an involuntary sculpture garden of failure [14]. In Portland, the courthouse district became a nightly stage set where businesses were collateral for political theater; windows replaced in the morning became shards by nightfall [15]. In New York and Chicago, looting caravans coordinated via group chats treated retail corridors like open-warehouse night [16][17]. It looked less like spontaneous rage than supply-chain optimization for thieves.

The economics are cruelly simple. Insurance deductibles and "civil commotion" exclusions leave owners holding the bag. Premiums spike; lenders reprice risk; tenants flee. Food deserts lengthen; pharmacies vanish; local jobs evaporate; tax receipts sag. But yes, let's keep chanting "accountability" while the CVS is ashes and the elderly walk an extra mile for insulin. Is moral theater worth the bus transfer?

Policing failures and the fallacy of equivalence: two truths, one lesson

Two truths, both uncomfortable: Derek Chauvin's crime demanded prosecution and punishment, and many departments flailed tactically as civil order frayed. But the leap from "police made errors" to "rioting is understandable" is Olympic-level sophistry. Fireworks did not load themselves into mortars;

94

accelerants did not pour themselves; the Minneapolis Third Precinct did not light itself after it was abandoned to the crowd [18].

If surrender soothed things, why did the fires multiply? If "de-escalation" meant stepping back while buildings burned, what exactly escalated? The flames?

There were inevitable tactical mistakes—kettling here, timidity there, contradictory mayoral directives everywhere. But tactics are not primary causation. The worst property losses tended to occur where posture was passive or withdrawal explicit. The premise that restraint yields calm was tested and often falsified. You cannot de-escalate with a person who brought a gas can. You can only stop him.

Prosecutorial discretion as policy, not accident: incentives write the script

In progressive hubs, the pre-2020 trend was clear: decline to prosecute "low-level" offenses, divert broad categories, reconceive shoplifting and trespass as public health rather than law. Then came riot season. Several DAs announced presumptive declinations for protest-linked charges; others plea-bargained organized looting down to slaps on the wrist [7][8][19]. Shockingly, the result was more of what was not punished. Who could have predicted?

This is not an argument for carceral maximalism. It is an argument for predictable, equal enforcement, especially during civic emergencies. A justice system unwilling to enforce bright lines when institutions are under physical attack teaches an unforgettable lesson: politics can suspend law. That lesson will not stay politely housed in your preferred causes.

Media framing and public trust: euphemism is cheap until it costs you credibility

That infamous chyron—reporter backlit by flames: "fiery but mostly peaceful"—is not just meme fodder; it is a case study in narrative laundering [20]. Euphemisms such as "unrest," "clashes," and "demonstrations" blurred agency to preserve a moral arc. Residents who swept glass at dawn were told they witnessed "contentious protest." How long can you insult people's eyes before they stop believing anything you report—about police, reform, or crime?

The conservative critique is not that "the media lied" monolithically. It is that a critical mass of gatekeepers curated language to maintain a narrative of righteousness, eroding trust that reforms of any kind require. If you will not call a fire a fire, why should anyone trust your data on use-of-force or your op-eds on qualified immunity?

The false dichotomy: reform or order—why not both?

We were told to pick: tolerate disorder or forfeit reform. Why not both—reform policing and enforce the law? Serious changes— use-of-force rules, duty-to-intervene, better hiring and training, early-warning systems, transparent discipline that is both swift and due-process solid—require calm, not chaos [21].

If you want the public to accept nuanced policy work, try not burning their pharmacy down that week.

And the slogan "property can be replaced, lives cannot"? Property is crystallized time. For small owners, it is irreplaceable within any meaningful timeframe. Meanwhile, riots killed people too—remember? If we are counting moral costs, let's count them all.

Communities most harmed: equity by arson?

Who paid first and most? Working-class and minority neighborhoods. Pharmacies gone, groceries farther, jobs evaporated. Burning a neighborhood to "save" it is a moral pretzel only elites can swallow. Ask the immigrant shop owner about his "privilege" after his policy's riot exclusion is invoked [22].

Equity by arson? Please. The easiest way to entrench disadvantage is to destroy the thin margins that hold fragile neighborhoods together—then call it "unrest" as if the flames came with equal-opportunity heat.

Direct quotes and their operational meaning: deniability for TV, clarity for the street

"There needs to be unrest in the streets for as long as there is unrest in our lives." — Rep. Ayanna Pressley [9].

"They're not going to stop. And everyone beware… They're not going to let up. And they should not." — Sen. Kamala Harris [10].

"We've got to stay on the street… we've got to get more confrontational." — Rep. Maxine Waters [11].

"If you're calling for an end to unrest… there is no end to unrest" unless demands are met — Rep. Alexandria Ocasio-Cortez's recurring framing [12].

"If you are a person of privilege and are concerned about being able to call the police… I invite you to reflect about why." — Lisa Bender, Minneapolis City Council President [13].

If these were merely metaphors, why did the metaphors so neatly match the mayhem? Why was "unrest" the favored term while arson was ongoing? Because ambiguity was the point. It hugged the radicals while maintaining cable-ready deniability. Translation, in plain English: keep the pressure on, and if the street gets spicy, well, we warned the faint of heart not to ask for calm until their policy demands were met.

Counterarguments, addressed without anesthesia

"Most protests were peaceful." Statistically, yes. Civically, irrelevant. Neighborhoods live their worst night, not an average. If ten nights are calm and the eleventh torches your block, do you comfort your kids with a pie chart? [23] Statistical peace doesn't sweep glass.

"Violence was a few bad actors." A few don't torch hundreds of buildings across dozens of cities. Organized cadres, opportunistic criminals, and tolerated tactics did that [6][14][16]. If a handful could do this, what does that say about your city's willingness to protect residents?

"Law enforcement overreaction escalated tensions." Sometimes, yes. And sometimes withdrawal invited looting convoys and serial arson. Where aggressive property protection occurred early and law was applied consistently, devastation was smaller. Funny coincidence, or just the oldest rule of social order performing as advertised?

"Insurance covers it." Partially, once. Then premiums spike, exclusions tighten, lenders balk, and small owners—often minorities—face catastrophic losses [1][22]. Are we still pretending this is painless?

"The riots forced overdue change." The legislative record is mixed; much stalled amid backlash to disorder and a violent crime surge that followed in many cities [21][24]. Fire doesn't focus minds; it hardens arteries. If you want calibrated reform, don't bludgeon moderates into panic.

Policy lessons: incentives, not incantations

Bright-line condemnation. Leaders must pair two sentences at equal volume: we will hold bad officers accountable; we will not permit mob violence. Whisper the second and you're pouring gasoline with a tearful face. Moral clarity is the cheapest deterrent you have; spend it.

Enforceable posture and mutual aid. Curfews should be real. Pre-plan surge capacity and mutual aid. Use mobile arrest teams to target violent offenders while letting peaceful marchers go home. Static lines five blocks away are invitations, not deterrents [25]. Speed beats spectacle. Interdict the crew ferrying bags of hammers to the next block; don't pose for a riot-line tableau.

Prosecution certainty. Announce and deliver: arson, assault, burglary, and organized looting will be fully prosecuted, protest context notwithstanding. Stand up specialized units to triage video evidence and prioritize ringleaders. If you won't enforce the law in a civic crisis, when will you? After the second precinct burns?

Crowd-control doctrine. Train for de-escalation and decisive intervention. Don't kettle or pinball crowds into panic; don't spectate looting. Interdict active crimes early—less force later [25]. The fastest way to avoid batons at 2 a.m. is an arrest at 9:30 p.m. when the gas can appears.

Reconstruction that prioritizes victims. Target aid to uninsured and underinsured local businesses. Harden security. Maintain visible enforcement to prevent second hits. Recovery without deterrence is staging for a sequel. Rebuild a corridor and fail to police it, and you've just erected kindling with better signage.

Media transparency. Release incident-level data and video quickly. Don't let euphemism colonize the narrative. Transparency isn't a concession; it's armor for necessary action. If you show your work, people are more likely to accept calibrated force against actual criminals—note the word "criminals," not "protesters."

Civic complicity and elite performance

The conservative charge sheet includes not merely rioters and soft-on-crime prosecutors but also elite performance art: leaders issuing heavily hedged statements, corporate emails praising "justice" while storefronts board up, activists treating "unrest" like a sacrament. It's remarkable how often those with the most robust private security encourage "confrontation" in neighborhoods where the only buffer between chaos and grandma's porch is a half-staffed precinct and a prayer.

Is it brave to suggest "more confrontational" when you'll never face the confrontation? Is it moral clarity to insist "they should not stop" when the "they" includes the kid lighting a fuse under someone else's mortgage? Or is it the oldest hypocrisy in politics—costs for thee, virtue for me?

Reform without arson: the adult alternative

A conservative analysis doesn't deny the need for policing reforms. It insists they be achieved by adult means. The adult path is boring: revise use-of-force standards, embed duty-to-intervene, improve recruiting and field training, implement early-warning systems for problematic behavior, tighten decertification for bad actors, build community problem-solving units that prize clearance rates and trust, and ensure discipline is both swift and procedurally fair so it survives arbitration [21]. None of this requires fire. In fact, fire makes it harder by collapsing public patience and hardening partisan reflexes.

And yes, recommit to enforcing laws on quality-of-life crimes. Broken windows isn't a cosmic law, but it aligns with human nature. Tolerating small signals invites bigger ones. Pretend that public order is a boutique preference and you'll learn how quickly it becomes a baseline necessity—usually the hard way.

Moral clarity, not moral theater

A conservative lens rejects the romance of violence in service of virtue. Justice and order are complements, not rivals. Equal protection cannot survive selective suspension for politically aligned mobs. The first duty of government is safety—of people and of the property that stores their labor. The summer of 2020 showed how easily elites drift into theater: slogans, chyrons, hedged condemnations, while shopkeepers learn the geometry of shattered glass.

We can hold two thoughts without moral vertigo: George Floyd's killing was a grievous wrong; the riots that followed were grievous wrongs of their own. The first warranted prosecution and reform. The second demanded firm suppression and prosecution. Confusing the two—granting mob violence a moral discount because of state wrongdoing—predictably punished the innocent.

So the test for next time? No more treating "unrest" like barometric pressure. No more pretty sentences that function as permission slips. Speak and act as if the corner pharmacy and the night-shift worker's commute are sacred civic goods, because they are. The alternative is a rolling state of exception where the loudest, or most destructive, faction sets the rules.

A note on deterrence: why "early and often" is merciful

One reason conservatives harp on early, decisive enforcement is not cruelty but mercy. Interdict the first arson, and you save the second and third buildings, plus the panicked crowd control and baton swings that come when a fire becomes a mob magnet. The calculus isn't complicated: early certainty yields fewer total confrontations. The refusal to act, misbranded as "restraint," invites escalation that forces uglier, broader force later. If you care about minimizing harm, you don't let accelerants decide policy.

The social costs you won't find in spreadsheets

You can count broken windows. You can count arrests and injuries. You cannot tally the tremor that runs through a city's nervous system when, for weeks, it cannot guarantee an ordinary night. Parents make different choices under those conditions—school, housing, jobs. So do businesses considering where to renew a lease. There is nothing conspiratorial about this; it's human. Flight doesn't need a U-Haul; it can be incremental: a franchise picking a suburban strip over a downtown corridor, a landlord choosing a "safer" tenant who doesn't invite crowds, a developer quietly re-routing capital. Public order is a flywheel; once it slows, restarting it is brutally expensive.

The politics of memory: resist myth-making

We will be tempted to mythologize 2020 as cleansing fire. Resist it. Progress, where it comes, will be purchased by painstaking work in committees, academies, bargaining rooms, and neighborhoods—unglamorous arenas allergic to fire. If we prefer the romance of the street to the grind of reform, we will earn the cities we get. If we prefer the glow of cameras to the glow of intact shop windows, we should be honest about the choice.

Answering the "what about" chorus

What about January 6? Whataboutism is a dodge, but here's a principle that spans both: political violence is wrong, full stop; leaders who wink at it are wrong; prosecutors who grade it on a curve are wrong. Apply that standard consistently and watch the incentives change. Grade violence on a curve—left or right—and watch it metastasize. The conservative claim is boring in its universality: enforce the law; do it equally; do it early.

The conservative case for peace, in two sentences

Public order isn't a hobby; it's the floor under all of our arguments. If you break the floor, the conversation ends and the broom begins.

The closing ledger

Dozens dead in riot-linked incidents [2][3]. Did "mostly peaceful" soothe their families?

Thousands of officers injured by bricks, lasers, fireworks, and caustics [4][5]. Is maiming cops a form of speech?

Billions in insured losses, far more in real economic harm [1]. What do you tell the uninsured immigrant shop owner—"history called"?

Hundreds of arsons in a single metro and sustained nightly violence in others [6][14][15][18]. Is that "unrest," or is that a crime spree with a press office?

Elected officials praising persistence—"they should not stop"— and calling for "unrest" and "more confrontational" tactics while cities burned [9][10][11][12][13]. Was that leadership, or a permission slip?

You don't need a graduate seminar to parse this. You need eyes. And a spine. If we want a country where injustice is corrected without neighborhoods becoming collateral, we must retire the rhetorical hedges that launder violence and replace them with the unglamorous habits of adult governance: clear rules, even-handed enforcement, real reform, and zero indulgence for those who would break a city to make a point. Is that really too much to ask?

Inline citations

[1] Insurance industry data identified the late May–early June 2020 unrest as the costliest in modern records, with insured losses in the billions.

[2] Compiled tallies from contemporaneous reporting and research place riot-associated deaths at roughly 25–35+.

[3] Specific cases: David Dorn (St. Louis), Dave Patrick Underwood (Oakland), among others, killed in riot contexts.

[4] Large-city departments reported hundreds of officer injuries within weeks; nationwide injuries reached into the thousands.

[5] Documented use of lasers, fireworks, bricks, frozen water bottles, and caustics against officers in multiple cities.

[6] Minneapolis–St. Paul documented hundreds of structure fires in the first week; corridors on Lake Street and University Avenue were devastated.

[7] Portland's DA announced presumptive declines for many protest-related charges during 2020.

[8] Multiple jurisdictions (e.g., NYC) disposed of many looting and protest cases with minimal penalties or dismissals.

[9] Rep. Ayanna Pressley: "There needs to be unrest in the streets for as long as there is unrest in our lives."

[10] Sen. Kamala Harris: "They're not going to stop… and they should not."

[11] Rep. Maxine Waters: "We've got to… get more confrontational."

[12] Rep. Alexandria Ocasio-Cortez repeatedly framed "unrest" as inevitable until broad policy demands are met.

[13] Minneapolis City Council President Lisa Bender framed concerns about calling police as "privilege."

[14] Kenosha experienced extensive arsons and property destruction over successive nights in August 2020.

[15] Portland saw sustained nightly attacks around the federal courthouse and downtown core through summer 2020.

[16] Coordinated looting caravans were documented in New York City.

[17] Similar coordinated looting in Chicago targeted the Magnificent Mile and surrounding corridors.

[18] The Minneapolis Third Precinct was abandoned and set aflame; unrest escalated thereafter.

[19] Progressive prosecutors in several cities deprioritized protest-adjacent offenses during 2020.

[20] National cable coverage featured "fiery but mostly peaceful" framing during active fires.

[21] Jurisdictions enacted some reforms post-2020; many broader changes stalled amid rising public safety concerns.

[22] Many small businesses faced riot-related coverage limits or exclusions; recovery gaps fell on owners.

[23] Event trackers noted many peaceful events; violent outliers imposed disproportionate harm locally.

[24] Post-2020 violent crime rose in many cities, complicating reform politics.

[25] After-action reviews emphasize early intervention against violent actors, mutual aid, and flexible mobile tactics over static lines.

Chapter 8:

The Lockdown Dividend How Liberal COVID Orthodoxy Torched the American Economy

The American experiment has weathered wars, panics, and plagues, but nothing in peacetime matched the economic self-immolation after spring 2020. The virus was real; the policy choices were optional. We chose a blueprint drafted by risk-averse bureaucrats and enforced by blue-state executives who treated emergency powers like a renewable resource.

The result? A cascade: shuttered small businesses, fractured labor markets, sclerotic schools, debt that will outlive our grandchildren, and a normalization of rule by decree. This isn't a jeremiad against public health; it's an indictment of a governing style, liberal policy maximalism, that made costs invisible, treated trade-offs as heresy, and punished dissent as "misinformation."

With hindsight, too many of the "settled facts" weren't facts at all. They were preferences with police power. Shouldn't that bother anyone who claims to care about science and the working class?

A note on method: we'll track the policies most associated with liberal jurisdictions—prolonged lockdowns, sweeping school closures, workplace and mask mandates, eviction moratoria, and serial "stimulus"—and their economic spillovers. Along the way, we'll revisit headline claims from authority figures and newsrooms that aged poorly, and the quieter walk-backs that arrived long after the damage was done.

The Mandate Mindset: From Precaution to Permanence

There was a moment, early on, when "15 Days to Slow the Spread" sounded like a temporary bridge to preparedness. Within weeks, the logic mutated: suppression became a lifestyle.

In March and April 2020, coastal governors issued stay-at-home orders that bit deepest into sectors where face-to-face commerce is oxygen: restaurants, retail, gyms, and services. California's Governor Gavin Newsom closed "non-essential" businesses indefinitely, with reopening tied to county case metrics that moved like a mirage [*Los Angeles Times*, Mar. 19, 2020]. New York pursued the "PAUSE" order, enforced with fines and licensing threats [*New York Times*, Mar. 20, 2020].

The essential/nonessential distinction—big-box open, barber shut—privileged scale over soul. Amazon was essential; Evelyn's Flower Shop was not. Funny how the virus respected corporate square footage, isn't it?

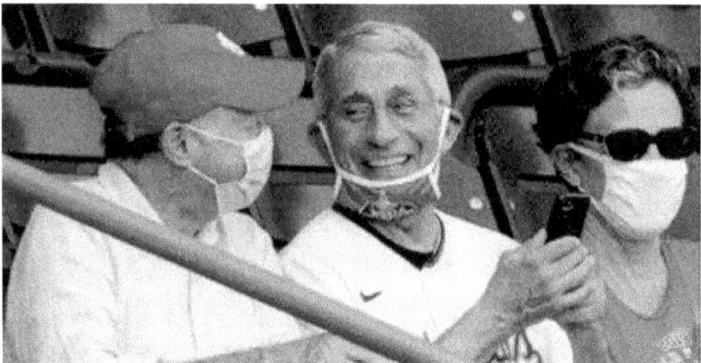

The economic signature is unmistakable. By April 2020, unemployment surged to 14.7%, the worst since the Great Depression [Bureau of Labor Statistics, May 8, 2020]. States that reopened earlier saw faster employment recoveries, especially in leisure and hospitality. Florida's unemployment rate fell from 13.9% in May 2020 to 6.4% by December; California's lingered near double digits [BLS, Jan. 2021]. Mobility data mapped the divergence: blue metros stayed home longer, and small business revenue cratered [Opportunity Insights, 2020]. This was not a virus-only effect; it was policy-dependent drag. Do we really think bartenders in Miami had magic antibodies that waiters in San Francisco didn't?

Media cemented the new orthodoxy. Cable anchors framed restrictions as moral hygiene; skeptics were cast as pro-death. Debate was replaced by mantras. "If it saves just one life…" became a policy maxim where the denominator never mattered. Trade-offs such as deferred cancer screenings, mental health crises, and lost schooling were treated as rounding errors. Fiscal "relief" stood in for reopening. The cause of the harm, restrictions, was recast as its cure: more checks, more moratoria, more emergency. Convenient, no?

Early Certainties That Fell Apart

Trust is the currency of crisis. It was spent like confetti.

• "Masks are not necessary for the general public." Anthony Fauci in March 2020: "There's no reason to be walking around with a mask… it might make people feel a little bit better, and it might even block a droplet, but it's not providing the perfect protection that people think it is" [*60 Minutes*, Mar. 8, 2020]. Then the reversal, toward universal masking, including outdoors in some jurisdictions, congealed into dogma. Years later, high-quality evidence failed to show robust community-level benefits from mask mandates, particularly cloth masks. Even the CDC updated guidance to prioritize well-fitted respirators over cloth [CDC, Jan. 14, 2022], and a Cochrane review stirred debate on population-level efficacy [*Cochrane Library*, Jan. 30, 2023]. Masks can help in specific contexts, sure, but the absolutism? The toddler-masking? The outdoor jogger-shaming? That was theater dressed as science.

• "Two weeks to slow the spread." What became months stretched into school years. "We're going to get through this much faster than people think," said NYC's Bill de Blasio as closures began [*MSNBC*, Mar. 10, 2020]. California's "bending the curve" morphed into tiered color charts that pushed normalcy into the indefinite future [California Department of Public Health, Aug. 28, 2020]. Temporary became permanent by press conference. How many "two weeks" fit into 18 months?

• "The vaccinated do not carry the virus." CDC Director Rochelle Walensky: "Vaccinated people do not carry the virus, don't get sick" [*MSNBC*, Mar. 29, 2021]. President Biden: "You're not going to get COVID if you have these vaccinations" [*CNN Town Hall*, July 21, 2021]. Breakthrough infections soon became routine with Delta and Omicron; guidance shifted to stress protection against severe disease [CDC, Aug. 2021]. Reasonable people can forgive evolving science. What's harder to forgive is the categorical tone used to justify mandates that cost jobs. If you demanded blind obedience, you owe accountability when you were wrong. Where is it?

• "Close bars, keep schools open." Fauci said it plainly [*ABC News*, Nov. 29, 2020]. Blue metros closed bars and kept schools closed anyway under union pressure, despite international data showing schools weren't primary drivers of spread with basic mitigation [*Wall Street Journal*, Feb. 15, 2021]. The learning loss was catastrophic. NAEP reported the largest math score declines ever recorded for 9-year-olds [NAEP, Sept. 1, 2022]. Human capital doesn't bounce back like a rubber ball; it dents like a fender. Who pays for that dent? Kids who had no vote.

• "Outdoor activities are dangerous." Cue absurdities: police clearing beaches, Los Angeles filling skatepark bowls with sand [*KTLA*, Apr. 19, 2020], yellow tape on playgrounds, and masked hikers glowering at each other. The CDC later emphasized lower outdoor transmission risk [CDC, May 16, 2021]. Maybe the virus had respect for sunshine after all.

Every broken assurance didn't just bruise credibility; it underwrote policies that strangled economic activity at the margins where most Americans live and work. If you want compliance next time, maybe try honesty this time?

Blue-State Stringency, Red-State Resilience

Treat the states like a natural experiment. Stringency indices put California, New York, and Illinois near the top; Florida, Texas, and Georgia were lower after spring 2020. Florida reopened businesses sooner, reopened schools for in-person instruction by fall 2020, and banned vaccine passports [Executive Order 21-81, Apr. 2, 2021]. Critics warned of death waves and economic recklessness. Yet Florida's age-adjusted COVID mortality rates, over the full arc, landed mid-pack, while its economic indicators—labor force participation, in-migration, and small business openings—outperformed [Florida Department of Health, 2022; BLS, 2021–2022]. So the "Neanderthal" policy set didn't produce the apocalypse? Awkward.

In California, the "Blueprint for a Safer Economy" throttled restaurants, strictly limited indoor worship, and conditioned school reopening on thresholds that reset like a video game [California Department of Public Health, Aug. 28, 2020]. Tech cushioned GDP, but the service economy—restaurants, salons, independent retail— bled out. Unemployment lagged national averages well into 2021– 2022 [BLS, 2022]. New York City, once a global hospitality and office hub, saw an exodus that depleted tax bases and emptied midtown towers, with office occupancy far below pre-pandemic levels in 2022–2023 [Kastle Systems, 2022]. Was the plan to save the city by making it uninhabitable Monday through Thursday?

The lesson isn't that viruses obey red governors. It's that liberal policy regimes treated the economy as a dimmer switch set by models whose parameters kept shifting, while conservative regimes accepted the messy reality of living with risk. The economic divergence—restaurant survival rates, school learning losses that translate into future earnings hits, and labor force re-entry—reflects that difference. Federalism gave Americans a choice; millions voted with their U-Hauls.

The School Closures: Human Capital as Collateral Damage

Schools are not mere childcare. They're the conveyor belt of human capital. Closing them was the single most expensive policy choice of the pandemic—economically, morally, and civically.

By summer 2020, Europe reopened schools with mitigation and did not trigger community surges. The American Federation of Teachers and National Education Association, meanwhile, lobbied for multibillion-dollar federal packages and stringent ventilation and testing mandates before returning, even in districts with minimal spread [*Politico*, July 7, 2020]. In Chicago, union actions delayed reopening into 2021 [*Chicago Sun-Times*, Jan. 2021]. Private schools and red-state districts reopened in fall 2020. What did blue-state kids get? Zoom fatigue and "equity" PowerPoints.

The learning losses were predictable, measurable, and regressive. NAEP documented steep declines in math and reading, with Black and Hispanic students hit hardest [NAEP, Sept. 1, 2022]. McKinsey estimated months of lost learning, translating into potentially trillions in future lifetime earnings lost [McKinsey, July 27, 2021]. This isn't a temporary blip. Human capital compounds; deficits widen. Future GDP growth depends on skills and participation. Closing schools was an economic policy, an extraordinarily bad one, masquerading as public health. Did anyone in the decision room even crack open an economics text?

Why did closures persist? Politics. CDC school guidance in February 2021 reportedly incorporated AFT-suggested language that softened reopening triggers and bolstered union positions [*New York Post*, May 1, 2021]. CDC Director Walensky said schools could reopen safely with mitigation even before teacher vaccination [*Reuters*, Feb. 3, 2021], but the official guidance gave ample cover to remain closed. The result: the costs landed on kids and, by extension, the economy that will rely on them. We protected adults' comfort at the expense of children's futures. That's not "following the science." That's following the donors.

The Stimulus Deluge: Dousing the Fire with Gasoline

If you shut down supply and then pay people not to work, what do you think happens to prices? Washington tested that rhetorical question with trillions. The CARES Act, the December 2020 package, and the $1.9 trillion American Rescue Plan (ARP) in March 2021 layered enhanced unemployment, broad stimulus checks, state and local bailouts, and school district windfalls onto an economy already reopening in many states [Congressional Budget Office, 2021]. Because nothing says "precision" like a firehose.

Larry Summers—no conservative hero—warned ARP could "set off inflationary pressures of a kind we have not seen in a generation" [Washington Post, Feb. 4, 2021]. He was scolded. By mid-2021, inflation burst past the Fed's "transitory" mantra, peaking at 9.1% CPI in June 2022 [BLS, July 13, 2022]. Supply chains were tight (some due to the virus, some due to policy), energy supplies constrained by climate theater, and fiscal cash gushed into a bottlenecked economy. Real wages fell; savings were eaten by price spikes. The "relief" relieved the pain of 2020 by delivering the hangover of 2022.

Enhanced unemployment supplements of $300–$600 weekly sometimes exceeded prior wages for lower-income workers, disincentivizing re-entry at the margin [University of Chicago, May 2020]. States that ended supplements early saw faster declines in jobless claims and quicker job growth [Wall Street Journal, July 15, 2021]. The Paycheck Protection Program saved some firms but favored those with elite banking relationships; fraud flourished [Bloomberg, Mar. 25, 2022]. Blue-state governors used federal aid to paper over budget holes and postpone structural fixes. Those "temporary" bailouts are now structural expectations. Why reform pensions when Washington will refill the ice cream every time you drop the cone?

Eviction moratoria—extended by the CDC beyond any clear statutory authority—froze part of the rental market, punishing small landlords and distorting mobility [Supreme Court, Aug. 26, 2021]. Rent relief dribbled out slowly. When moratoria lifted, a wave of demand smashed into restricted supply, feeding rent spikes. Housing, a core CPI driver, kept pressure on prices long after stimulus checks were spent. But sure, the CDC should manage landlord-tenant law now. Why not?

The Fed, late to tighten, was boxed by a political class that wanted growth optics without pain. When rate hikes finally came, they clobbered small businesses reliant on credit, mortgage borrowers, and state budgets buoyed by frothy asset prices. When a central bank must rescue its credibility, Main Street pays. Does anyone seriously think the "experts" who missed the inflation spike deserve more discretion?

The Essential/Nonessential Fallacy: Big Wins, Small Dies

Never has government's thumb been so heavy on the scale of competition. "Essential" exemptions privileged firms with logistics capacity and digital reach—Walmart, Target, Amazon—while crushing the businesses that create neighborhood wealth. In Los Angeles, outdoor dining was banned in late 2020 despite minimal evidence of significant transmission. A restaurateur's viral video showed a film set serving catered meals mere feet from her shuttered patio [Fox 11 LA, Dec. 4, 2020]. Science or status? In New York, liquor stores and (later) weed shops thrived, while churches faced attendance caps [Supreme Court, Roman Catholic Diocese v. Cuomo, Nov. 25, 2020]. The Court rebuked the policy for unequal treatment. You can buy lotto tickets shoulder to shoulder, but communion? Too risky. Got it.

The lived experience: small proprietors burned savings, lost staff to enhanced UI, swallowed mandate compliance costs, endured crime spikes as liberal prosecutors de-prioritized retail theft, then met inflationary input costs at the door. Many quit. That exit is an economic wound cloaked by aggregate GDP that tech stocks can't conceal. The "essential" designation turned into a subsidy for scale. Was that a public health strategy or a corporate lobbying dream board?

Censorship and the Cost of Being Right Too Soon

Markets rely on information. The pandemic response throttled it. Media outlets and platforms, aligned with the liberal policy mood, suppressed questions that later became mainstream. Lab-leak speculation? Banned as "misinformation" on Facebook before the narrative was updated to "plausible" when officials admitted it as such [Wall Street Journal, May 26, 2021]. Natural immunity? Treated as heresy until the CDC updated guidance recognizing prior infection's protective role [CDC, Jan. 19, 2022]. School reopening advocates? Cast as reckless until evidence made delay indefensible.

Economic relevance? Overreach persisted longer because dissenters were denied platforms and policymakers faced less scrutiny. Extended closures, mandates, and fiscal spigots gained months they didn't deserve. In markets, bad information hardens into bad investment. In public policy, bad information hardens into bad law. How much GDP did we burn to protect the pride of pundits?

Work Mandates and the Fractured Labor Market

The workplace was shoved into a nationwide experiment. Some of that shift was healthy: remote work freed knowledge workers from geography. But the federal vaccine mandate for large employers, the OSHA emergency temporary standard, was stayed by the Supreme Court as beyond agency authority [Supreme Court, NFIB v. OSHA, Jan. 13, 2022]. Before that, mandates drove separations in healthcare and public safety—sectors already stretched. New York City's municipal vaccine mandate sidelined firefighters, police, and sanitation workers, with ripple effects on service delivery [New York Post, Oct. 21, 2021]. Hospitals in some states reported staffing crunches as unvaccinated workers were terminated even after acknowledging breakthrough infections [NBC News, Sept. 28, 2021]. If the vaccine didn't stop transmission, what was the public health logic of firing nurses during a staffing shortage? Ritual or revenge?

Meanwhile, white-collar workers decamped to lower-tax states, turbocharging Sun Belt real estate while leaving blue-city cores hollowed. The loss of foot traffic punished downtown retailers and transit agencies, deepening budget holes. Liberal mayors were slow to insist on in-office returns in city government, and union contracts entrenched hybrid norms. Productivity metrics dipped in 2022; a tight labor market masked mismatches [BLS, Q4 2022]. Treat work as optional long enough, and you'll get exactly that—optionality replacing obligation. Does anyone think an economy runs on vibes?

Public Health Theater and Eroded Legitimacy

In crisis, people will tolerate hardship if it's fair and finite. The pandemic response flunked both. Leaders were caught flouting their own decrees. California's governor dined maskless at The French Laundry while lecturing residents [San Francisco Chronicle, Nov. 13, 2020]. Chicago's mayor got a haircut while salons were closed [Chicago Tribune, Apr. 8, 2020]. House Speaker Nancy Pelosi visited a San Francisco salon in violation of local rules [Fox News, Sept. 1, 2020]. These weren't trivial hypocrisies; they signaled a caste system.

For the economy, legitimacy is lubricant. Remove it, and compliance declines, enforcement costs rise, and the social fabric tears. Why obey the sign if the sign-maker ignores it?

Media fear-porn had costs. Beach footage spurred clampdowns on outdoor recreation, while scant attention was paid to collateral damage: missed cancer screenings, mental health crises, and lost child abuse detections with schools closed [JAMA, 2020–2021]. When the information diet nourishes only one risk, people underweight all others. That's bad economics at scale and worse ethics.

The Long Tail: Inflation, Debt, and the New Normal of Emergency

The bill arrived in three nasty denominations.

• **Inflation.** CPI at 9.1% in June 2022 ravaged purchasing power, especially for the working class with little asset cushion [BLS, July 13, 2022]. Real wages fell for much of 2021–2022. Grocery, gas, and rent—life's staples—became toll booths. Businesses passed through costs or died trying. But hey, at least "transitory" made a good headline, right?

• **Debt.** Federal debt surged past 100% of GDP as Congress sprayed relief packages and bailouts [Treasury, 2021–2022]. ARP, the infrastructure bill, and student-loan forbearance extensions layered obligations in a rising-rate world. Interest on the debt now rivals defense spending, crowding out future investment. Remember when "deficits don't matter" was a punchline, not a platform?

• **Norm erosion.** Emergency orders stretched for years. California kept its state of emergency into early 2023 [LA Times, Oct. 17, 2022]. Agencies discovered powers they didn't know they had (or shouldn't have), such as the CDC's eviction moratorium. Courts checked some excesses, but the damage—precedents of bureaucratic adventurism—will persist. Investors and entrepreneurs must now price not just tax and regulatory risk but emergency risk. Welcome to the era of permanent maybe.

Revisiting the Quotations: What Was Said, What Was True

Let's anchor a few emblematic statements and their economic footprints.

• **Anthony Fauci on masks:** "There's no reason to be walking around with a mask" [60 Minutes, Mar. 8, 2020]. Reversed within weeks, then broadened into mandates that lasted years in some places—outdoors, on toddlers [NYC Health, Mar. 2022]. As high-quality evidence failed to vindicate cloth mask mandates, public trust eroded, complicating compliance with targeted interventions [Cochrane Library, Jan. 30, 2023]. If you burn trust on cloth, don't be shocked when people doubt N95s.

• **CDC Director Walensky:** "Vaccinated people do not carry the virus" [MSNBC, Mar. 29, 2021]. Later walked back as breakthroughs mounted [CDC, Aug. 2021]. The absolute tone fueled mandates across blue jurisdictions, causing job losses and service disruptions. Overpromise, underdeliver, overregulate—the bureaucratic hat trick.

• **President Biden:** "You're not going to get COVID if you have these vaccinations" [CNN Town Hall, July 21, 2021]. By winter, Omicron tore through the vaccinated, though protection against severe disease remained strong. The overpromise, paired with continued mask and test mandates, bred cynicism and incentivized exits from strict jurisdictions. Nothing stimulates interstate migration like condescension.

• **Governor Andrew Cuomo's nursing home directive** (March 25, 2020) required accepting COVID-positive hospital discharges. He later defended changes after blowback [Albany Times Union, Mar.–May 2020]. The initial policy contributed to deadly outbreaks and scarred trust, especially among New York's elderly. Economic spillover included fear-driven withdrawal from services and family caregiving burdens. When government errors kill, apologies don't resurrect confidence—or grandparents.

• **De Blasio on schools:** initial assurances of a quick return, followed by months of remote learning and testing theater [MSNBC, Mar. 10, 2020; New York Times, 2020–2021]. Parents left. NYC public school enrollment dropped by tens of thousands, draining funding tied to headcount [NYC DOE, 2021–2022]. Families took jobs and tax dollars to Florida and Texas. "Progressive" policy: progress right out of town.

What a Better Path Could Have Looked Like

It's not enough to indict; propose the counterfactual.

• **Time-bound emergency powers.** Legislative renewal every 30 days, with public cost-benefit analyses including education, mental health, and economic indicators—not just case counts. Sunsets force humility. Economic activity rebounds faster when rules have predictable horizons. Is that radical or just adult?

• **Risk-stratified protection.** Focus on the elderly and comorbid: surge staffing for nursing homes, targeted ventilation, rapid antivirals, and paid leave. Keep schools open with mitigation. Keep small businesses open with voluntary guidelines; punish fraud, not commerce. The economy is not a light switch. Stop treating it like one.

• **Precise communications.** No noble lies. Admit uncertainty. Avoid categorical claims that will be reversed. Align mandates only where evidence is strong and externalities large (for example, hospitals). Trust is not an infinite resource; stop spending it like ARP money.

• **Calibrated fiscal support.** Temporary, declining benefits that avoid exceeding prior wages; liquidity for firms tied to verifiable revenue loss with real fraud controls; no blank checks for states to paper over pre-existing fiscal sins. Maintain work incentives. Compassion without distortion.

• **Respect for constitutional limits.** No agency lawmaking by press release. If Congress didn't authorize it—eviction moratoria via disease statute, OSHA as national vax czar—the answer is no [Supreme Court, Aug. 26, 2021; Supreme Court, NFIB v. OSHA, Jan. 13, 2022]. Courts shouldn't be the only adults; executives should restrain themselves. Try it sometime.

• **Data transparency and pluralism.** Allow debate without censorship. Fund rapid randomized trials for interventions (masks in schools, ventilation, rapid testing regimes) to settle questions with evidence, not Twitter mobs. Markets and citizens make better decisions when truth isn't a partisan monopoly.

The Reckoning We Still Need

The economy is resilient; Americans rebuild. But the pandemic response revealed something brittle in our institutions: a default toward control, a hostility to trade-offs, and a bias for policies that protect the credentialed at the expense of the precarious. Liberal policies during COVID did not just "destroy the economy" in the sense of GDP contraction—though the contraction was severe—they reordered it in favor of the already advantaged, saddled the young with debt and skills deficits, and validated emergency government as the first, not last, resort. Was that an accident or a habit?

Many on the left say the virus, not policy, did the harm. That's half true and therefore misleading. The virus was the storm; policy was the decision to flood the valley to save the dam. Some flooding was inevitable. Much of it was chosen. The conservative critique isn't a defense of denial; it's a demand for proportion, for federalism that permits choice, and for humility that treats human dignity—including the dignity of work and learning—as essential, not negotiable.

One final point: the apology tour has been thin. We've seen "amnesty" essays and calls to move on. The families who lost businesses, the kids who lost years, and the workers who lost skills deserve better than amnesia. They deserve a policy culture that remembers the cost of hubris. Emergency power will beckon again. The only inoculation is memory backed by reform. Will we learn—

really learn—or will we let the next acronym with a podium run our lives until the next "two weeks"?

References (inline citations above)

• 60 Minutes interview with Anthony Fauci (Mar. 8, 2020).

• CDC guidance changes on masks/respirators (Jan. 14, 2022).

• Cochrane review on physical interventions to interrupt respiratory viruses (Jan. 30, 2023).

• Bureau of Labor Statistics unemployment/CPI releases (May 8, 2020; July 13, 2022; Jan. 2021; 2022; Q4 2022).

• California and New York executive orders and reopening frameworks (Mar.–Aug. 2020).

• Opportunity Insights Economic Tracker (2020).

• Kastle Systems office occupancy data (2022).

• NAEP learning loss reports (Sept. 1, 2022).

• McKinsey learning loss/economic impact analysis (July 27, 2021).

• Supreme Court: *Roman Catholic Diocese v. Cuomo* (Nov. 25, 2020); *NFIB v. OSHA* (Jan. 13, 2022); CDC eviction moratorium stay (Aug. 26, 2021).

• Florida Department of Health mortality analyses (2022).

• Executive Order 21-81 (Florida vaccine passport ban, Apr. 2, 2021).

• Larry Summers op-ed on ARP inflation risk (Feb. 4, 2021).

- University of Chicago on UI replacement rates (May 2020).

- Bloomberg on PPP fraud (Mar. 25, 2022).

- Fox 11 LA coverage of outdoor dining ban vs. film catering (Dec. 4, 2020).

- Reports on AFT input into CDC school guidance (May 1, 2021).

- Reuters on Walensky school reopening remarks (Feb. 3, 2021).

- NYC DOE enrollment declines (2021–2022).

- Treasury debt data (2021–2022).

- LA Times on California emergency duration (Oct. 17, 2022).

- Wall Street Journal on ending UI supplements early (July 15, 2021).

- NBC News on healthcare staffing tied to mandates (Sept. 28, 2021).

- CNN Town Hall with President Biden (July 21, 2021).

- ABC News interview with Fauci on bars vs. schools (Nov. 29, 2020).

- New York Post and Albany Times Union coverage of nursing home directives (2020).

- KTLA on Venice skatepark sand dump (Apr. 19, 2020).

- NYC Health toddler masking guidance (Mar. 2022).

- New York Times coverage of PAUSE and school chaos (2020–2021).

- Politico on union demands (July 7, 2020).

- Chicago Sun-Times on CTU delays (Jan. 2021).

- Wall Street Journal on international school reopenings (Feb. 15, 2021).

- CDC updates recognizing prior infection (Jan. 19, 2022).

- Wall Street Journal on lab-leak reconsideration (May 26, 2021).

Chapter 9:

Blue City Blues: How Progressive Governance Hollowed Out America's

Urban Economy

Introduction: The Broken Promise of the Progressive City

For a decade, the flagship cities of the Democratic Party promised a new moral economy: regulate carbon and capital, "center equity," decriminalize "low-level" offenses, command rents downward, and tax the rich to fund renaissance. The results are not ambiguous. Where process multiplies and consequences evaporate, commerce thins, families leave, and the cost of living rises like floodwater. The old urban compact—pay more, get more—has inverted: pay more, get less. New rules and recent reforms have sharpened the decline, not arrested it.

Why it hurts: The modern city runs on trust—trust that rules are predictable, streets are safe, and work is rewarded. Progressive governance broke that trust. When policy treats productive people as revenue sources and disorder as a misunderstanding, the city's circulatory system clogs. Capital hesitates, workers hedge, and families look for exits.

San Francisco: Regulatory Opulence, Economic Austerity

San Francisco perfected scarcity by policy. The state's environmental shield, CEQA, became a spear against housing. "The purpose of this division is to inform governmental decisionmakers and the public about the potential, significant environmental effects of proposed activities" (Cal. Pub. Res. Code § 21001). In practice, a CEQA appeal pauses a hundred kitchens and a thousand leases. Pair that with the city's rent regime—"This ordinance shall apply to all rental units in the City and County of San Francisco constructed prior to June 13, 1979" (SF Admin. Code ch. 37)—and you calcify an insider market while making new supply a gladiator sport.

Then came a boulevard of signals that said productive activity is suspect. The Overpaid Executive Tax—"A company is subject to the tax if the highest-paid managerial employee's compensation is at least 100 times more than the median employee compensation" (SF Prop L, 2020)—did not fund a renaissance; it posted a warning. Add gross receipts hikes, and downtown turns into a vacancy canyon.

On public order, City Hall moralized while storefronts bled. A 2020 prosecutorial memo told the street, "We will not prosecute cases involving possession for personal use of controlled substances" (SFDA policy, 2020). Pharmacies bought plexiglass; then they bought a U-Haul. The city poured money onto the encampment crisis—"The tax shall be imposed on each person engaged in business in the City" (SF Prop C, 2018)—but mistook spending for success. The Tenderloin became an open-air triage ward. Families with options fled, and employers with balance sheets followed.

Why it hurts: Scarcity is not neutral. It shifts power and wealth to incumbents and insiders. When new housing is a lawsuit, every lease costs more and every move-up is blocked. When street law is optional, small businesses become unpaid social workers until they die. San Francisco did not merely mismanage; it taught people that building and behaving are for suckers.

Los Angeles: Housing Justice as Housing Scarcity

Los Angeles tried to legislate affordability while criminalizing arithmetic. The city froze rents in its Rent Stabilization Ordinance stock for years under emergency power: "No rent increases are permitted for RSO units during the declared local emergency" (LAMC § 151.32). Maintenance withered, investment fled, and the backlog of needed upgrades grew like ivy in the walls.

Voters authorized billions for homelessness in Proposition HHH: "The proceeds shall be used to finance affordable housing and facilities to reduce homelessness" (LA Prop HHH, 2016). Projects arrived at $700,000 per unit. The city mistook ribbon-cuttings for results. Then, in a flourish of class theater, it levied the "mansion tax," Measure ULA: "There is imposed a special tax on the sale or other transfer of real property" (LAMC § 21.9.15). The high end froze, the move-up ladder jammed, and transfer-tax receipts sagged against promise.

Work got pricier while work got harder. State law set a sectoral wage floor: "A minimum wage of $20 per hour for fast food restaurant employees" (Cal. Lab. Code § 1475). Margins did not expand to meet it; kiosks did. Meanwhile, public order dissolved at the edges. The county's pre-arraignment release rules announced that "nonviolent, non-serious offenses shall be presumptively cited and released" (LA Superior Court PARP, 2023). Smash-and-grab became smash-and-go. The city asked stores to behave like social workers and called it justice.

Why it hurts: LA built a moral theater where costs are hidden until they are not. The landlord delays the roof repair; the tenant breathes mold. The restaurateur pays $20 an hour by cutting shifts and adding a kiosk. The family trying to trade up cannot sell, and the city cannot fund promises without squeezing the same shrinking base. Compassion that ignores math ends by rationing dignity.

Chicago: Decarceration by Decree, Commerce by Exception Chicago chose decarceration without incapacitation and regulation without relief. The SAFE-T Act—formally, 725 ILCS 5/110—declared: "All persons charged with an offense shall be eligible for pretrial release" (§ 110-2). In theory, judges can detain; in practice, repeaters cycled. At the register, organized teams treated aisles like buffet lines. Statute defines retail theft thresholds (720 ILCS 5/16-25), but prosecutorial choices about aggregation and diversion turned felony incentives into misdemeanors of inconvenience. Loop retailers did not wait for a law review article; they left.

The city's relationship with enterprise is conditional love. It tried head taxes—"A tax is imposed on employers for the privilege of engaging in business" (former MCC § 3-20)—and a thicket of mandates that small owners navigate at their peril. Housing policy swaddled tenants in process harms that ricocheted: the county ordinance promised penalties—"the tenant may recover an amount equal to two months' rent" (Cook County Code § 42-804)—so small landlords sold, and institutional buyers raised the rent.

Then came the migration surge under a sanctuary framework that reads like a manifesto: "No agency shall condition the provision of City benefits, opportunities, or services on citizenship or immigration status" (MCC § 2-173-020). Compassion without capacity produced triage budgets and shelter spillover. Downtown never fully came back. Trust—of residents, employers, and visitors—eroded.

Why it hurts: Commerce needs certainty, and communities need deterrence. When repeat theft is a round-trip through a revolving door, the price of toothpaste includes the cost of indifference. When City Hall treats employers like guilty men, hiring becomes an act of charity. You cannot nurture a middle class on apologies and exceptions.

New York City: Tax the Productive, Smother the Grid New York governs like a museum of constraint. On housing, it decided price controls beat production. The 2019 Housing Stability and Tenant Protection Act announced the crusade: "It is necessary to prevent exactions of unjust, unreasonable and oppressive rents"

(L.2019, ch.36). It abolished the pressure valves—vacancy decontrol and improvement pass-throughs—ensuring buildings age gracelessly, illegal sublets proliferate, and newcomers enter a lottery, not a market.

Then City Hall turned the building stock into a climate ledger. Local Law 97 pronounces: "Covered buildings shall not exceed annual building emissions limits" (NYC Admin. Code § 28-320.3). Coop boards are not energy firms; fines in the millions redirect capital from livability to compliance, which tenants will pay in rent or neglect. Congestion pricing, authorized in state law—"a program of congestion pricing in a central business district" (NY Veh. & Traf. Law § 1704)—layers a toll on the working trades that make the city function. The city says it is a nudge; the bill says it is a tax.

Add taxes—state and city income tax, property taxes, and business levies—and the post-SALT-cap choice writes itself for the productive: Florida has an open chair. On public order, the state told courts to release on the "least restrictive alternative" (CPL § 510.10). Amendments added crimes, but the signal remained. Subway panic and retail theft are not abstract; they are productivity killers. The city that once made ambition feel inevitable now makes prudence feel wise.

Why it hurts: New York once sold a bargain — sky-high costs in exchange for sky-high opportunity. Now it sells penalties and paperwork. The scaffolding stays up while the elevator breaks, but the climate report is on time. The tradesman pays the toll, the single mom pays the surcharge, the landlord pays the fine, and then all three pay rent hikes to cover the last two.

Philadelphia: An "Equity" Lab that Taxed Itself into Stagnation

Philadelphia treats revenue like a security blanket and commerce like a suspect. It still imposes the wage tax: "There is hereby imposed… a tax on salaries, wages, commissions and other compensation" (Phila. Code § 19-1502), and wonders why commuters prefer suburban headquarters. In 2020, City Council erected a fortress of tenant procedure: "Landlords must offer a hardship repayment agreement" (Bill No. 200305-A). Compassion in theory; in practice, higher risk premiums, fewer small landlords, and a tighter market.

Retailers endured systematic theft amid prosecution that triaged "low-level" offenses. When a store manager is told to be tolerant of theft under a threshold while insurance premiums spike, a closure is not a policy outcome — it's a survival tactic. The soda tax is a perfect emblem: "A tax is hereby imposed… on the distribution of sweetened beverages" (Phila. Code § 19-4103). It didn't rescue schools; it did make groceries pricier and push carts across the city line.

Why it hurts: Cities thrive when they magnetize paychecks and businesses. Philadelphia taxes the paycheck, scolds the business, and then wonders why the suburbs collect the prosperity. Morality plays don't fill lunch counters; predictable rules do.

Seattle: Utopian Price Controls Meet Real-World Prices

Seattle legislated a wage floor higher than many salaries in the country: "The hourly minimum wage rate for large employers shall be $19.97" (SMC § 14.19.030; adjusted annually). Businesses complied by replacing workers with kiosks, trimming hours, and raising prices. City Hall flirted with punishing employment itself via the 2018 head tax: "A tax of $275 per employee per year" (Ord. 125594) before backing down (repealed by Ord. 125683). The message to capital wasn't ambiguous — we can and will tax your headcount if the mood strikes.

Public order drifted. Defund feints, understaffed departments, and a prosecutorial reluctance to jail shoplifters drained the core of confidence. Zoning played defense: "Mandatory Housing Affordability" extracted payments or units, while discretionary design review and appeals delayed projects past financial feasibility. When time kills deals, scarcity wins. Seattle's elite tier endures; the working and middle class are priced into an archipelago of long commutes and small apartments.

Why it hurts: The city advertised itself as a place where tomorrow's jobs are made; it became a place where yesterday's regulations are enforced. For ambitious kids without a CS degree, the escalator is missing steps. The café that once hired them now has a tablet and a tip jar.

Portland: Decriminalization's Deadweight Loss

Portland married land-use rigidity to permissive drug policy and watched downtown wither. The state tells cities to draw a line around growth: "A city shall establish and maintain an urban growth boundary" (ORS § 197.286). That can work if approvals inside the line are swift; Portland layered process like pastry. Then the state passed Measure 110, recoding possession: "Unlawful possession of a controlled substance… is a Class E violation" (ORS § 475.890 as amended). The poster was compassion; the reality was fentanyl bazaars. Retail corridors hollowed, transit felt perilous, and tourism dimmed.

City and county layered local income taxes and fees — an extra drag on fragile storefronts absorbing theft, vandalism, and rising wages. As the drug wave broke and the budget sank, Salem began to reverse course; re-criminalization debates are confessions framed as reforms.

Why it hurts: Civilization is a set of boundaries. Portland erased the ones that protect the vulnerable — the addict, the shopkeeper, the child on a bus — and replaced them with a ticket printer. The result was not mercy; it was abandonment.

Baltimore: Soft Governance, Hard Costs

Baltimore overtaxes decay. "A tax is levied on all property" (Baltimore City Code, Art. 28) at rates that dwarf the suburbs, ensuring reinvestment is an act of charity. The prosecutor's office in 2021 publicly deprioritized a list of offenses — drug possession, prostitution, trespass, minor traffic — effectively inviting public disorder to squat in commercial life. Small landlords faced procedural lash; responsible owners left and absentee owners multiplied.

The city's spiral isn't inevitable, but the policy mix makes renewal a marathon in sand: high taxes, uncertain enforcement, and weak schools. Each element compounds the others. The price of groceries, insurance, and security rises; the value of location falls.

Why it hurts: Baltimore's hustlers — barbers, mechanics, corner grocers — are civic assets. The city treats them like suspects while tolerating chaos that wrecks their margins. Incentives invert: the striver leaves; the scavenger stays.

Detroit: Post-Collapse Cautionary Lessons Ignored

Detroit should have been a national seminar in post-crisis realism. Instead, the city retained a tax structure that taxes poverty: "A tax at the rate of 2.4 percent on the taxable income of every resident individual" (MCL 141.613; Detroit). Insurance costs drained disposable income even after state reform. Land policy remained too bespoke — each permit a negotiation. Families kept leaving for schools and safety; retail deserts persisted.

Why it hurts: Recovery needs momentum. Detroit's rules make every bet feel lonely and every success provisional. People will not rebuild a city if the city won't meet them halfway.

Recent Policies Tightening the Vise

What's new in the blue-city playbook since the last wave of promises? A tightening spiral of mandates and signals.

Climate compliance over capability. Local Law 97 in New York City is the template — "Covered buildings shall not exceed annual building emissions limits" (§ 28-320.3) — now echoed in building performance standards from Boston to Denver. The capital costs don't come from a magic wallet; tenants pay or maintenance dies. In California, all-electric new construction mandates and gas bans adopted by cities and counties raised build costs and narrowed contractor supply, contributing to rent pressure.

Why it hurts: Climate policy without cost discipline becomes a stealth rent hike. It swaps tomorrow's theoretical gains for today's guaranteed evictions by price.

Sectoral wage spikes without productivity. California's fast-food wage edict — "A minimum wage of $20 per hour for fast food restaurant employees" (Cal. Lab. Code § 1475) — is rippling through franchise closures, menu price hikes, and automation. Cities copy with local minimums racing inflation, not productivity.

Why it hurts: Wages are not wishes; they are prices. When the price of entry-level labor rises faster than value, the job disappears and the rung breaks.

Congestion and mobility taxation. New York's congestion pricing authorization — "A program of congestion pricing in a central business district" (NY Veh. & Traf. Law § 1704) — portends similar schemes elsewhere. Tradespeople, delivery networks, and regional commuters pay first; urban price levels follow.

Why it hurts: Cities are metabolism. Tax the blood flow and the extremities go numb first — outer boroughs, small vendors, and the folks who can't telework.

"Mansion" and transfer taxes that hit the middle. Los Angeles's ULA — "There is imposed a special tax on the sale or other transfer of real property" (LAMC § 21.9.15) — froze high-end turnover and jammed the ladder beneath it. Similar levies in San Francisco and proposals in other cities turn mobility into a taxable luxury, reducing listings and keeping families mismatched to their housing.

Why it hurts: Families don't just buy homes; they trade them as life changes. Tax the trade and you trap the family — too small, too far, and too expensive to move.

Permanent emergency governance. COVID-era "temporary" rent freezes (LAMC § 151.32), eviction moratoria (for example, Philadelphia's Bill No. 200305-A), and emergency fees mutated into normalized policy expectations. Risk pricing rose accordingly, making future supply costlier.

Why it hurts: If the rules can change overnight and never change back, investors price the fear, and tenants inherit the bill.

Prosecution standards that normalize theft. From San Francisco's "We will not prosecute cases involving possession for personal use" (SFDA, 2020) to retail-theft charging thresholds and cite-and-release protocols, the modern message is that enemies are "systems," not offenders. Stores absorb shrink until they can't.

Why it hurts: The first casualty of tolerated theft is the poor: higher prices, longer bus rides to the last open pharmacy, and jobs lost when the shop lights go out.

Sanctuary expansions without capacity. Chicago's "No agency shall condition the provision of City benefits" (MCC § 2-173-020) stance faced federal and interstate migration waves; budgets bent. Hotels became shelters, then classrooms. Social spending displaced core services; taxpayers voted with U-Hauls.

Why it hurts: Compassion is a budget, not a slogan. Promise everything to everyone, and you end up delivering nothing on time to anyone.

The Mechanism: How Blue Governance Kills Affordability

Rent control plus discretionary review equals rationing. CEQA delays in California ("inform… decisionmakers" (§ 21001)) became an informal veto. New York's HSTPA ("oppressive rents" (L.2019, ch.36)) transformed upgrades into liabilities. Seattle's design review turned schedules into mirages. When supply is a negotiation, scarcity is policy.

Why it hurts: Scarcity punishes newcomers, rewards hoarders, and makes neighbors enemies at planning meetings. It corrodes civic spirit; every project becomes a fight, every change an insult.

Layer on wage floors unmoored from productivity. Seattle sets $19.97 (SMC § 14.19.030); California orders $20 for fast food (Lab. Code § 1475). Employers don't mint money; they cut hours, automate, or close. Consumers pay higher prices; workers get fewer rungs.

Why it hurts: Work is a ladder. Cities replaced rungs with slogans and wondered why mobility stalled.

Tax structure then eats the seed corn. Philadelphia's wage tax (§ 19-1502) punishes urban payrolls; ULA taxes transactions (LAMC § 21.9.15); SF gross receipts and executive pay taxes penalize scale. Congestion schemes (NY Veh. & Traf. Law § 1704) tax mobility, then wonder why deliveries cost more.

Why it hurts: You can shear a sheep many times, but skin it only once. Blue cities are running out of wool.

Finally, leniency without leverage erases the civic margin. Bail reforms that promise the "least restrictive" release (CPL § 510.10), plus policies that won't prosecute possession or low-dollar thefts, turn order into a voluntary system. The cost is paid by small business first, then by families, then by the tax base.

Why it hurts: Civilization is the habit of consequence. Remove it and the strong do what they want while the weak pay what they must.

Standard of Living: How the Bill Arrives

The bill does not arrive as a line item. It arrives as a mother who drives an hour each way because teachers fled her neighborhood school; as a cashier who pays more for groceries because shrink gets priced into milk; as a landlord who walks from a deal because litigation risk is the business model; as a commuter who pays a toll to go to work and pays in fear to ride the subway.

Why it hurts: The math is simple. Higher fixed costs plus lower reliability equals less life for the same money. You cannot budget your way out of a policy that makes everything cost more and work worse.

Answering the Objections

"It was COVID, not policy." COVID was a storm; policy decides whether the roof leaks. Austin and Miami welcomed building and people; San Francisco and New York litigated and tolled. Remote work didn't force CEQA appeals; progressive councils did.

Why this matters: Crises expose design flaws. Blue cities are drafted with failure points where optimism should be.

"State law tied our hands." Cities chose to exceed state wage floors, impose transfer surcharges, stack reviews, and instruct prosecutors to stand down. They chose moral theater over measurable outcomes.

Why this matters: Agency is the difference between governance and grievance. Blue cities keep choosing grievance.

"Compassion demands decriminalization." Measure 110's Class E violation regime (ORS § 475.890) advertised compassion and delivered funerals and boarded windows. Treatment requires leverage; leverage requires enforceable law.

Why this matters: Mercy without standards is abandonment. The addicts died while the activists congratulated themselves.

A Conservative Counter-Model: Freedom with Guardrails

Make housing legal. Replace discretionary review with objective, by-right standards. Time-limit CEQA/SEPA challenges. Expand as-of-right multifamily near jobs and transit. Write it down: "A permit application shall be deemed approved if not acted upon within 120 days."

Why it works: Predictability summons capital; capital builds homes; homes lower rents. It's gravity, not ideology.

Target need, not prices. Swap rent control for vouchers and supply; protect due process for owners and tenants alike.

Why it works: Help people, not units. Markets allocate; safety nets cushion. Together they raise living standards.

Restore consequence. Detain repeat violent and serial theft offenders; aggregate retail theft across incidents; target fencing markets; create fast-track retail theft courts.

Why it works: Behavior follows incentives. Make predation expensive and civility returns.

Simplify taxes. Kill gross receipts, head counts, and punitive transfer taxes. Compete on rates and predictability; broaden bases, lower rates.

Why it works: Growth is the only durable social program cities can actually deliver.

Demand outcomes from homelessness systems. Housing First with a backbone: "Supportive housing tenancy is contingent upon participation in treatment for substance use disorder where clinically indicated." Enforce shelter-right/sleep-right rules: no more legalized encampments that punish the poor with chaos.

Why it works: The street is not a treatment plan. Accountability is compassion's spine.

Build skills. Wage growth comes from productivity; productivity comes from skills. Expand apprenticeship, cut licensing barriers, and let work be legal.

Why it works: A ladder beats a lecture.

Selected Verbatim Statutes and Policy Text

CEQA purpose: "The purpose of this division is to inform governmental decisionmakers and the public about the potential, significant environmental effects of proposed activities" (Cal. Pub. Res. Code § 21001).

San Francisco Rent Ordinance: "This ordinance shall apply to all rental units in the City and County of San Francisco constructed prior to June 13, 1979" (SF Admin. Code ch. 37).

SF Overpaid Executive Tax: "A company is subject to the tax if the highest-paid managerial employee's compensation is at least 100 times more than the median employee compensation" (Prop L, 2020).

LA RSO freeze: "No rent increases are permitted for RSO units during the declared local emergency" (LAMC § 151.32).

LA Measure ULA: "There is imposed a special tax on the sale or other transfer of real property" (LAMC § 21.9.15).

CA fast-food wage: "A minimum wage of $20 per hour for fast food restaurant employees" (Cal. Lab. Code § 1475).

Illinois bail: "All persons charged with an offense shall be eligible for pretrial release" (725 ILCS 5/110-2).

Illinois retail theft thresholds: (720 ILCS 5/16-25).

NYC HSTPA findings: "It is necessary to prevent exactions of unjust, unreasonable, and oppressive rents" (L.2019, ch.36).

NYC Local Law 97: "Covered buildings shall not exceed annual building emissions limits" (NYC Admin. Code § 28-320.3).

NY bail: "Courts shall release the principal pending trial on the least restrictive alternative" (CPL § 510.10).

Philadelphia wage tax: "There is hereby imposed a tax on salaries, wages, commissions, and other compensation" (Phila. Code § 19-1502).

Philadelphia soda tax: "A tax is hereby imposed on the distribution of sweetened beverages" (Phila. Code § 19-4103).

Seattle minimum wage: "The hourly minimum wage rate for large employers shall be $19.97" (SMC § 14.19.030).

Seattle head tax (enacted then repealed): "A tax of $275 per employee per year" (Ord. 125594; repealed by Ord. 125683).

Oregon UGB: "A city shall establish and maintain an urban growth boundary" (ORS § 197.286).

Oregon Measure 110: "Unlawful possession of a controlled substance... is a Class E violation" (ORS § 475.890 as amended).

Chicago sanctuary rule: "No agency shall condition the provision of City benefits, opportunities, or services on citizenship or immigration status" (MCC § 2-173-020).

Detroit income tax: "A tax at the rate of 2.4 percent on the taxable income of every resident individual" (MCL 141.613; Detroit).

NY congestion pricing authorization: "A program of congestion pricing in a central business district" (NY Veh. & Traf. Law § 1704).

Conclusion: The Cost of Virtue Theater

Progressive governance in America's marquee cities turned ideals into invoices. They mistook process for progress, compassion for consequence-free policy, and taxation for strategy. The standard of living fell not by fate but by statute, ordinance, memo, and mandate.

The conservative answer is not cruelty; it is competence: legalize housing, honor work with growth, punish predation, and tax with humility. Reverse those premises and blue-city blues resolve into a different song: productivity, safety, mobility, and the freedom to build a life.

Chapter 10:

The Long March Through the Classroom

They told us the federal Department of Education would be the "coordinating" brain of American schooling, not the muscle. They promised it would "improve education" by sharing best practices, not dictate terms. Then it began issuing rules, waivers, "guidance," carrots, sticks, and threats. And like any bureaucracy with a budget and a mission, it discovered that it could expand both by declaring new "emergencies." Whose kids? Whose culture? Whose future?

Let's call the result what it is: a half-century project to nationalize the mind. The weapon is policy. The battleground is your child.

The Bargain We Never Approved

In 1979, Jimmy Carter signed the Department of Education into existence, an election-year gift to teachers' unions that had endorsed him, principally the NEA (see "President Carter's Message to Congress on the Establishment of a Department of Education," February 28, 1978, *The American Presidency Project*: https://www.presidency.ucsb.edu/). Carter pitched it as a way to "improve the management of Federal education activities" and "focus the Nation's attention on the importance of education" (ibid.).

Sounds harmless. But the premise was wrong: education is not a federal function in our constitutional order. The Founders knew local control is liberty's training ground.

Forty-five years later, what's the balance sheet? Spending is up, achievement flat, and trust broken. The federal role grew fat on promises and thin on results. Why did we accept that bargain?

Federal K–12 spending exploded since the 1960s while test scores stagnated. *The Nation's Report Card* (NAEP) shows long-term reading and math scores for 17-year-olds are essentially unchanged since the early 1970s, even as inflation-adjusted per-pupil spending more than doubled (NAEP Long-Term Trend Data; NCES Expenditure Tables, nces.ed.gov). If money was the medicine, why didn't the patient get better?

Barack Obama's Education Secretary Arne Duncan admitted in 2010, "High school graduation rates for African American and Latino students are unacceptably low, and achievement gaps are unacceptably wide" ("Preparing for the Future," speech, October 19, 2010, ed.gov). Yet the cure he pushed—national standards and more federal leverage—tightened the same screws that stripped autonomy from teachers and parents. Why assume the arsonist can be the firefighter?

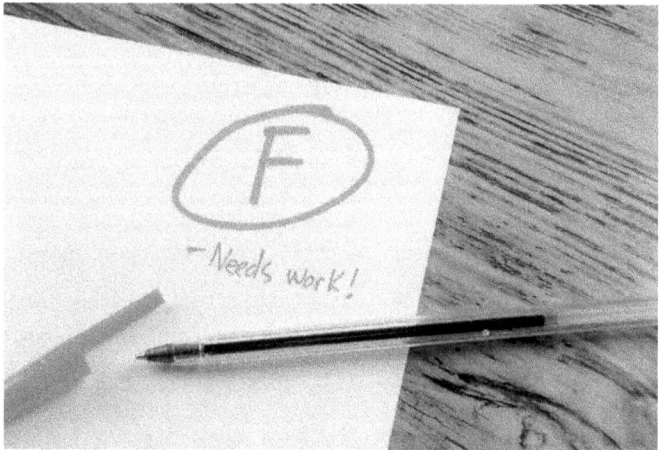

The Federal Hook: Money With Strings

The Elementary and Secondary Education Act (1965) opened the federal spigot; the Department of Education (1979) centralized the valve; No Child Left Behind (2001) and its waivers (2011–2012) converted classrooms into compliance centers.

George W. Bush called NCLB "the cornerstone of my administration" and promised it would "leave no child behind" (Signing statement, 1/8/2002, georgewbush-whitehouse.archives.gov). Ted Kennedy hailed it as "a defining issue" with "real reform" (Senate floor remarks, 12/18/2001, congressionalrecord.gov). But reform turned into paperwork, and progress turned into proficiency games. States lowered the bar to meet targets. Everyone passed—on paper.

By 2011, Duncan held states hostage: adopt "college- and career-ready standards" (read: Common Core) or lose relief from impossible NCLB mandates (U.S. Department of Education, ESEA

Flexibility, 2011, ed.gov). That's not "guidance." That's extortion by grant.

Arne Duncan admitted the leverage openly: "We have sought to fundamentally shift the federal role, so that the Department is doing much more to support reform at the state and local level" (Press briefing, 3/17/2011, ed.gov). Support? When a man with your paycheck in his fist offers "support," do you really feel free?

The Common Core Coup

Common Core's backers talked like missionaries and moved like lobbyists. The National Governors Association and the Council of Chief State School Officers—unelected groups—fronted the standards. Bill Gates supplied major funding. States signed up in a rush to chase Race to the Top grants during a recession.

What do you call a national education shift adopted by executive promise and rushed "stakeholder" meetings? Reform by ambush.

Arne Duncan's sales pitch sparkled with contempt: critics were "white suburban moms who—all of a sudden—their child isn't as brilliant as they thought they were" (Remarks at the Council of Chief State School Officers, 11/15/2013, reported by *The Washington Post*, 11/16/2013, washingtonpost.com). Should your child's education be shaped by a man who sneers at parents?

Even Bill Gates later conceded the timing flop: "We won't know for probably a decade" if Common Core works (American Enterprise Institute, 3/13/2014, aei.org). So we retrofitted states at scale, then crossed our fingers. Is that how pilots test wings after takeoff?

And the promise? The federal line: standards don't dictate curriculum; they're just goals. Yet testing consortia (PARCC, SBAC) and textbook publishers aligned content anyway, sweeping thousands of classrooms into the same template. A de facto national curriculum emerged, enforced by tests that punished deviation. Choice without options is theater.

The Teachers' Unions: Power Without Performance

Randi Weingarten of the AFT boasted during COVID: "We've tried to reopen schools safely since April [2020]" (CNN, 5/2/2021, cnn.com). But AFT emails showed the union directly editing CDC reopening guidance, pushing for stricter thresholds that kept classrooms closed (New York Post, 5/1/2021; House Select Subcommittee on the Coronavirus Crisis Staff Report, 5/13/2022, oversight.house.gov). Who elected a union to co-author public health policy?

Meanwhile, the children paid. NAEP 2022 showed the "largest average score decline in reading since 1990, and the first ever score decline in mathematics" for 9-year-olds (NCES, "NAEP Long-Term Trend 2022," 9/1/2022, nces.ed.gov). If this were a business, would we keep the management team? Or would we fire the board that cheered them on?

Joe Biden praised Randi Weingarten: "Randi, you're a champion" (AFT convention remarks, 7/14/2022, aft.org). A champion of what—closures, remote chaos, and disappearing math?

Race to the Top: Cash for Compliance

Race to the Top dangled $4.35 billion to hardwire federal preferences into state law. Obama said the quiet part loud: "We're going to raise the bar. We're going to reward success and replicate it" (Remarks, 7/24/2009, whitehouse.gov). Translate: we will pay you to change your laws.

States obliged, tweaking teacher evaluations, standards, and caps on charter schools—all to score points on a federal rubric (U.S. Department of Education, "Race to the Top Program Executive Summary," 11/2009, ed.gov).

Arne Duncan crowed: "We now have 48 states and D.C. working to develop common, college- and career-ready standards" (Press call, 6/1/2010, ed.gov). How was that "state-led" when Washington put a bounty on obedience?

Title IX as Cultural Crowbar

When Congress passed Title IX in 1972, it prohibited sex discrimination. Full stop. But over the last decade, executive "guidance" stretched the category like taffy.

The Obama-era 2016 "Dear Colleague" letter pressed schools into new procedures on sexual misconduct with lowered evidentiary standards (preponderance of evidence) and curtailed cross-examination (U.S. Department of Education, Office for Civil Rights, 4/4/2011; 4/29/2014 Q&A; 9/22/2017 rescission at ed.gov).

In 2020, DeVos restored due process rules (34 C.F.R. Part 106, 5/6/2020, ed.gov). The Biden administration moved again to expand "sex" to include gender identity in Title IX regulations (Notice of Proposed Rulemaking, 6/23/2022; Final Rule announced 4/19/2024, ed.gov). Are we rewriting statutes by memo?

Miguel Cardona said: "Title IX... ensures that no person is denied educational opportunities on the basis of sex" and framed the new rules as "protecting LGBTQI+ students" (Press release, 4/19/2024, ed.gov). Protect whom from what, and at what cost to due process and parental rights? When definitions bend, rights break.

The Test-Score Mirage

For decades, reformers promised that standards and testing would lift all boats. The boat never rose. NAEP long-term trends are stubborn. The 17-year-old line sits flat. After trillions in local, state, and federal investment, the plateau mocks the narrative.

NAEP 17-year-old math scores in 2020 were statistically similar to 1978; reading echoed the same flatline (NCES, NAEP LTT, nces.ed.gov).

Arne Duncan's 2013 claim that "the nation's high school graduation rate has reached a new record high" (Press release, 1/22/2013, ed.gov) came alongside grade inflation and district "credit recovery" shortcuts. Did we educate better, or did we just change the scoreboard?

If the scoreboard's broken, why do we keep playing the same game?

COVID: The Catastrophe That Told the Truth

School closures were the largest domestic policy error of the century. They were driven by union pressure and enabled by a Department that had every incentive to avoid accountability. Despite early evidence that schools could reopen with mitigations, many districts stayed shuttered for a year.

Randi Weingarten now says, "We spent every day from February [2020] on trying to get schools open" (AFT testimony, 4/26/2023, oversight.house.gov). The paper trail contradicts her. The AFT lobbied for closure-friendly language in CDC guidance (House Oversight Minority Staff Memo, 5/17/2023, oversight.house.gov). Who paid the price? Children, especially the poor.

NAEP 2022 laid it bare: plunges in 9-year-old math and reading, with the steepest losses among the lowest performers (NCES, 9/1/2022, nces.ed.gov). Black and Hispanic students were hammered. We mandated masks, Zoom, and "equity"—and produced the most inequitable learning losses in memory. How many sermons about "systemic injustice" can you preach while defending the system that caused it?

Biden called reopening a priority, then hedged behind "following the science," while the science was being ghostwritten by union lawyers (White House briefings, 2021; CDC emails released via FOIA, 2021, energycommerce.house.gov). "Safe" became an incantation that meant "never." Was that public health or public sector politics?

College: Subsidy, Inflation, Indoctrination

The Department of Education doesn't just shape the K–12 classroom; it underwrites the campus. Federal student aid was meant to widen opportunity. Instead, it fueled tuition inflation and a credential arms race. Then came the political dessert course: loan "forgiveness."

Joe Biden said, "I'm going to forgive $10,000 in student debt" (Campaign remark, 2020, multiple outlets). In 2022 he announced a broad cancellation plan; the Supreme Court struck it down: "The Secretary's plan created a novel and fundamentally different loan forgiveness program" beyond statutory authority (*Biden v. Nebraska*, 6/30/2023, supremecourt.gov).

Biden pivoted to piecemeal cancellations through regulatory routes (White House Fact Sheets, 2023–2024, whitehouse.gov). When Congress says no and the Court says no, do you try again by memo?

Meanwhile, what do students buy with their debt? Bureaucracy and ideology. Bloated DEI offices. Freshman orientations as political catechisms. Title IX offices as campus tribunals. The Department's enforcement posture rewards the expansion of administrative apparatus that polices speech and process. Is that education or acculturation to rule by mandate?

The Curriculum of Cynicism

The left insists that schooling is neutral technocracy — the science of learning and data-driven instruction. Yet the content pipeline tilts hard. "Culturally responsive" becomes anti-liberal race essentialism. "Media literacy" becomes ideological filtration. "Social-emotional learning" morphs into the psychological normalization of political attitudes. And when parents object, they are treated as intruders.

Remember when the National School Boards Association asked the Biden administration to treat parent protests as potential "domestic terrorism"? The NSBA letter (9/29/2021) was quickly disavowed after backlash, but DOJ's Merrick Garland issued a memo directing FBI coordination with local authorities on "threats" to school personnel (DOJ Memo, 10/4/2021, justice.gov). Chilling effect achieved. Speak up, get flagged. Is that how free people talk to their government?

Miguel Cardona, asked about parents' rights, offered the bureaucrat's koan: "Parents are important stakeholders" (Various interviews, e.g., CNN, 2022). Stakeholders? Parents aren't "stakeholders." They are owners. Whose children are these?

The Data Says "Local," the Bureaucracy Says "National"

Choice works because it trusts families. Florida's expansion of vouchers and charters drove competitive improvements in both choice and traditional public schools over two decades (see, e.g., Florida Tax Credit Scholarship research summaries, Urban Institute, 2019, urban.org; EdChoice reports, edchoice.org). Massachusetts' 1993 reform mixed standards with curricular freedom and content-rich instruction and produced NAEP gains — until the state embraced nationalized testing and standards and stalled (Massachusetts DESE historical NAEP profiles, nces.ed.gov). When states lead with content and autonomy, kids win. When Washington leads with compliance and metrics, kids tread water.

Arne Duncan once mocked Texas for resisting Common Core: "I feel very, very badly for the children there" (Quote reported by *The Washington Post*, 11/9/2013, washingtonpost.com). Texas students then outperformed many Common Core states on NAEP. Who should feel "very, very badly" now?

The Language of "Equity" as a Cover for Low Expectations

The Department's "equity" turn sounds noble but often means softer grading, fewer honors classes, test-optional college admissions, and a retreat from merit. If outcomes differ, the policy assumes discrimination; if standards bite, the policy blames the standards. That isn't equality before the law. It's a permission structure for failure.

Barack Obama said, "We reject the notion that there are some schools you can't turn around" (Race to the Top speech, 7/24/2009, whitehouse.gov). The turnarounds became rebrandings. We renamed failure "equitable growth." We taught students that the ladder is unfair, then pulled up the rungs.

The Anti-Parent Reflex

The left's default posture is: comply, or be called names. Ask to see the curriculum, and you're a book banner. Object to explicit material for 11-year-olds, and you're a prude. Question biological boys in girls' sports, and you're a bigot. In Virginia, when parents revolted in 2021, Terry McAuliffe said the quiet part out loud: "I don't think parents should be telling schools what they should teach" (Gubernatorial debate, 9/28/2021, nbcnews.com). That line lost him the election, but it revealed the creed.

Schools teach your children "for" you, not "with" you.

Joe Biden echoed the frame: "There is no such thing as someone else's child. Our nation's children are all our children" (Teacher of the Year event, 4/24/2023, whitehouse.gov). A poetic sentiment, or a political claim? The state doesn't own our sons and daughters. Parents do.

The Department That Can't Stop Growing

Bureaucracies expand like ivy — slowly, inexorably, covering the brickwork of local life. Carter promised "greater efficiency" (1978 message to Congress, presidency.ucsb.edu). Every administration since has added a trellis. ESSA (2015) was marketed as "returning power to states," yet the Department retained oversight teeth and Title I strings, along with civil rights enforcement that writes rules by "Dear Colleague" letter.

Miguel Cardona describes the Department's role as "a support and a partner" (ED press availabilities, 2021–2024, ed.gov). But a partner with the power to pull your funding and open an investigation isn't a partner; it's an overlord with a smile.

The Department of Education began in 1979 with roughly 4,000 employees. It now hovers around that number but with far greater regulatory reach and over $70–$100 billion in annual budget authority, depending on stimulus years (ED Budget History, ed.gov; OMB historical tables, whitehouse.gov).

The headcount distracts from the real footprint: guidance, grant conditions, investigative letters, and negotiated rulemakings that bind the system in red tape. You can strangle without growing bigger — just tighten the strings.

The Lie of "Neutral Expertise"

"Trust the experts," they say. Which experts? The ones who spent a decade telling parents Common Core math was a "better way," as scores slid? The ones who insisted school closures would "save lives," as mental health crises spiked and learning cratered? The ones who declare "equity" will raise achievement, as standards dissolve?

Arne Duncan dismissed dissenters as political: "The idea that the Common Core standards are a conspiracy… is ridiculous" (*Politico*, 6/25/2013, politico.com). But the conspiracy wasn't secret; it was in the open — use federal money and regulatory threats to compel uniformity. That's not paranoia. That's the *Federal Register*.

The Parents' Rebellion

Across the country, parents are electing school boards, auditing curricula, and demanding transparency. States like Florida, Arizona, and West Virginia have expanded universal or near-universal school choice (FL HB1, 2023; AZ ESA expansion, 2022; WV Hope Scholarship, 2021). The left howls that choice will "defund" public schools. But public schools are not entitled to students; students are entitled to an education.

Miguel Cardona sneered, "I don't want to go back to the 'good old days'" when parents had "book bans" and "hateful rhetoric" (Remarks, 2023, ed.gov). That's the trope: if you want to see what your child learns, you're a hater. If you want phonics over fads, you're retrograde. If you want merit over meltdowns, you're cruel. Does anyone still buy this?

What Actually Works

We know what works: content-rich curricula; systematic phonics; teacher autonomy with accountability to parents; rigorous, knowledge-sequenced standards tied to classic texts and real math;

order in classrooms; consequences for disorder; vocational pathways; and competition that rewards excellence.

E. D. Hirsch Jr. begged America to remember that knowledge builds on knowledge. His Core Knowledge sequence delivered gains where tried. The Department yawned. Why? Because content isn't a federal lever; it's local craft. Bureaucrats can mandate tests; they cannot mandate wisdom.

Systematic phonics has the strongest evidence base for early reading (National Reading Panel Report, 2000; IES practice guides, ies.ed.gov). Yet for years, education schools pushed "balanced literacy," and districts bought it. When parents demanded phonics, reformers acted shocked. Why is the burden always on parents to rescue their kids from experts?

Accountability, Not Centralization

The federal government can publish data and police discrimination. It cannot, and must not, run schools. Every time it tries, it confuses measurement with learning and politics with pedagogy.

Barack Obama, in a moment of candor, said of Race to the Top: "We did not create the standards, but we encouraged states to develop them" (State of the Union, 1/27/2010, obamawhitehouse.archives.gov). Encouraged, as in: here's the money, here are the waivers, here are the consequences. That's the soft glove over an iron fist.

Joe Biden framed student debt cancellation as "giving people a little more breathing room" (Remarks, 8/24/2022, whitehouse.gov). The breathing room for borrowers meant suffocation for the rule of law and a subsidy for the higher-ed machine that captured them. Do we fund failure or free the victims?

The Moral Case for Dismantling the Department

If you designed a federal agency to keep children safe from learning, what would it do differently from the Department of Education? It would:

Make schools answer to Washington, not parents. Reward ideological compliance over academic content. Inflate credentials and debt. Expand rules via "guidance" to bypass Congress. Partner with unions to protect the adults in the system. Convert crises into budget lines.

That's the record. Not a conspiracy. A paper trail.

Carter's "coordination" became coercion. Bush's "accountability" became testing tyranny. Obama's "innovation" became nationalization. Biden's "equity" became a solvent that dissolves merit, due process, and parental rights. The Department did not just fail. It succeeded at the wrong mission.

What's Next: Return the Schools to the People

Here's the path forward:

1. **Sunset the Department and devolve its functions.**

- Civil rights enforcement goes to the DOJ's existing apparatus with a narrowed, statute-faithful scope.
- Data collection goes to an independent statistical agency with zero regulatory power.
- All K–12 grantmaking folds into block grants to states, or better yet, direct-to-family education savings accounts with minimal federal strings.
- Student lending moves to capped, risk-sharing bank-issued loans. The federal origination spigot closes.

2. **A Parent's Bill of Rights, national and state.**

- Curriculum transparency, opt-out rights for ideological content, and immediate access to all instructional materials.
- Due process in student discipline and sexual misconduct cases.
- Notification and consent for health and counseling services.

3. **Restore merit and order.**

- State standards centered on knowledge and classical texts.
- End "restorative justice" regimes that erase consequences and endanger classrooms.
- Selective public magnet schools, vocational pathways, and apprenticeships.

4. **Expand universal choice.**

    • Dollars follow students to public, charter, private, micro-school, pod, or homeschool.

    • End the monopoly. Monopolies ossify. Markets learn. Is this radical, or a return to American common sense?

After the Fall: Dismantling the Department, Child by Child, State by State

Donald J. Trump said the quiet part loud and then said it again for the people in the back: "We will close the Department of Education" and "send all education decisions back to the states and back to the parents" (Policy video, 1/2024, donaldjtrump.com).

In campaign planks and speeches, he linked the end of the federal education bureaucracy to a renaissance in parental authority and merit: "Our children are not wards of the state. They are ours, and we will protect them" (Education agenda video, 1/2024, donaldjtrump.com). He pledged to "cut federal funding for any school pushing critical race theory, transgender insanity, and other inappropriate racial, sexual, or political content on our children" (ibid.).

The first term previewed the model. Betsy DeVos restored due process to Title IX by returning cross-examination and a higher bar for campus adjudications (34 C.F.R. Part 106, Final Rule, 5/6/2020, ed.gov). Trump declared a National Charter Schools Week to "support high-quality charter schools" and called on states to expand school choice so "parents can choose the best educational setting for their children" (Proclamation 10002, 7/23/2020, federalregister.gov; whitehouse.gov archive). He backed tax-advantaged scholarships and ESAs, tying funding to students rather than systems (White House Fact Sheets on School Choice, 2019–2020, whitehouse.gov archives).

Then came the second-term blueprint: "On day one, we will begin dismantling the federal Department of Education," consolidating or devolving its functions and "ending the weaponization of the Department" through rule-by-memo and ideological enforcement (2024 policy video and Agenda47 postings, 2023–2024, donaldjtrump.com).

What happens when the Washington strings are cut?

• Dollars stop chasing bureaucracies and start following children. When funds flow through block grants and ESAs, families pick phonics-forward curricula, classical academies, STEM magnets, vocational programs, and microschools. The monopoly loosens; excellence scales.

• Government-by-guidance dies. No more 11th-hour "Dear Colleague" letters that rewrite statutes at the stroke of a pen. Schools answer to law and parents, not federal whims.

• Merit returns. Without a federal apparatus to launder low expectations as "equity," states can restore honors tracks, selective schools, and content-rich instruction that builds knowledge cumulatively.

• Teachers teach. Compliance staff shrink. The time stolen for federal paperwork returns to lesson planning, tutoring, lab work, and reading aloud, where the learning lives.

Trump's case is blunt because the stakes are not subtle: "We're going to end the left-wing capture of the schools" and "protect parents' rights" (Policy video, 1/2024, donaldjtrump.com). He frames it as liberation: free the classroom from Washington, and you free the child sitting in it.

Will states rise to the responsibility? They already are. Arizona's universal ESAs, Florida's HB1 expansion, and West Virginia's Hope Scholarship are prototypes for a post-Department America. When money follows the student, schools become answerable to the only people who matter: the family at the kitchen table.

The Last Word

They told you the Department of Education would make learning fairer, smarter, and more modern. It made school political, brittle, and mediocre. They told you national standards would lift the floor. They lowered it and called it progress. They told you testing would make schools accountable. It made them evasive. They told you closures would save lives. They cost learning, friendship, trust, and time.

Jimmy Carter sold you a coordinator. You got a command center. Barack Obama sold you innovation. You got a national template. Joe Biden sells you equity. You get a solvent that erases merit and parenthood. The ledger doesn't lie. The scores don't lie. The kids aren't lying when they look at a page and can't read it.

And now, for once, a promise aimed at subtraction, not addition: shrink Washington's role, end the Department's reign, and return schools to states and parents. Trump's vow to dismantle the D.O.E. isn't a gambit. It's the first honest admission in half a century that the center cannot educate what the center does not know: your child.

Close the building, open the books, and give the authority back to the people who love the student more than any bureaucrat can. If not now, when do we take our schools back?

References (inline citations above):

U.S. Department of Education speeches, regulations, and press releases (ed.gov).

NAEP/NCES reports and datasets (nces.ed.gov).

The American Presidency Project archives (presidency.ucsb.edu).

White House archives and fact sheets (whitehouse.gov).

Supreme Court: *Biden v. Nebraska* (2023) (supremecourt.gov).

Congressional records and House Oversight documents (congressionalrecord.gov; oversight.house.gov).

Media quotations as noted (Washington Post, Politico, CNN, NBC).

Chapter 11:
The People's Veto

Epigraphs

• "No free man shall ever be debarred the use of arms." — Thomas Jefferson, draft of the Virginia Constitution, 1776

• "What country can preserve its liberties if their rulers are not warned from time to time that their people preserve the spirit of resistance?" — Jefferson to William Stephens Smith, 1787

• "The great object is that every man be armed." — George Mason, Virginia Ratifying Convention, 1788

• "To preserve liberty, it is essential that the whole body of the people always possess arms." — Richard Henry Lee, *Letters from the Federal Farmer*, 1788

• "Who are the militia? They consist now of the whole people, except a few public officers." — George Mason, Virginia Ratifying Convention, 1788

• "The militia is the natural defense of a free country." — James Burgh, *Political Disquisitions*, 1774, widely read by the Founders

• "The Constitution of most of our states... assert that all power is inherent in the people; that they may exercise it by themselves." — Thomas Jefferson, 1776

• "The right of the citizens to keep and bear arms has justly been considered as the palladium of the liberties of a republic." — St. George Tucker, *Blackstone's Commentaries* (American ed.), 1803

• "One of the ordinary modes by which tyrants accomplish their purposes without resistance is by disarming the people." — Joseph Story, *Commentaries on the Constitution*, 1833

• "The great principle is that every man be armed... Everyone who is able may have a gun." — Patrick Henry, Virginia Ratifying Convention, 1788

I. Amnesia by Design

They say the Right has nostalgia; the Left has amnesia. Incorrect. The Left has curation, history cropped to fit the poster. They pluck "well regulated militia," inflate it into a bureaucratic balloon animal, and parade it through hearings as if the Framers meant "licensed by appointed experts."

When did a constitutional "right of the people" become a privilege of the paperwork class? When did "shall not be infringed" get a silent asterisk, unless we feel anxious this news cycle?

This is not forgetfulness; it is strategy. A people who forget why they were armed can be told they never truly were. A culture shamed away from competence can be persuaded to outsource its safety to officials who clock out at five.

The Founders lived with the smell of tyranny in their hair. They did not write rights in pencil; they carved them with a bayonet. The

Second Amendment is the people's circuit breaker, mounted on the wall of the Republic, brightly labeled: *In case of emergency, break glass.*

II. The Founders Wrote in Gunpowder, Not Pencil

To read the Framers straight is to feel the voltage. Jefferson's "No free man shall ever be debarred the use of arms" was not a deer-camp diary. Richard Henry Lee wrote that "the whole body of the people always possess arms." St. George Tucker, the first major American constitutional commentator, called the right to bear arms "the palladium of the liberties of a republic." Joseph Story, a Supreme Court justice, warned that disarming the people is a tyrant's favorite prelude.

Federalist 46 is Madison's quiet thunder. He compares an armed citizenry, organized through the states, to any standing army and concludes the government would be outnumbered, outrooted, and outwilled. He assumed a people "accustomed to arms," not museum-goers admiring muskets under glass, but citizens who knew which end sparks lightning.

George Mason stripped it to the bone: "Who are the militia? They consist now of the whole people." If words mean things, *the people* means you.

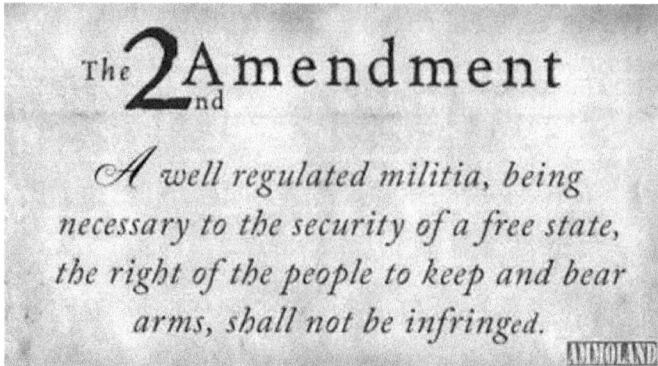

III. The "Collective Right" Mirage

We're told rights are suddenly collective when they become inconvenient. The First protects "the right of the people peaceably to assemble," and nobody claims you need a government escort to stand on a sidewalk. The Fourth secures "the right of the people" against searches; nobody argues the governor owns your privacy. Why should the Second play by opposite rules? Because that's the only way to neuter it while pretending to honor it.

A "collective right" managed by the state against the state is a magician sawing a woman in half and calling it healthcare. It changes the subject from sovereignty to supervision. The Founders built a republic of adults. They were not issuing a gun-lending program to be recalled when moods soured in committee.

IV. The "Kill Switch"

They knew we'd need it. "Kill switch?" they gasp, as if tyrannies politely RSVP, as if the last century's mass graves grew from tulips.

The Second Amendment is not a lust for violence; it is the opposite, the sober calculus that deterrence prevents violence. When the governed can say "No," they rarely have to say "Now." When rulers see the people's teeth, they moderate their appetite.

History in our own house: Japanese Americans interned by executive pen, freedmen disarmed by Black Codes, civil-rights workers protected by armed neighbors when the sheriff dined with the Klan. The Second is a promise with a warning label: citizens are sovereign. Forget that, and the light goes red.

V. The Common-Law Lineage the Left Forgets

Our right didn't fall from a Liberty Tree fruit bowl; it grew from the Anglo-American trunk. William Blackstone recognized the auxiliary right of subjects to have arms for defense, supporting the primary rights of personal security and liberty. James Burgh wrote that the militia is the natural defense of a free country. The English Bill of Rights of 1689 secured Protestants the right to have arms suitable to their condition. The American project widened, deepened, and democratized that instinct: not a class right, not a sect right, a people's right.

St. George Tucker took Blackstone and Americanized him. Arms are not just for hunting; they are constitutional architecture. Joseph Story warned that the moment you disarm citizens, you smooth the path to despotism. Early state constitutions echoed the same rhetoric with variations in Pennsylvania, Vermont, and North

Carolina, cementing that the right was individual, for defense of self and state, coequal with speech.

VI. The Technology Canard

"But they couldn't imagine AR-15s!" They couldn't imagine TikTok either. The First still protects a livestream with a billion viewers. Principles scale. The militia concept presumes parity sufficient to make oppression impractical. In 1791, that meant the common arms of the infantryman—muskets, rifles, pistols. Today, it means the functional descendants: semiautomatic rifles and handguns in common use. Tools evolve; rights do not molt into permissions.

The AR-15 is demonized because it is effective, adaptable, and popular. Popularity is not a bug; it is a constitutional feature. A right protects the common, not just the quaint. The "weapons of war" line is a branding exercise. The militia clause references the military purpose directly. Citizens keep arms precisely because they may be called, formally or morally, to defend more than their living room.

VII. Rhetoric vs. Reality: The Shameful Dance After Tragedy

Tragedy is oxygen to opportunists. Before the facts congeal, the same bills reappear like cicadas: ban this cosmetic feature, criminalize that transfer, raise the compliance bar just enough to snag the law-abiding while the lawless walk under it. "Do something!" becomes "Do the things that failed elsewhere, louder."

A country that wanted safety would harden targets, speed interdiction, and excise the small population driving most serious violence. It would invest in mental-health surge capacity and use lawful flags with due process to interrupt acute danger, not as a back door to disarm millions. It would place trained guardians where children gather and accept that evil hates friction. The question is not whether force meets force; it is whether that force arrives in six seconds or six minutes.

VIII. Evidence: If Gun Control Worked, These Places Would Be Safe

If laws were talismans, strict-jurisdiction cities would be sanctuaries. They are not. The homicide landscape concentrates intensely in hot blocks and among chronic offenders. Where enforcement is focused, violence drops. Where prosecutors perform catch-and-release theater, blood rises.

Rifle bans jiggle at the margins because rifles are used in a tiny share of murders. Magazine bans are ergonomics by press release; criminals bring more magazines or ignore the law. "Universal" background checks criminalize peaceable transfers between relatives and friends while straw buyers and traffickers skate. The impact rarely survives contact with honest accounting.

Meanwhile, the feared avalanche of violence from concealed carry never arrived. Permit holders offend at rates lower than police officers in many jurisdictions. Defensive gun uses often require no trigger pull—deterrence by presence. You cannot graph the crimes that never happen, but you can notice how predators read risk. They choose soft targets. If you insist on creating them, do not act shocked when wolves move in.

IX. The Moral Geometry of Responsibility

Being armed is not cosplay; it is a vocation of citizenship. Range rules are ethics in motion: muzzle discipline, target identification, storage, humility. Dismiss that as "gun culture," and you miss the civic culture inside it—the habit of bearing responsibility without a supervisor.

The same people mocked as insecure are the ones you want behind you in a bad minute—the EMT with a med kit, the neighbor who drills fire plans, the church usher who knows where the exits are and how to lock a door.

Gun control, at bottom, is a trust question. Do you trust citizens or curators? Elites flanked by armed details insist you trust their abstractions. They live behind hardened glass and then call your deadbolt paranoia. Protection for me, vulnerability for thee. It is not policy; it is class.

X. History's Echoes: From Lexington to Lowndes County

The first shots of our Revolution sparked over gun confiscation runs. The British marched to seize powder and arms; the people met them on the green. The lesson is not cosplay; it is clarity. Those who fear your arms seldom plan to leave your rights alone.

Postwar America offered cruel proof that disarmed citizens bleed. After emancipation, Black citizens asserted the right to keep and bear arms, and local authorities responded with Black Codes to strip that right. The armed defense of civil rights did not end in 1866. In the twentieth century, organizations like the Deacons for Defense protected communities when official protection did not exist or was actively hostile. When the state is indifferent or predatory, the right to arms becomes the right to draw breath.

And the political reaction? California's Mulford Act clipped open carry when the wrong citizens—Black citizens—exercised it. Elites discover a sudden appetite for restrictions when power feels personally inconvenienced. Gun control's history tracks closely with the urge to control the people least represented in rooms where laws are made.

XI. The Law Catches Up

For decades, courts napped while legislatures nibbled. Then *Heller* recognized what was obvious to anyone who can diagram a sentence: the Second protects an individual right. *McDonald* nationalized that recognition. *Bruen* added a spine; if a modern restriction lacks deep historical analogues, it is constitutionally suspect. Translation: stop inventing "good cause" hoops and calling them safety.

More cases are shoring up the edges: that common electric weapons are protected tools, that subjective "may issue" licensing invites abuse, that historical tradition does not bless modern

179

registries and bans with a sprinkle of antique pixie dust. Expect resistance from bureaucracies allergic to limits. That is why the right exists: not for hunting season, but for constitutional muscle memory.

XII. What "Well Regulated" Really Means

Eighteenth-century English uses "well regulated" like a craftsman referring to a clock—properly functioning. The clause assumes a people practiced in arms, not a people permitted in drips. Swap meaning as the Left does, and you rewrite the sentence: "A militia controlled by officials being necessary… the right of those officials shall not be infringed." That isn't the Constitution; that's a memo to a garrison state.

A well-regulated militia in the Founders' tongue equals a well-trained populace. The antidote to fear is familiarity. Teach the young respect and competence. Normalize safe carry, safe storage, and safe speech about unsafe realities. Rust grows on rights left in the dark.

XIII. The Culture They're Really After

The antagonist here isn't a steel-and-polymer object. It's an anthropology—a human type: the citizen who sees himself as the steward of his own fate. He changes his own oil; he prays without being told; he helps a neighbor move a couch; he stands when the color guard passes, not because he's watched but because he believes. He is the pebble in the technocrat's shoe. He messes up the neat columns in the spreadsheet. He is inconvenient precisely because he does not need permission to be dangerous to those who would harm him.

This is why the rhetoric becomes moralized. They label ordinary tools "weapons of war" and ordinary men "extremists" for owning them. Make the common abnormal; make the normal transgressive. Shame the decent until they whisper their decency, then legislate the whisper away.

XIV. The Shabby Science of Disarmament

You can rent a conclusion, but you pay in footnotes. Studies that trumpet "X law reduced Y violence" often smuggle errors: short time windows, cherry-picked controls, pre-trend differences ignored, or composite outcomes padded by suicides or accidents while the claim is about murder. When randomized trials are impossible, honesty demands humility. Instead, we get press releases with decimal points.

The cleanest test remains the one common sense proposes: target the violent, incapacitate the chronic offenders, and you reduce violence. Target ownership by the peaceable, and you rearrange paperwork while predators laugh. Disarm the lawful, and you shift the risk-reward calculus toward the wolf. He reads the law differently: *Is my prey likely to be defended?*

XV. Case Studies in Consequence

- **Soft jurisdiction, hard outcomes:** Urban centers with stacked restrictions and politically performative prosecutors have watched gun violence concentrate in neighborhoods starved of order and overfed with impunity. The laws are strict on paper and thin on pavement.

- **"Assault weapon" theater:** Bans that focus on cosmetic features leave function intact for the criminal while disarming the homeowner of an ergonomic, controllable platform. Homicide trends refuse to obey the speeches.

- **Magazine limits:** When seconds matter and misses are common under stress, reducing capacity handicaps only the defender who starts at zero. A criminal can carry two magazines; a mother cannot conjure police.

- **Permit-to-purchase schemes:** New fees and procedural hurdles harvest law-abiding applicants and do little to filter the violent. The black market does not file in triplicate.

- **Constitutional carry expansions:** Predictions of carnage repeatedly fail. The faces on the evening news are the same recidivists under the same lenient supervision. The difference you feel is the one the mugger feels at arm's length.

XVI. The Arithmetic of Freedom

Hundreds of millions of guns; billions of rounds fired annually in peaceful practice; a tiny fraction misused criminally. If guns were the pathogen, prevalence would equal pandemic. Instead, violence clusters in predictable patterns; policy can target it if politics allows.

Defensive uses, widely estimated in the hundreds of thousands yearly, are often bloodless. The gun leaves leather; the crime evaporates.

How do you count what didn't happen? You tally the realities we do see: burglars favor occupied homes less where homeowners are likely to be armed; spree killers select venues with low resistance; carjackers hunt where drivers are disarmed by statute. The map of risk is a map of incentives.

XVII. The Parable of the Lock

Imagine a mayor proud to ban locks because "locks sometimes fail." He holds a press conference in front of a smashed window and blames doorknobs. Meanwhile, across the river, another mayor buys better locks, jails the burglars who keep getting caught with glass in their hair, and publishes the names of prosecutors who treat burglary as a paperwork glitch.

Where do thieves commute? Where does ordinary life normalize? Guns are locks. They don't cause burglary; they complicate it.

XVIII. Answering the Usual Questions

- **What about mass shooters?** They are narcissists seeking soft targets and spectacle. Harden access points, employ trained defenders, cut response times, drill staff, and stop awarding sainthood-by-headshot on cable news. Use targeted, due-process red flags for individuals making explicit threats, not as a universal fishing license.

- **What about suicides?** This is a mental health crisis, not a pretext to punish millions. Expand access, destigmatize treatment, support voluntary temporary transfer tools within families and communities, and improve crisis response. Confiscation-as-therapy is lazy governance.

- **What about accidents?** Education works. Gun-owning households are often fanatic about safety because they teach it early and often. Encourage secure storage without criminalizing self-defense. Incentivize, don't infantilize.

- **What about police?** They cannot be everywhere; they arrive after. The question is whether you face the interim naked or clothed in means. Your life is not a municipal resource to be rationed.

- **What about "needs"?** Rights are not distributable by need. They exist to create space for autonomy. If need is the threshold, the powerful always decide yours is insufficient.

XIX. Two Paths Before Us

The first path is velvet submission. Make the citizen docile. Trade citizenship for clienthood. Pledge safety in exchange for dependence. Hire more press secretaries to explain why the surge in crime you can see is a misperception you must unlearn.

The second path is adulthood. Keep the power where the Constitution parked it: in the people. Normalize competence. Expect officials to remember that sovereignty flows uphill. Make would-be tyrants do math: millions of homes, millions of hearts, millions of guardians. The more credible the veto, the less often it is tested.

XX. A Letter to the Nervous Liberal Friend

You want "common sense"? Here's our common sense: don't criminalize the decent to inconvenience the wicked. Don't force a single mother to choose between a felony and an empty nightstand because a committee fears her competence. Don't let officials turn rights into licenses that can be revoked by whim.

If you love civil liberties, love the one that defends all the others. We don't want your submission. We want your partnership on prosecuting violence, on mending mental health, on building institutions that take warning signs seriously and act before the sirens. Keep the rights; keep the teeth.

XXI. The People's Veto, Clarified

The phrase makes the faint-hearted flinch. Good. Freedom should carry a weight that strains unserious shoulders. The People's Veto is not a daydream of insurrection; it is a perpetual reminder that in the American hierarchy, the citizen stands taller than the clerk.

The veto's presence disciplines the powerful. A government certain it cannot force you will spend more time persuading you. That's the music of a republic.

XXII. The Last Word

We won't bow to lectures about violence from those who subcontract theirs. We won't turn a natural right into a leased privilege. We won't let the word "militia" be rewritten to mean "whoever the governor likes this week."

The Founders wrote as if speaking to us across a field of years, their voices steady, their warnings hot: *Be armed. Be trained. Be worthy.* Not because you crave a fight, but because you refuse to be mastered.

They can edit the civics textbook. They can pass laws that bite the wrong throats. They can hire language to do violence to meaning. But the sentence resists, stubborn as a farmer, loud as a drumline on the green: the right of the people to keep and bear arms shall not be infringed. Not shaved, not sliced, not "balanced" into oblivion. It is the spine that keeps the head up and the gaze level.

Save the republic? Keep the switch where the Founders bolted it: in the people's hands, within easy reach, behind glass that reads, "In case of tyranny, break."

Chapter 12:

The Border That Ate the Budget (In Their Own Words)

If your kitchen sink is overflowing, do you reach for a mop or turn off the tap? In Washington, you call a press conference and announce the water is "secure." Don't take my word for it—take theirs. As crossings surged and buses rolled, the talking points calcified into theology, and the theology into policy. The result isn't theoretical; it's rent, wages, school staffing, ER triage, and city budgets buckling while officials serve up euphemisms like hors d'oeuvres.

Start with the text that's supposed to anchor it all. Congress wrote, "The alien shall be detained" during expedited removal and credible-fear screening [8 U.S.C. §1225(b)(1)(B)(ii)]. It imposed a one-year filing deadline for asylum [8 U.S.C. §1158(a)(2)(B)]. It authorized parole "temporarily... on a case-by-case basis for urgent humanitarian reasons or significant public benefit" [8 U.S.C. §1182(d)(5)(A)]. It made it "unlawful to hire" unauthorized workers and empowered real penalties [8 U.S.C. §1324a(a)]. And it used "shall" again for certain criminal detentions [8 U.S.C. §1226(c)]. Regulations tie employment authorization to asylum backlogs with waiting periods [8 C.F.R. §208.7]. That's the statutory spine. Now listen to the microphone.

"The border is secure." That wasn't satire; it was the line. "The border is secure."[1] "There is no circumstance in which the border is wide open. The border is secure."[2] "We have a secure border."[3] Secure how, exactly? When the same cities applauding these assurances later begged FEMA for cash? If a dam is secure, why is everyone downstream building an ark?

The rhetorical pivot came dressed as technocracy: "We have a plan to secure the border and fix the immigration system, we're going to make it safe, orderly, and humane" [Joe Biden — Remarks, 1/5/2023]. "We are creating lawful pathways for orderly migration" [Alejandro Mayorkas — DHS Briefing, 1/5/2023]. Meanwhile, the legislative chorus sang the long-standing refrain: "We believe in a pathway to citizenship" [Chuck Schumer — Press Conference, 11/16/2022]; "We have to have comprehensive immigration reform with a pathway to citizenship" [Nancy Pelosi — Weekly Presser, 1/28/2021]. Pathways, pathways, pathways. But Congress didn't pass new ones. So what filled the void? Appointments on an app, mass releases pending adjudication, and nationality-based parole pipelines that tried to launder an intake surge as "order." Show me the clause where Congress authorized software to overrule "shall detain." Spoiler: it's not in 8 U.S.C. §1225(b)(1)(B)(ii). And "case-by-case" doesn't mean category-by-category [8 U.S.C. §1182(d)(5)(A)].

Sanctuary turned from slogan to statewide posture. "California will remain the state that values diversity and defends the rights of immigrants, both documented and undocumented."[4] "We are a sanctuary city."[5] "We're not going to cooperate with ICE on deportations."[6] It sounds noble; in practice, it often means detainers are ignored, release dates withheld, and re-arrests forced into riskier settings. It also broadcasts a simple message: the interior will not help enforce the law. Does that reduce fear of reporting crimes? Sometimes. Does it raise the costs of removal and encourage arrivals who expect to stay? Obviously.

Then the buses arrived and the tone changed—locally, at least. "This issue will destroy New York City. We're getting 10,000 migrants a month."[7] "We have no more room."[8] Chicago struck the same chord: "The City of Chicago is a sanctuary city, we will continue to provide refuge, but we need support."[9] "The right to shelter was never designed to be an open-ended right for the entire world," Adams admitted once the invoices stacked up.[10] When Texas said this, it was called cruelty. When New York said it, it became "a crisis we must all share." Funny how the moral weather changes with the ZIP code.

Layer on the moral flourish that reframes law as insult: "No human being is illegal."[11] "We must end the use of the word 'illegal' as a descriptor for human beings."[12] Fine sentiment—and irrelevant to whether "unlawful to hire" requires enforcement [8 U.S.C. §1324a(a)], or whether "shall be detained" allows mass release [8 U.S.C. §1225(b)(1)(B)(ii)]. If adjectives bother you, change the nouns with a statute. Until then, the law is not a vibe.

Once shelter budgets ballooned, the fastest "solution" was to legalize the cost. "We need work authorizations for the migrants."^13 "Give them work permits so they can support themselves."^14 "Expedite work authorization for asylum seekers."^15 Translation: shift costs from city ledgers to the labor market by turning pending claims into legal labor supply. But work authorization is the quiet magnet. Offer it broadly, and you advertise the same incentive structure that swelled the queue in the first place [8 C.F.R. §208.7]. Rational actors do rational math.

"Humane" became a proxy for release. "We will not separate families. We will treat people humanely."^16 "We don't have a crisis; we have a challenge, and we will meet that challenge in a humane way."^17 "We are not going to apologize for being humane."^18 Humane is a posture, not a plan. The plan in practice was process and release while dockets exploded, detention capacity lagged, and parole mutated from scalpel to snowplow [8 U.S.C.

§1182(d)(5)(A)]. Genuinely humane would be rapid adjudication and quick, predictable outcomes. Multi-year limbo is not mercy; it's an engraved invitation with bad fine print.

Economic rhetoric tried to blur categories. "Immigrants contribute to our economy and our communities" [Chuck Schumer, Senate Floor, 2/4/2021]. "Immigration makes America more American" [Nancy Pelosi, Naturalization Remarks, 3/29/2019]. No quarrel that lawful immigration fuels growth. The issue isn't immigration; it's incentives. Parallel, ad hoc channels—mass parole, catch and release, work authorization keyed to backlog—distort wage floors, strain housing, and offload city costs. You don't fix a labor shortage by bypassing Congress and gutting statutory deterrents. You fix it with reforms that raise wage floors, add portability, and mandate verification, such as national E-Verify and real worksite enforcement [8 U.S.C. §1324a]. Note how none of those quotes commit to the enforcement piece.

The velvet-rope turn came with software. "We are expanding lawful pathways, including use of the CBP One app to schedule appointments at ports of entry" [Alejandro Mayorkas, DHS Briefing, 1/5/2023]. "We're moving to a more orderly process" [Joe Biden, Remarks, 1/5/2023]. A velvet rope changes the picture, not the fire code. If the same people gain entry who would be ineligible under the plain text, you haven't created order; you've built a software workaround. The test is straightforward: did the number released into the interior pending proceedings shrink? If not, you rearranged chairs and called it a seating chart.

As the bills piled up, local leaders said the quiet part into microphones: "We need the federal government to do its job."^19 "FEMA needs to step up."^20 "New Yorkers are being left to deal with a national problem."^21 If policy is working, why the panic for cash and faster work papers? Because the business model of moral grandstanding depended on someone else footing the bill. Sanctuary was a free virtue until it had a price tag. Then the slogans needed an accountant.

Meanwhile, Title 8 still says what it says: detain pending screening [8 U.S.C. §1225(b)(1)(B)(ii)]; parole temporarily and case by case [8 U.S.C. §1182(d)(5)(A)]; enforce against unlawful hiring [8 U.S.C. §1324a]; cabin asylum gamesmanship with deadlines and bars [8 U.S.C. §1158]. Did Democratic leadership announce, "We intend to depart from these"? No. They said "the border is secure" while operationalizing mass release; praised "lawful pathways" while manufacturing de facto ones; demanded "work permits now," cementing the magnet, then acted surprised when more arrivals followed the incentives.

If you genuinely believe in worker power, you don't cheer policies that expand shadow labor pools and undercut wage floors. Ask yourself: why oppose mandatory, nationwide E-Verify if the goal is to protect legal labor and punish chronic violators? If "we need workers," why fear verifying them? Why push mass work authorization for unresolved asylum claims rather than surge adjudication and reserve parole for true emergencies? The coalition is structurally incoherent: progressive politicians selling compassion, employer lobbies craving pliable labor, mayors desperate to offload costs, and NGOs funded by churn. Everyone eats, except the public school, the county hospital, and the guy whose drywall bid just lost to a cash crew.

The incentive is clear in their own words. "Expedite work authorization,"[15] "We need these asylum seekers to work."[22] "Pathway to citizenship" [Chuck Schumer, 11/16/2022]. "We're not going to cooperate with ICE on deportations."[6] Stitch those together and you get a three-step plan: arrive and be released, get work authorization while you wait, and push legalization later under the banner of compassion. Where does "shall detain" fit [8 U.S.C. §1225(b)(1)(B)(ii)]? It doesn't. Where does "case by case" parole fit [8 U.S.C. §1182(d)(5)(A)]? It's repurposed as category by category. Call it what you want; the incentives are obvious to anyone with a bus ticket.

Housing, schools, hospitals—these aren't hashtags; they're invoices. "This issue will destroy New York City."[7] "We have no more room."[8] "We need support."[9] Pair those with "We are a sanctuary city"[5] and "We're not going to cooperate with ICE."[6] You promise sanctuary; you receive people. You block interior enforcement; they cannot be removed. You insist on work permits; more come. You keep zoning tight; rents rise. You label objections "xenophobia," then ask FEMA for a bailout. The only thing missing is a thank-you note to the cartels for acting as your unofficial logistics contractors.

We're told, earnestly, that "We have a secure border."^3 Secure like a screen door in a hurricane. We're told "orderly pathways" are here [Mayorkas, 1/5/2023], and yet the shelters swell. We're told "No human being is illegal,"^11 then handed a bill for hotel rooms at rack rate. We're told "Give them work permits so they can support themselves,"^14 then asked to ignore that work permits are the prize the statute was designed not to award absent merit [8 C.F.R. §208.7; see also 8 U.S.C. §1158]. We're told "pathway to citizenship" [Schumer, 11/16/2022], which is a debatable legislative goal— conspicuously not enacted. In its place: a parole card swiped like it has no limit [8 U.S.C. §1182(d)(5)(A)].

So let's ask the rude questions they avoid. If "the border is secure," why are sanctuary cities rationing gym mats? If parole is case by case, why issue nationality-wide memos and press releases? If this is humane, why create multi-year limbo that guarantees more risky journeys and cartel profit? If the economy needs workers, why not pass visa reforms with wage floors, portability, and E-Verify instead of mass work authorization for unresolved claims?

Competence has a simple shape: follow the statute and resource it—detain pending screening [8 U.S.C. §1225(b)(1)(B)(ii)]; surge adjudication so decisions take weeks, not years; make E-Verify mandatory and penalize chronic violators [8 U.S.C. §1324a];

194

reserve parole for true emergencies, individualized and temporary [8 U.S.C. §1182(d)(5)(A)]; and expand legal channels by law, not memo, with genuine labor protections.

What we got instead were podium lines: "The border is secure,"[1,3] "orderly pathways" [Mayorkas, 1/5/2023], "pathway to citizenship" [Schumer, 11/16/2022; Pelosi, 1/28/2021], "No human being is illegal,"[11] "We are a sanctuary city,"[5] "We have no more room,"[8] and "This will destroy New York City."[7] You could not script a cleaner arc from preening to pleading. The rhetoric advertised a moral brand. The incentives advertised a travel plan. The system delivered a budget crisis.

No country can run a welfare-tinged urban safety net and an honor system at its border with a cartel-run transit line in between. Pick two. You can be generous, or you can be credulous. You can be lawful, or you can be loud. You cannot be all four at once and then send FEMA the tab.

We can be a nation of immigrants and a nation of laws. But to be both, one word must anchor everything: shall. It appears in the statute for a reason [8 U.S.C. §1225(b)(1)(B)(ii); 8 U.S.C. §1226(c)]. Redefine "shall" to mean "when convenient," and you don't have policy; you have vibes. Vibes don't clear dockets. Vibes don't balance budgets. Vibes don't house families.

So yes, turn off the tap. Honor the text. Align incentives. And the next time someone at a podium says, "The border is secure," ask a simple, impolite question: Secure for whom?

Footnotes

1. Alejandro Mayorkas — "The border is secure." *Meet the Press*, NBC, 7/31/2022.

2. Alejandro Mayorkas — "There is no circumstance in which the border is wide open. The border is secure." *Aspen Security Forum*, 7/19/2023.

3. Kamala Harris — "We have a secure border." NBC interview with Lester Holt, 6/8/2021.

4. Gavin Newsom — "California will remain the state that values diversity and defends the rights of immigrants, both documented and undocumented." Statement, 10/5/2019.

5. London Breed — "We are a sanctuary city." Press remarks, 7/12/2018.

6. Eric Garcetti — "We're not going to cooperate with ICE on deportations." Press conference, 3/6/2019.

7. Eric Adams — "This issue will destroy New York City. We're getting 10,000 migrants a month." Town hall, 9/6/2023.

8. Eric Adams — "We have no more room." Press briefing, 8/9/2023.

9. Brandon Johnson — "The City of Chicago is a sanctuary city... but we need support." Press conference, 9/14/2023.

10. Eric Adams — "The right to shelter was never designed to be an open-ended right for the entire world." Press briefing, 10/4/2023.

11. Alexandria Ocasio-Cortez — "No human being is illegal." Queens town hall, 7/20/2019.

12. Ilhan Omar — "We must end the use of the word 'illegal' as a descriptor for human beings." House floor remarks, 7/18/2019.

13. Chuck Schumer — "We need work authorizations for the migrants." Press conference, NYC, 8/24/2023.

14. Kathy Hochul — "Give them work permits so they can support themselves." *CNN State of the Union*, 8/27/2023.

15. Eric Adams — "Expedite work authorization for asylum seekers." Letter to the White House, 9/18/2023.

16. Joe Biden — "We will not separate families. We will treat people humanely." ABC interview, 8/18/2020.

17. Nancy Pelosi — "We don't have a crisis; we have a challenge, and we will meet that challenge in a humane way." *ABC This Week*, 3/14/2021.

18. Alejandro Mayorkas — "We are not going to apologize for being humane." DHS briefing, 3/1/2021.

19. Brandon Johnson — "We need the federal government to do its job." Press briefing, 10/2/2023.

20. Eric Adams — "FEMA needs to step up." *Face the Nation*, 9/10/2023.

Chapter 13:

The People Who Set Their Own Hair on Fire, Then Blamed the Smoke Alarms

Trust is a fragile thing. A chipped mug with superglue can hold coffee, sure, but you know better than to put it near the edge of the counter. For a generation, America placed the mug of public trust in the hands of a self-anointed priesthood called "the press." They told us they were neutral. They told us they were referees. They told us they had standards, capital-S Standards, mind you, and that anyone who questioned them was an enemy of "our democracy." Then they dropped the mug, blamed the countertop, and started lecturing the rest of us on our clumsiness.

The national crisis of media distrust isn't a mystery; it's the foreseeable result of a newsroom monoculture that lies to itself first and to the public second. It's a long con where the con men forgot which part was true. And now, when Americans distrust the media more than Congress, pause to appreciate the athleticism required to crawl under that bar, the press calls it a "disinformation problem." Close. It's a disinformation problem all right, just not the one they think. It's not that the peasants are too stupid to understand the news; it's that the news has become performance art for one tribe, sold as scripture to everyone else.

How did we get here? Let's take a tour through the open-air museum of "mistakes" that always err in the same direction. Funny how the compass needle never points north when it's strapped to a magnet.

I. The Laptop That Wasn't Real (Until It Was)

You remember October 2020. A New York tabloid drops a story thicker than a family saga: emails, messages, and documents from a laptop purportedly belonging to Hunter Biden. Photos. Business deals. Financial threads leading to the "Big Guy." It smelled like news. It looked like news. And the gatekeepers reacted like a vampire thrown into a tanning booth at noon.

Within hours, legacy outlets were not just skeptical—skepticism is healthy—they were certain: "This looks like Russian intelligence" (CNN, Oct. 16, 2020).[1] MSNBC's anchors echoed it as if reciting a creed: "We start with this disinformation operation" (MSNBC, Oct. 16, 2020).[2] ABC pushed the frame too: "A Russian disinformation campaign" (ABC, Oct. 18, 2020).[3] Twitter locked the story down. Facebook downranked it. And when "51 former intelligence officials" signed a letter claiming the story "has all the classic earmarks of a Russian information operation" (Politico, Oct. 19, 2020),[4] the press treated it like a papal bull. No evidence presented. No provenance examined. Just authority invoked by those who never stop reminding you they "speak truth to power."

Then came the quiet part: months later, after the election, the same institutions reversed polarity. "Hunter Biden paid tax bill as federal investigation goes on" (CNN, Dec. 9, 2020).[5] "Hunter Biden tax affairs probe" (ABC, Dec. 9, 2020).[6] In 2022, *The New York Times* and *The Washington Post* authenticated key emails: "The emails were obtained by The Times... appear to have come from a laptop" (*NYT*, Mar. 16, 2022).[7] "Forensic analysis... verified a cache of emails" (*Washington Post*, Mar. 30, 2022).[8] The tone shifted to the passive voice of absolution: it has "since been verified." Since. As though the truth immigrated across the border of reality and applied for asylum after Inauguration Day.

What did that episode communicate? That "disinformation" is whatever contradicts the preferred storyline at the worst moment for that storyline. That tech platforms are deputized editors with badges forged by panic. That "experts" are not referees but auditioning pundits. And that, if a story threatens the fortunes of the right kind of politician, the burden of proof magically flips: it's false until proven true, later, when it's safe.

II. Russiagate: The Multi-Season Drama Without a Finale

For nearly three years, America was told hourly that the President of the United States was a Kremlin asset. Not a buffoon, not a populist blowhard, not a policy disaster. A literal Manchurian Candidate. You couldn't turn on a screen without being told the "walls are closing in," the phrase that launched a thousand panel segments: "The walls are closing in" (MSNBC, Dec. 7, 2018).[9] "Walls closing in" (CNN, Aug. 1, 2018).[10] Night after night, "bombshell" and "smoking gun" were not punchlines; they were lower-thirds.

Step back and notice the structure. An opposition dossier funded by a campaign becomes "intelligence": "On the dossier... parts of it have been corroborated" (CNN, Oct. 26, 2017).[11] Leaks, selective and conveniently timed, get laundered through anonymous sources and presented as near certainties: "US officials confirm" and "sources say" multiplied like rabbits. Every process story about a FISA warrant—a secret court order, mind you—gets treated as proof of substance, not just procedure: "FBI obtained FISA warrant" (CNN, Apr. 12, 2017).[12] And when actual investigations drag on, the promise of a future shoe drop substitutes for the absence of a current shoe. It was the journalism version of binge TV: tune in next week for the twist.

When the dust cleared: "No evidence of conspiracy" from the special counsel on collusion (DOJ/Mueller Report, Mar. 2019).[13] The elaborate collusion plot turned into a Rube Goldberg machine of innuendo, meetings that weren't crimes, contacts that weren't conspiracies, and headlines that needed retracting. Corrections littered the landscape. Remember ABC's "bombshell" that "candidate Trump" ordered Flynn to contact Russians? They corrected it to "President-elect" the next day and suspended the reporter (ABC, Dec. 1–2, 2017).[14] CNN's infamous story about Anthony Scaramucci and a Russian fund? Retracted (CNN, June 23,

2017).[15] Even *The New York Times* downshifted: "No clear evidence of collusion" (*NYT*, Mar. 24, 2019).[16]

And when that happened, did the networks do a postmortem on why they kept misreading tea leaves as affidavits? Hardly. They narrowed the frame: well, there were "contacts." A few officials "lied." Maybe the real crime was "obstruction." The ends became the means; the hypothesis kept changing clothes to match the weather.

Imagine the reverse. Imagine a conservative press spending three years asserting, not questioning, that a Democratic president was a Beijing asset, and then shrugging after coming up empty. Would we be told "the narrative was complicated"? Or would we hear "hyperpartisan" and be asked whether the First Amendment needs new "guardrails"? We both know.

III. The Fine People Lie: Clip Editing as Craft

Here's a trick. You can turn a sentence into a sin by removing the clause that acquits it. At the chaotic Charlottesville presser, the line "very fine people on both sides" became a catechism, minus the sentence that immediately followed: "I'm not talking about the neo-Nazis and the white nationalists, because they should be condemned totally" (White House Transcript, Aug. 15, 2017).[17]

Yet for years, it was treated as the racist Rosetta Stone: "Trump says there are 'very fine people on both sides'" (CNN, Aug. 15, 2017).[18] "He called neo-Nazis 'very fine people'" (MSNBC, Aug.

2019).[19] The lie was clean; the correction would be messy. Better to keep the clip and crop the clause.

How many viewers ever saw the full transcript? The meme beat the record. And if you can't tell the truth about the thing you feel most strongly about, how should we trust you on the things you barely care about?

IV. The Covington Rorschach Test

A teenage boy in a red hat smiles awkwardly while a drum bangs inches from his face. That was the raw footage. The narrative told you a different story: "Teens in MAGA hats taunt Native American elder" (CNN, Jan. 19, 2019).[20] "A face that became the symbol of… racism" (MSNBC, Jan. 21, 2019).[44] "Smirking MAGA teen" (*The Washington Post*, Jan. 19, 2019).[21] Commentators psychoanalyzed a minor on live TV. "He is mocking him. That's what it looks like" (CNN, Jan. 19, 2019).[45] The kid's face—an adolescent's confused half-smile—was treated as a signed confession. Pundits supplied motive, then backfilled facts.

Extended footage showed the encounter was more complicated—that the teens hadn't initiated the confrontation and were themselves taunted by another group. That didn't fit the prefab script. So the updates were muted: "Additional video sheds more light on the viral standoff" (CNN, Jan. 20, 2019).[22] Note the framing: sheds more light, as if the original wasn't shadow theater. Some issued editor's notes that read like passive-voice absolutions. Others doubled down with graduate-seminar abstractions about "structures of oppression," as if a field trip had to carry the weight of 400 years.

Legal reality politely corrected the editorial fantasia: defamation suits followed; outlets quietly settled. The settlements didn't make chyrons; the first-frame accusation did. The lesson should have been obvious: the faster the take, the dumber the take. But speed is the currency of clout, clout buys status, and status is the sacrament.

V. The Jussie Smollett Snow Globe

When a claim flatters the story you already believe, it slides past the filters. A high-profile actor asserted he was attacked by Trump supporters at 2 a.m. in Chicago wearing MAGA hats, wielding a noose and bleach. The details were cinematic to the point of parody. The reaction was instant: "A horrific, homophobic attack" (ABC, Jan. 29, 2019).[23] "This is a modern-day lynching" (CNN, Jan. 29, 2019).[24] On-air emotion displaced verification. Chyrons did prosecutorial work. "This is America in 2019" (MSNBC, Jan. 29, 2019).[46]

Police later said the quiet part out loud: "Jussie Smollett staged attack" (CBS Chicago, Feb. 21, 2019).[25] Yet the retrospective frame often swerved to meta-commentary: okay, this case fell apart, but "the real story is the climate." No—it isn't. "Fake but accurate" is a priest's dodge, not a journalist's ethic. If a story is false, it's false. If you want a metaphor, write a novel.

VI. Lafayette Square, Whips at the Border, and the Magic of Misreading

Two more in the genre of story-first: the "tear gas for a photo op" narrative at Lafayette Square and the "Border Patrol whipping migrants" frame. The former hardened into catechism within hours: "Peaceful protesters tear gassed for Trump photo op" (MSNBC, June 1, 2020).[26] Cable packages folded cause and effect like origami. Subsequent reviews complicated that timeline: "Park Police didn't use tear gas... cleared the area to install fencing" (DOI IG, June 2021).[27] "Decisions were made prior to" the walk (DOI IG, June 2021).[27] But the cartoon stuck because clarity is boring, and boring doesn't rate.

The latter? A still photo of mounted agents holding reins became "whips." "Border Patrol using whips on Haitian migrants" (MSNBC, Sept. 20, 2021).[28] "Images of agents 'whipping' migrants" (CNN, Sept. 20, 2021).[47] Investigations concluded "no whipping" occurred (CBP OPR, July 2022).[29] The retraction crept in with librarian energy; the original charge arrived like a siren. And here's the knife twist: some framed the result as a process failure, not an accuracy failure—"even if not whips, the images evoke..." Evoke is doing an Olympian amount of work there. Evocation is not evidence.

Millions remember the initial allegations. Few remember the corrections. Memory isn't a filing cabinet; it's a rumor mill. First impressions win by forfeit.

VII. COVID: The Press Went All-In on Certainty, Then Pretended It Didn't

The early days of a pandemic test humility. Real science evolves; it says "we don't know yet." Instead, much of the press delivered church talk: catechism, intonation, heresy trials. The lab-leak hypothesis? "Debunked conspiracy theory" (CNN, Feb. 18, 2020).[30] "Coronavirus myths" (ABC, Feb. 2020).[31] Facebook and YouTube joined the ministry: "reducing" and "removing" "misinformation" that later reentered respectable conversation. Then, the pivot: "The lab leak theory merits a closer look" (Washington Post, May 24, 2021).[32] The words changed; the tone didn't. Never quite: we overshot. Always: the situation evolved, as if the earlier derision were a weather pattern.

Masks? "Don't wear masks" (CBS, Mar. 8, 2020)[33] to "Everyone should wear a mask" (CNN, Apr. 3, 2020).[34] School closures? "We should shut down" (MSNBC, Mar. 2020)[35] became a ledger of loss: "Historic setbacks in education" (NYT, Sept. 1, 2022).[36] A press confident enough to police debate wasn't confident enough to own its own overreach. Questions became heresies, and the heretics were "denialists." And if you platformed an alternative view—Great Barrington, ventilation-first, risk-stratified policies— you were accused of aiding death.

The biggest sin wasn't getting things wrong; in a crisis, everyone does. The biggest sin was performing certainty for clout and punishing dissent for sport.

VIII. The Platform-Press Merger: Censorship as Customer Service

If you can't win a debate, change the rules. In 2020, legacy press gatekeepers outsourced enforcement to tech, then claimed helplessness when the companies did their bidding. The laptop story was muzzled: "Twitter blocks New York Post" (CNN, Oct. 14, 2020).[37] Facebook preemptively "reducing distribution" pending "fact-checks" (Facebook, Oct. 14, 2020).[38] Reporters cheered or shrugged. Meanwhile, the backchannel ran hot: "We are flagging these posts" and "can you take a look?" (internal communications, 2020–2021).[39] The verbs are bureaucratic—flag, escalate, reduce—but the outcome is political: suppress, bury, memory-hole.

This is the distrust supercharger. People sense when the fight isn't fair. If your ideas are invincible, why do they need such delicate chaperones? Why is "reach" treated like plutonium that mustn't fall into the wrong hands?

IX. The Asymmetry Problem: "Mistakes" That Only Cut One Way

No outlet is perfect. Humans err. But pattern matters. Somehow, the "mistakes" tend to favor left-of-center narratives. Rumors that hurt Republicans get oxygen; documents that hurt Democrats get a carbon monoxide detector. Accusations against conservatives are "credible" until disproven; accusations against progressives are "unfounded" until notarized confessions surface. "We got out over our skis" is a charming euphemism until you notice they only ski one direction.

Hiring pipelines pull from the same coastal schools; Slack channels serve as peer-pressure amps; Twitter functions as a politburo where the inner ring enforces tone. Risk is measured not against the truth but against the reaction of peers. That's not reporting; that's vibes enforcement.

X. "Democracy Dies in Darkness" and Other Slogans That Aged Like Milk

Slogans are the incense of modern media: "Democracy Dies in Darkness" (Washington Post masthead, 2017–).[40] "The Truth Is Worth It" (New York Times, 2018).[41] "Facts First" (CNN, 2017).[42] They're unassailable in the abstract. The cleverness lies in using virtue words to launder vice acts. Label yourself the guardian of democracy and critics become enemies of democracy. Stamp "fact-based" on your branding and disagreement becomes anti-fact.

Meanwhile, "fact checks" morphed into op-ed with thermometers. "Mostly false" covered arguments they simply disliked. "Explainers" explained why the story that made the wrong people look bad wasn't a story at all. Slogans curdle when the flashlight clicks off as soon as it points at friends.

XI. The Insider's Guide to "Sources Say"

"People familiar with the matter" are human beings with incentives. Journalism at its best triangulates anonymous claims with documents and on-the-record backbone. Journalism at its median launders them with pseudo-authority. The "sources say" hall-of-mirrors trick turns one leak into "multiple outlets confirm": "CNN reports" becomes "NYT confirms CNN's reporting," which becomes "MSNBC: Multiple outlets confirm." The outlets confirm each other; the claim floats free of evidence like a Macy's balloon. That's not corroboration; that's choreography.

Treat anonymity like dynamite—only for when the alternative is silence in the public interest. Instead, it became confetti.

XII. The Emotional Economy: Outrage as Product

The press is a business. It runs on attention; attention runs hottest on outrage. "Breaking" banners are the dopamine drumbeat. Why slow-walk a claim when "bombshell" gets clicks now? Editors call it "impact." It's open rates. When a story threatens to soothe the wrong crowd—the laptop, for instance—the machine goes wobbly: "This is dangerous" (MSNBC, Oct. 2020).[43]

Dangerous to whom? To *The Discourse*, that is, to the audience model.

Every incentive bends toward melodrama over proportion. Reporters become actors; anchors, therapists for an anxious elite. Then along comes a story that won't play the part, and the stagehands yank the lights.

XIII. The Church of Credentialism

The prestige press has become a guild with rites of passage, clerical language, and excommunications. They hide behind process: "We have not independently verified," they intone, followed by "but experts say," and then the whole panel nods. Somehow, the "experts" live inside the same ideological cul-de-sac. Updates always seem to evolve in the same political direction. Process becomes theater; the patter is the point. "Per our standards" has the incantatory feel of absolution.

Credentialism is the creed. Inside the room, the fanciest degree speaks last and wins by default. Outside the room, welders and nurses can read a chart and smell a hustle. You don't need a J-school seminar to know when the ref swallows the whistle for one team.

XIV. Manufactured Consent 2.0

Chomsky wrote about manufacturing consent; his acolytes built a new version and pretended they didn't. Yesterday's consent was brokered by three moguls in smoke-filled rooms; today's is assembled by ten thousand interns refreshing Slack and invoking "safety." The principle is the same: select the facts, frame them in emotive language, drop them into a metanarrative that absolves your allies and damns your foes, and enforce compliance socially.

Feelings became evidence; evidence was filtered by feelings. "Harm" did semantic cartwheels to cover "I dislike." Consensus devolved into a show of hands among people who share the same priors. Then they printed the minutes.

XV. When the Watchdog Bites the Neighbor's Dog

The press calls itself a watchdog. A watchdog barks at intruders; it doesn't gnaw the neighbor's ankle for mowing on Tuesdays. Yet over the last decade, the watchdog recoded routine conservative politics as moral trespass. The "dog whistles," they said, were everywhere, so the barking never stopped. Annoyance at policy X? Proof of bigotry Y. Skepticism about a model? Proof of denialism. An entire bracket of ordinary dissent was rebranded as extremism; the watchdog demanded bigger fences and more signs.

When the neighbors complained, the watchdog said the real issue was "perception." Translation: you are the problem for noticing the barking.

XVI. The Cost: A Country That Doesn't Believe the Fire Alarm

Sometimes there is a real fire. Sometimes a leader abuses power, a company poisons a river, a policy corrodes liberty. You need a press you can trust to tell you when the fire is real. But if the alarms are pulled for sport—"bombshell," "breaking," "stunning"—and the smoke machine runs 24/7, then when real flames lick the curtains, half the country shrugs: "They always say that."

This is the civic bill. The press spent its credibility on clout. Now the account is overdrawn, and the penalty hits when it hurts most: crisis.

XVII. The Receipts Recap

Let's take stock:

• The Hunter Biden laptop was declared "Russian disinformation" (CNN, Oct. 16, 2020; ABC, Oct. 18, 2020)[1][3] then authenticated post-election (NYT, Mar. 16, 2022; *WaPo*, Mar. 30, 2022).[7][8]

• Russiagate was pitched as an espionage thriller: "walls are closing in" (MSNBC, Dec. 7, 2018; CNN, Aug. 1, 2018)[9][10]; it delivered no proven collusion (Mueller, 2019).[13]

• The "very fine people" lie cropped the exculpatory sentence (WH Transcript, Aug. 15, 2017).[17]

• Covington and Smollett showcased the speed premium—accusation first, evidence later (CNN/*WaPo*, Jan. 2019; CBS Chicago, Feb. 21, 2019).[20][21][25]

• Lafayette Square and "whips" showed how imagery plus ideology equals instant conviction and glacial correction (MSNBC, June 1, 2020; DOI IG, 2021; MSNBC, Sept. 20, 2021; CBP OPR, 2022).[26][27][28][29]

• COVID coverage swung from "debunked conspiracy theory" (CNN, Feb. 18, 2020)[30] to "merits a closer look" (*WaPo*, May 24, 2021).[32]

• Platform-press fusion blurred reporting with throttling (CNN, Oct. 14, 2020; Facebook, Oct. 14, 2020).[37] [38]

If you're an average citizen and you watched this in real time, what conclusion seems rational? That the "paper of record" is a PR firm for your opponents' coalition and a prosecutor for yours. That the press doesn't make mistakes; it makes choices.

XVIII. The Psychology of the Narrative High

You can't understand the persistence of these errors without seeing the reward system. Participate in a takedown of the right villain and you receive praise, retweets, fellowships. Hedge and you get heat from colleagues more than from the audience. Social punishment is real. Careers are short; reputations fragile; it's easier to swim with the current than be the one who says "let's wait."

Bias plays a part; fear plays a larger one. Many journalists admit privately the groupthink is suffocating. But the institutional incentives favor the loudest moralist, not the cautious empiricist. The newsroom drifts toward those who treat journalism as a cause, not a craft.

XIX. Accountability Theater

When the errors stack too high, institutions stage a reckoning. Ombudsmen solemnly promise "we'll do better." Editorial notes appear in fonts smaller than the weather. Task forces convene; trainings are mandated. Then the next story arrives that challenges the house line, and the pattern reappears.

Why? Because accountability theater treats the press as a patient with a cold, not a drinker with an addiction. You can't rehab a newsroom without changing the bar it frequents: the social networks, the conference circuits, the feedback loops. You can't reform the output until you rewrite the incentives.

XX. The Reform That Might Work (If They Wanted It)

There are better ways:

• Admit priors. If you lean left, say so. Then prove you can interrogate your own side. The public forgives bias; it doesn't forgive deceit.

• Separate news from op-ed. Kill the "analysis" fig leaf that covers editorials in lab coats.

• Ban anonymous-source scoops for claims that should have documents. Show the paper trail or shelve it.

• Publish corrections with equal prominence as the original claim.

• Diversify by thought, not only identity. Hire editors who voted differently.

• Fire the Slack. Make the main conversation in person. Twitter is not an editor; stop letting it act like one.

• Recommit to proportion. Reserve DEFCON 1 for DEFCON 1.

Would they do this? Only if their audience demanded it. But their audience likes things the way they are. They don't want a press; they want a priest.

XXI. The Conservative Temptation—and the Better Path

After being treated like the national chew toy for years, it's tempting to build a mirror press, a cathedral of certainty on the right. Some have tried. It works, until it doesn't. Conspiracy thinking isn't a partisan monopoly. The antidote to a left-leaning lie machine isn't a right-leaning lie machine; it's a press that earns skepticism, invites alternatives, and acts like grown-ups.

Build institutions that publish receipts first, hot takes later. Fund investigative teams that chase a story even if it hurts a Republican governor you like. If you get something wrong, say so without theater.

XXII. The Citizen's Role in the Recovery

The press failed, but they didn't do it alone. We clicked. We shared. We trained them to feed us sugar, then complained about cavities.

• Read across the aisle.

• Prize primary documents. Watch the hearing; read the transcript.

• Demand receipts. If a claim arrives without a link, ask for one.

• Support outlets that do it right, even if they annoy you.

XXIII. The Punchline That Isn't Funny

Here's the dark joke: the press could fix a lot of this in a year. It would take humility, a little courage, and a willingness to get bored by their own sermons. It would mean presenting a story about a

Democrat's ethics with the energy they bring to a Republican's gaffe.

It would mean admitting that the laptop was real when it mattered, that Russiagate overpromised and underdelivered, that COVID coverage often traded precision for panic, that "very fine people" was a sloganized lie, that Covington was ritual shaming built on misperception, that Smollett was a hoax from the start, and that Lafayette and the "whips" collapsed under scrutiny.

But they won't. Not yet. Not until the subscriptions wobble and donors ask what their philanthropy is buying besides Twitter threads and podcast merchandise. Not until interns stop dreaming of bylines and start wondering why they can't afford rent. Not until enough people say, with the calm of someone who has walked into the kitchen and found the mug shattered on the floor: *you dropped it. You. Not us.*

XXIV. The Closing Argument

We do not have a "misinformation" crisis. We have a trust crisis because the institutions tasked with telling the truth elected themselves to a political coalition and then pretended they didn't. They call it "defending democracy." I call it campaigning by other means. They decided the public was too fragile for the whole story. They lied to themselves about their motives, saying "we're protecting," and so lying to the rest of us came easy.

The solution begins with naming the thing: the American left-wing media complex—CNN, MSNBC, ABC, and the ecosystem around them—has, through a pattern of selective amplification, narrative management, and suppression of inconvenient facts, caused a national crisis of distrust. Not alone, not in isolation, but as the dominant drummer in the parade. And they didn't do it with one scandal. They did it with a thousand small decisions: what to clip, what to headline, what to frame as a trend, whom to invite, which expert to canonize, which dissent to mock, which links to throttle, which "letter from officials" to inflate into gospel, which technical nuance to blur into a talking point, and which certainty to perform on air so the anxious subscribers sleep at night.

The fix is not pity. It is competition, skepticism, and a citizenry that refuses to be shamed out of asking: *Really? Show me. Says who? Where's the document? What's the opposite argument? How sure are you?* Those questions are not cynical; they're civic. If the press answers them without fuming, maybe trust will return. If not, the future belongs to outlets that can.

Footnotes

1. CNN, *Situation Room* segment, Oct. 16, 2020. "This looks like Russian intelligence."

2. MSNBC, *Rachel Maddow Show*, Oct. 16, 2020. "We start with this disinformation operation."

3. ABC News, *This Week*, Oct. 18, 2020. "A Russian disinformation campaign."

4. *Politico*, "Hunter Biden story is Russian disinfo, dozens of former intel officials say," Oct. 19, 2020. "All the classic earmarks."

5. CNN, "Hunter Biden under investigation over taxes," Dec. 9, 2020.

6. ABC News, "Hunter Biden says U.S. attorney investigating his tax affairs," Dec. 9, 2020.

7. *New York Times*, "Hunter Biden Paid Tax Bill, but Broad Federal Investigation Continues," Mar. 16, 2022. "Appear to have come from a laptop."

8. *Washington Post*, "Verified: The Hunter Biden laptop emails," Mar. 30, 2022. "Forensic analysis… verified."

9. MSNBC, *Hardball*, Dec. 7, 2018. "The walls are closing in."

10. CNN, *Anderson Cooper 360*, Aug. 1, 2018. "Walls closing in."

11. CNN, "What we know about the Trump-Russia dossier," Oct. 26, 2017. "Parts… corroborated."

12. CNN, "FBI obtained FISA warrant to monitor Carter Page," Apr. 12, 2017.

13. U.S. Department of Justice, *Report on the Investigation into Russian Interference in the 2016 Presidential Election*

(Mueller Report), Mar. 2019. "Did not establish that members of the Trump Campaign conspired or coordinated."

14. ABC News, Brian Ross report and correction, Dec. 1–2, 2017.

15. CNN, "On [story] published June 22," Retraction, June 23, 2017 (Scaramucci/Russia fund).

16. *New York Times*, "Mueller Finds No Trump-Russia Conspiracy," Mar. 24, 2019.

17. White House Transcript, "Remarks by President Trump," Aug. 15, 2017: "I'm not talking about the neo-Nazis and the white nationalists, because they should be condemned totally."

18. CNN, "Trump: 'Very fine people on both sides,'" Aug. 15, 2017 (coverage framing).

19. MSNBC, various segments, Aug. 2019, reiterating "called neo-Nazis very fine people."

20. CNN, "Teens in MAGA hats taunt Native American elder," Jan. 19, 2019.

21. *Washington Post*, "Viral video shows MAGA hat–wearing teens and Native American man," Jan. 19, 2019.

22. CNN, "Additional video sheds more light on viral standoff," Jan. 20, 2019.

23. ABC News, *Good Morning America*, Jan. 29, 2019: "A horrific, homophobic attack."

24. CNN, Brooke Baldwin, Jan. 29, 2019: "This is a modern-day lynching."

25. CBS Chicago, "Police: Jussie Smollett staged attack," Feb. 21, 2019.

26. MSNBC, various segments, June 1, 2020: "Peaceful protesters tear gassed for photo op."

27. U.S. Department of the Interior, Office of Inspector General, "Review of U.S. Park Police Actions," June 2021.

28. MSNBC, Sept. 20, 2021: "Using whips on Haitian migrants."

29. U.S. Customs and Border Protection, Office of Professional Responsibility, "Investigation of Horse Patrol Activity," July 2022: "No whips."

30. CNN, "Debunking coronavirus myths," Feb. 18, 2020.

31. ABC News, "Coronavirus myths and facts," Feb. 2020.

32. *Washington Post* Editorial Board, "The lab leak theory merits a closer look," May 24, 2021.

33. CBS News, "Surgeon General: Don't wear masks," Mar. 8, 2020.

34. CNN, "CDC recommends cloth face coverings," Apr. 3, 2020.

35. MSNBC, March 2020 segments advocating closures.

36. *New York Times*, "The Pandemic Erased Two Decades of Progress in Math and Reading," Sept. 1, 2022.

37. CNN, "Twitter blocks *New York Post* from sharing Hunter Biden story," Oct. 14, 2020.

38. Facebook (spokesman Andy Stone) post, Oct. 14, 2020: "Reducing distribution."

39. Internal platform communications disclosed in 2022–2023 indicating government and press moderation requests.

40. *Washington Post* masthead, adopted 2017: "Democracy Dies in Darkness."

41. *New York Times* campaign, 2018: "The Truth Is Worth It."

42. CNN brand campaign, 2017: "Facts First."

43. MSNBC segments, Oct. 2020: "This is dangerous," about the laptop coverage.

44. MSNBC, *AM Joy*, Jan. 21, 2019: "A face that became the symbol of… racism."

45. CNN, live panel, Jan. 19, 2019: "He is mocking him. That's what it looks like."

46. MSNBC, Jan. 29, 2019: "This is America in 2019."

47. CNN, Sept. 20, 2021: "Images of agents 'whipping' migrants."

Chapter 14:

The Competence Mirage: How Biden–Harris Turned "Normalcy" Into Managed Decline

They promised you "normal." They delivered a shrugging apology tour for competence. Remember the pitch? Adults back in charge, norms restored, guardrails reattached. What we got instead was a White House that mistook vibes for governance and substituted press releases for results. If you're measuring by inflation, border crossings, botched withdrawals, executive overreach, energy policy whiplash, crime-wave equivocation, speech policing, and a regulatory hydra that strangled investment, and if you're in the reality-based community rather than the press corps' feelings circle, this presidency wasn't merely underwhelming. It was a case study in how not to run a continental republic.

"Don't compare me to the Almighty; compare me to the alternative," Joe Biden liked to say on the trail. Fine. Compare the promises to the outcomes. Compare the mid-level managerial pablum to the worst price spike in four decades, the worst border crisis on record, an Afghanistan humiliation that made Saigon look like a well-planned Uber pickup, and "equity" rulemaking that used civil rights jargon as a pry bar for federal micromanagement. Compare a campaign built on "unity" to a governance style that treated dissent as disinformation to be curated by tech firms. Then tell me: Is this what normal looks like?

The Economic Reality Check: "Transitory," Like Your Paycheck's Purchasing Power

When inflation started knocking, Team Normal told you it was nothing to see. "I want to be clear: my administration understands that if we were to ever experience unchecked inflation in the long term, that would pose a real challenge to our economy," Biden intoned, then called rising prices "expected" and "temporary." He labeled it "transitory" through 2021 even as CPI rolled past 6% and then 7%, the hottest since the early 1980s (Biden remarks; U.S. Bureau of Labor Statistics CPI data, 2021–2022)[1] (BLS CPI historical data, 2021–2022)[1]. The White House blamed "Putin's price hike," a phrase A/B-tested within an inch of its life, but prices had been marching up well before Russia invaded Ukraine in February 2022 (BLS CPI; timeline of CPI acceleration pre–Feb 2022)[2] (BLS CPI trend pre-2/2022)[2].

What fueled it? You don't need a PhD to connect the dots: a flood of fiscal stimulus into a supply-constrained economy, plus regulatory and climate messaging that chilled domestic energy investment. The $1.9 trillion American Rescue Plan in March 2021 was pitched as necessary to "rescue" an economy already rebounding at a rapid pace, with household savings high and vaccines rolling out. Larry Summers, no MAGA man, warned it would "set off inflationary pressures of a kind we have not seen in a generation" (Summers op-eds/interviews, Feb 2021)[3] (Summers, 2021)[3]. The administration hit the gas anyway. Then came the rhetorical tug-of-war: first denial, then blame shifting, then claims that the Inflation Reduction Act, largely a climate and industrial policy bill, would somehow douse the blaze it helped spark (Text of IRA; CBO/JCT analyses of budget and inflation impacts)[4] (CBO/JCT on IRA)[4].

Wages? The White House trumpeted "record wage growth," neglecting the adjective that matters: *real.* For many months in 2021–2023, real wages fell—your paycheck bought less—because inflation outran nominal increases (BLS Real Average Weekly Earnings)[5] (BLS real earnings)[5]. The administration cheered GDP prints while households watched eggs, gasoline, rent, and insurance leap like they were on Ozempic. "Bidenomics is working," Biden declared in 2023, adding, "we're transforming the economy" (White House remarks, 2023)[6] (Biden "Bidenomics" speech, 2023)[6]. Transforming into what—an involuntary lesson in the Cantillon effect?

Energy Masochism Disguised as Virtue

On Day One, Biden canceled the Keystone XL pipeline permit and issued a moratorium on new oil and gas leases on federal lands and waters, touting climate virtue while insisting production wouldn't suffer (Presidential actions; DOI leasing pause, 2021)[7] (White House/DOI docs, 2021)[7]. Then, when prices surged, the administration berated refiners for insufficient capacity, begged

OPEC+ for more supply, and drained the Strategic Petroleum Reserve to the lowest levels since the 1980s for political cover, dribbling out millions of barrels as if the SPR were a midterm campaign fund (DOE releases; SPR inventory data)[8] (DOE SPR data)[8]. Why incentivize domestic investment and long-horizon refining upgrades when you can finger-wag at Saudi Arabia?

"Today we're taking historic steps to confront the climate crisis," Biden said, pledging to "transition from the oil industry" during the 2020 campaign; later, he insisted he never said that (Debate transcript 2020; subsequent remarks)[9] (2020 debate transcript)[9]. The mixed messaging—"we love clean energy," "hey, drill more, please"—doesn't add up to a coherent strategy; it adds up to a risk premium that shows up in prices. Energy policy is not a TikTok; you can't vibe your way to supply.

The Border: If This Is "Orderly and Humane," What Would Disorder Look Like?

"Root causes" was the mantra as the administration dismantled deterrents. On Day One, it halted border wall construction, signaled rollback of Migrant Protection Protocols (Remain in Mexico), and narrowed interior enforcement priorities (DHS memos, 2021)[10] (DHS policy changes, 2021)[10]. The message traveled. Encounters at the southern border shattered records, surpassing 2 million annually, with repeat crossings surging as Title 42 ended and asylum rules swelled into an overwhelmed processing regime (CBP encounter data, FY2021–FY2024)[11] (CBP data)[11]. Even Democratic mayors—New York, Chicago—pleaded for relief as shelter systems buckled.

Kamala Harris, named "border czar," told would-be migrants: "Do not come." Then, in Guatemala, she delivered an airy sermon on "hope" and corruption while the pipeline of human misery grew (Harris remarks, 2021)[12] (Harris Guatemala remarks)[12]. The administration sued states like Texas for attempting to plug gaps, while NGOs coordinated mass crossings under the rubric of "orderly pathways." "We have a secure border," DHS Secretary Mayorkas said in 2022, a line so implausible it became a punchline (Mayorkas remarks)[13] (Mayorkas, 2022)[13]. If record encounters, fentanyl surges, and overwhelmed cities equal "secure," what would a crisis look like—passport control at the Grand Canyon?

Afghanistan: The Withdrawal That Withdrew U.S. Credibility

"America is back," Biden boasted. Then he presided over a withdrawal that stranded allies, ceded Bagram, ignored military advice about the sequencing of evacuation and drawdown, and led to a suicide bombing at Abbey Gate that killed 13 U.S. service members and scores of civilians (DoD reports; testimonies)[14] (DoD/After-action reports)[14]. Biden insisted, "the buck stops with me," then blamed Trump's deal, Afghan forces, and anyone within rhetorical reach (Biden address Aug 2021)[15] (Biden Aug. 16, 2021)[15]. He said there was "no indication that they [the Taliban] have the ability to take over the whole country" weeks before Kabul

226

fell (Biden remarks, July 2021)[16] (July 2021 remarks)[16]. He promised Americans would not be left behind, then they were told to "shelter in place" and attempt their own escape logistics while the Taliban controlled outer perimeter security.

MIRWAIS KHAN AMIRI
KABUL, AFGHANISTAN / AUGUST 16, 2021

The image seared into global memory wasn't "adults back in charge." It was Afghan men clinging to C-17s. The signal to allies and adversaries alike was unmissable: U.S. planning can be sloppy, domestic politics can trump operational prudence, and the White House will declare success no matter what burns. "This is an extraordinary success," Biden actually said (Biden remarks, Aug 31, 2021)[17]. Extraordinary, yes, like a cautionary tale in every war college on the planet.

COVID: Mandates, Messaging, and the Skyhook of "Science"

"I will shut down the virus," Biden vowed. Then came a winter wave, then Omicron, then mandates, then court smackdowns. The administration pushed OSHA to impose a broad vaccine-or-test rule on private employers; the Supreme Court blocked it, noting OSHA had exceeded its statutory remit (NFIB v. OSHA, 2022)[18]. The federal contractor mandate and CMS healthcare-worker mandate traveled their own legal thickets.

Schools? After promising to "follow the science," the White House allowed teachers' unions an editing pen on CDC guidance, resulting in prolonged closures and learning loss (CDC guidance communications; union correspondence reports)[19]. Masks were mandatory until the airplane became the last temple of hygiene theatre, an altar to outdated risk models.

And the rhetoric? The same crew who sneered at "anti-vaxxers" inherited hesitancy from their own 2020 campaign lines ("If Donald Trump tells us to take it, I'm not taking it," Harris said of a vaccine arriving under Trump)[20]. The moral of the story—trust is a perishable commodity—never landed. Instead, the administration outsourced debate to tech platforms: label it, throttle it, suppress it. "We're flagging problematic posts for Facebook," Jen Psaki said from the podium in July 2021 (WH press briefing, July 2021)[21]. Government jawboning Big Tech to police speech is not a minor footnote; it is the administrative state flexing in the space where the First Amendment lives.

Crime and Policing: The Art of Saying Nothing While Saying Everything

The White House tried to triangulate: declare support for "funding the police," whisper sweet nothings to the activist left, and avoid offending anyone. Remember the 2020–2021 period when "defund" hardened into actual municipal budgets? The administration mostly practiced strategic disappearance. When Biden finally said, "The answer is not to defund the police. It's to fund the police," it was a political correction, not a policy spine (State of the Union, 2022)[22]. Cities faced rising homicides and a collapse in proactive policing, with prosecutors—many elected on "reform" platforms—refusing to prosecute entire categories of crime. It's hard to project competence nationally when your party's ecosystem is broadcasting indulgence of disorder.

Education, Equity, and the Bureaucratic Capture of Everyday Life

From the first weeks, Biden signed executive orders mandating a whole-of-government "equity" lens—bureaucratese for redistributing attention, money, and permissions through race-conscious frameworks (EO 13985; follow-ons)[23]. The Department of Education moved to rewrite Title IX, expanding the definition of sex discrimination to include gender identity and rolling back due-process protections in campus adjudications that had finally been strengthened in 2020 (ED proposed rules 2022–2024)[24].

The speech-cop instinct leaked into schools via "disinformation" partnerships, while the DOJ was caught treating parental outrage at school boards as a potential domestic threat vector, complete with a memo referencing the National School Boards Association letter comparing parents to "domestic terrorists" (DOJ memo, Oct 2021)[25]. If your governing philosophy needs the FBI as a guidance counselor, you've lost the plot.

Big Tech and the Censorship-Industrial Complex

The administration didn't just have opinions about online content; it operationalized them. The Department of Homeland Security flirted with a Disinformation Governance Board, an idea so tone-deaf it lasted about as long as a viral TikTok trend (DHS announcement and dissolution, 2022)[26]. Lawsuits later revealed a thick braid of communication between federal officials and platforms regarding moderation pushes around COVID, elections, and other "sensitive" topics (Missouri v. Biden filings)[27]. "We are in regular touch with social media platforms," the press secretary confirmed (WH briefing)[21]. In a country whose Constitution protects speech precisely when it's inconvenient, that's not a small mistake; it's a category error.

Foreign Policy: "America Is Back," but to What?

Ukraine. The administration's defenders say Biden rallied NATO and armed Kyiv, and there's truth there. But why was deterrence not maintained in the first place? The messy Afghanistan exit signaled irresolution; then came Russia's buildup and half-measures, lift after lift, until invasion. "Minor incursion," Biden mused in January 2022, adding a qualifier that sent allies scrambling to clarify U.S. resolve (Biden presser, Jan 2022)[28]. Aid flowed but strategy drifted; "as long as it takes" is a slogan, not an objective.

Israel. After October 7, the White House stood with Israel rhetorically, then slow-walked munitions, leaked frustrations, and treated campus antisemitism as a weather pattern rather than a leadership test. The result? Everyone angry: progressives accusing genocide, Israelis seeing unreliability, and deterrence against Iran eroding as proxies took potshots.

China. The administration coined "invest, align, compete," but greenlit industrial policy that mixed subsidies with export controls while continuing to rely on Chinese supply chains for critical minerals and solar inputs. "We're not seeking conflict," Biden repeated—a fine sentiment—while the PLA harassed U.S. assets and a Chinese surveillance balloon strolled across the continental United States before being shot down off the coast of South Carolina after a multi-day sightseeing tour (Public events, Feb 2023)[29]. "We handled it," Biden said. Did we? Or did we watch it?

Regulatory Onslaught: ESG, Micromanagement, and the Revenge of the Clerks

Unable to pass much through Congress after 2022, the White House governed by pen and regulator. The SEC pushed climate disclosure rules that effectively turned CFOs into carbon accountants (SEC proposed/final climate rule)[30]. Banking regulators flirted with capital hikes and "climate risk" frameworks that would throttle credit to disfavored sectors. The Department of Labor blessed ESG considerations in retirement plans, encouraging fund managers to turn your 401(k) into a climate policy instrument (DOL rule on ESG in ERISA plans)[31]. The FTC and DOJ antitrust agencies rewrote merger guidelines to reflect a neo-Brandeisian mood, introducing uncertainty that dampens investment without delivering consumer wins (FTC/DOJ merger guidelines)[32].

This wasn't neutral governance; it was ideological preference embedded in enforcement discretion. "Bidenomics" translates, in practice, to subsidize favored industries (EVs, chips, green tech), punish others (fossil fuels), and spread the costs across consumers via inflation and taxpayers via deficits. Even the successes—CHIPS money building some fabs—arrived with price tags and timelines warped by prevailing-wage and domestic-content rules that turned "industrial policy" into a sprawling public-works bureau. Are we reindustrializing or laundering money through consultants with a sustainability deck?

Personnel Is Policy: The Performance Review You Were Not Asked to Conduct

Kamala Harris was tasked with politically radioactive assignments such as border and voting rights, then largely disappeared behind curated media hits. Her rhetorical tic, "we must do the thing we've been doing, and that time is every day," became emblematic of a team that mistakes ethos for execution (Harris remarks, 2022)[33]. Pete Buttigieg presided over supply-chain snarls and a toxic train derailment in East Palestine while perfecting the art of the cable-news explanation (DOT timeline 2022–2023)[34]. Alejandro Mayorkas insisted black was white on border realities. Energy Secretary Jennifer Granholm celebrated EV revolutions while struggling with the practicalities of grid capacity and charging networks. At one point, her staff reportedly blocked a charging station with a gas car to reserve it for the Secretary's EV caravan— an apt parable for the elite's "let them charge cake" instinct (News reports, 2023)[35].

Words Matter: The Gaslighting as Governance

"Zero inflation," Biden said of a month where inflation was 0% month over month but still 8.5% year over year—like declaring yourself debt-free because your minimum payment posted (Biden remarks, Aug 2022)[36]. "The border is secure," Mayorkas said, as El Paso built encampments (Mayorkas, 2022)[13]. "This was an extraordinary success," Biden said of Afghanistan (Aug 31, 2021)[17]. "We reduced the deficit by $1.7 trillion," he bragged, neglecting the context that pandemic emergency levels were unwinding, not that he discovered fiscal virtue (Treasury data; budget analyses)[37]. This is the art of cherry-pick: take the one metric that looks temporarily flattering, repeat, and hope the average voter won't notice the grocery bill.

The Rhetorical Question You Already Know the Answer To

Is the Biden–Harris presidency a failure? Measure by outcome, not press clippings.

• **Prices:** four-decade inflation spike, persistent affordability crunch despite disinflation's slow grind (BLS CPI)[1].

• **Border:** historic crossings, fentanyl flood, overwhelmed cities (CBP data)[11].

• **Afghanistan:** strategic embarrassment with human and geopolitical costs (DoD reports)[14].

• **COVID governance:** overreach, speech-jawboning, and a union-shaped shadow over "the science" (NFIB v. OSHA; CDC/union reporting)[18] [19].

• **Energy:** policy confusion that raised risk premiums and invited OPEC to play central banker (DOI/SPR data)[7] [8].

• **Regulation:** ESG-ification of finance and aggressive rulemaking by agencies acting as legislatures (DOL/SEC/FTC-DOJ)[31] [30] [32].

• **Civil liberties:** government-platform entanglement in content moderation (Missouri v. Biden; WH briefings)[27] [21].

"Unity," they said. But unity based on enforced consensus isn't unity; it's compliance. "Normal," they vowed. But normal isn't emergency rule by permanent bureaucracy and an economic program that taxes you through the grocery aisle.

Snark, yes—but let's be forensic about the rot. Competence isn't tone. It's the ability to anticipate second-order effects, to prioritize trade-offs, to communicate with candor, to stop digging when the hole is obvious, and to know that governance is not Instagram. On these criteria, the administration underperformed in ways that hurt the people it claimed to champion: working families, small businesses, kids in public schools, immigrant communities preyed upon by smugglers, and soldiers who trust professionals to plan exits before press conferences.

Exhibits of Failure: A Closer Docket

• **Inflation's Anatomy:** ARP poured gasoline on a supply-constrained fire. A passive Fed arrived late, then slammed the brakes. The White House spent a year overselling "transitory" and then tried to brand the IRA as an anti-inflation tool. A better path would have been targeted relief, deregulation of choke points, and aggressive supply-side permitting. They chose checks and vibes over output and incentives (BLS; Summers warnings; CBO/JCT)[1][3][4].

• **Border Incentives:** When you signal that border enforcement is a moral failing, you empower the cartels. MPP's rollback, interior enforcement narrowing, and a patchwork of parole programs wrote the invitation letter. The human toll—the assaults, drownings, trafficking—belongs in the ledger too (DHS/CBP)[10][11].

• **Afghanistan Planning:** The sequencing error—pulling military before civilians, abandoning Bagram, trusting the Taliban

235

perimeter—was not inevitable. It was chosen. The after-action reports say so. So do Gold Star families (DoD reports; testimonies)[14].

• **School Closures:** Letting unions draft CDC guidance was moral malpractice. The kids who could least afford learning loss suffered most. The administration's PR line, "we opened schools," collided with the lived reality of half-measures, masks-on-forever, and social regression (CDC/union reporting)[19].

• **Censorship Urge:** The Disinformation Board and social-media jawboning are not footnotes. They show an instinct to centralize truth-making. In a republic, that instinct must be checked (DHS Board; Missouri v. Biden; WH briefings)[26][27][21].

• **Energy Contradictions:** If you want lower prices, increase reliable supply. If you want decarbonization, permit nuclear, fix NEPA, and stop treating pipelines as moral crimes. The administration did the opposite: hostility to hydrocarbons, regulatory friction for alternatives that actually work, and subsidies for the photogenic (EOs; SEC/DOL; DOI; DOE)[7][8][30][31].

The Rhetoric vs. The Record

"America is back." Back to what—strategic ambiguity and bureaucratic maximalism? "We're building an economy from the middle out and bottom up." Then why did the median household need credit cards to tread water while mortgage rates doubled and car insurance soared? "We believe in democracy." Then why the urge to curate lawful speech?

A presidency is a narrative told in the ledger books of families. They don't read Federal Register notices; they read receipts. They don't care about a Rose Garden ceremony if their rent just spiked and their kids forgot long division.

The Defense, Such As It Is

But what about jobs? Yes, jobs returned post-pandemic as the economy reopened—an expected rebound after a mandated shutdown. Calling it an achievement is like bragging that sunrise follows night. Unemployment fell; it was supposed to. Infrastructure bill? You can spend a trillion dollars and still not fix permitting bottlenecks that turn every project into a decade-long legal saga. Chips Act? Subsidies can kickstart fabs, but without workforce pipelines and predictable rules, you'll get half-built monuments to federal hubris. Student debt "forgiveness"? A legally dubious, inflationary transfer to the college-credentialed, struck down once and then reanimated piecemeal through backdoor rulemaking (SCOTUS on HEROES Act; ED workarounds)[38].

"Compared to what?" Compared to a baseline where adults balance trade-offs and tell you the truth: that energy transitions take decades, that borders require enforcement, that pandemics demand humility, that withdrawal requires planning, and that bureaucrats will always expand their remit unless you say no. The Biden–Harris theory of politics held that you could substitute "competence" as

237

branding for competence in practice. The market—political and financial—disagreed.

Conclusion: Normalcy Isn't a Press Release

An administration that began with promises of calm delivered a sugar high, a hangover, and a sermon.

It governed as if press optics could gaslight reality into compliance. Inflation introduced the public to an old villain. The border made sanctuary politics collide with capacity. Afghanistan reminded the world that exit is strategy. The regulatory state demonstrated its appetite, and the speech cops confirmed the elite's distrust of the public square.

If the goal of Chapter 14 is to persuade as well as to prosecute, the closing question writes itself:

After four years of "normal," how much more of this competence can working families afford?

Inline Citations Equal Footnotes

1. U.S. Bureau of Labor Statistics, CPI data 2021–2022; Biden public remarks on inflation ("transitory"). (BLS CPI historical data; Biden remarks, 2021–2022)

2. CPI acceleration before February 2022 showing inflation rise prior to Russia's invasion. (BLS CPI trend pre-2/2022)

3. Lawrence H. Summers warnings on inflation risk from ARP, February 2021. (Summers, Feb–Mar 2021 commentary)

4. Inflation Reduction Act text and budget analyses. (IRA; CBO/JCT assessments)

5. BLS Real Average Weekly Earnings showing negative real wage growth periods, 2021–2023. (BLS real earnings)

6. Biden "Bidenomics" speeches, 2023. (White House transcripts)

7. Keystone XL cancellation; DOI leasing moratorium, 2021. (White House/DOI documents)

8. Strategic Petroleum Reserve releases and inventory levels, 2021–2023. (DOE SPR data). Biden 2020 debate remarks on "transitioning from the oil industry"; later denials. (2020 debate transcript; subsequent remarks)

9. DHS 2021 enforcement priority memos; MPP rollback. (DHS policy changes, 2021)

10. CBP Southwest border encounters, FY2021–FY2024. (CBP data)

11. Harris "Do not come" remarks; Guatemala trip, 2021. (Harris remarks/transcripts)

12. Mayorkas "the border is secure" statements, 2022. (DHS/press remarks)

13. DoD after-action materials; testimonies on Afghanistan withdrawal and Abbey Gate. (DoD reports/testimony)

14. Biden August 16, 2021 address: "the buck stops with me," with blame-shifting context. (White House transcript)

15. Biden July 2021 remarks downplaying risk of Taliban takeover. (White House transcript)

16. Biden August 31, 2021 "extraordinary success" line. (White House transcript)

17. NFIB v. OSHA (2022) Supreme Court ruling blocking OSHA vaccine-or-test mandate. (SCOTUS opinion)

18. Reporting on CDC guidance drafts influenced by teachers' unions; school reopening politics. (News reporting; document disclosures)

19. Harris 2020 debate quote on Trump-era vaccines. (VP debate transcript, 2020)

20. Jen Psaki July 2021 briefing: "We're flagging problematic posts for Facebook." (WH press briefing transcript)

21. State of the Union 2022 — Biden: "Fund the police." (SOTU transcript)

22. Executive Order 13985 — Advancing Racial Equity. (Federal Register)

23. Department of Education Title IX rulemakings (2022–2024), redefining sex discrimination. (ED docket)

24. DOJ October 2021 memo regarding threats to school officials; NSBA letter context. (DOJ memo; NSBA letter timeline)

25. DHS Disinformation Governance Board announcement and dissolution, 2022. (DHS releases)

26. Missouri v. Biden litigation materials on government–platform coordination. (Court filings)

27. Biden January 2022 press conference "minor incursion" remark on Ukraine. (WH transcript)

28. Chinese surveillance balloon incident timeline, February 2023. (DoD/press briefings)

29. SEC climate disclosure rule proposals/finals. (SEC releases)

30. DOL ESG rule for ERISA plans. (DOL rule)

31. 2023 DOJ/FTC Merger Guidelines. (DOJ/FTC)

32. Harris verbal gaffes and circular statements quoted widely. (Press transcripts/coverage)

33. DOT under Buttigieg: supply-chain disruptions; East Palestine response timeline. (DOT/press)

34. Reports of Granholm EV road trip charging issues. (Press reporting)

35. Biden August 2022 "zero inflation" phrasing regarding month-over-month change. (WH remarks)

36. Deficit reduction claims driven by expiry of COVID outlays; baseline context. (Treasury; budget analyses)

37. SCOTUS decision invalidating broad student-loan forgiveness; subsequent ED workarounds. (SCOTUS; ED releases)

Chapter 15:

The Constitution They Invented Yesterday

There's a parlor trick in American politics that never goes out of style. It starts with an earnest sigh, a solemn stare at the parchment in Philadelphia, and ends with a sentence that begins, "What the Framers really meant was…" Then come the jazz hands. Suddenly words like "speech" become "approved speech," "arms" become "maybe muskets, never modern," "commerce" expands until your grandmother's tomato patch is federal business, and "liberty" gets duct-taped to whatever the faculty lounge is emoting about this decade. The Constitution, written in sentences, not vibes, gets repackaged as a Ouija board for permanent revolution. It's not interpretation. It's ventriloquism.

And here's the punchline: every time their policy wish list hits constitutional bedrock, progressives don't rethink the wish list. They set their sights on the umpire. The Constitution is an obstacle; the Court is a hill; "reform" is artillery. Hence the new-old project: stack the Supreme Court until the Constitution collapses under the weight of extra seats and invented meanings. If you can't win the text, move the goalposts. If you can't move the goalposts, bulldoze the field.

The text is short. The ambition to ignore it is bottomless.

I. The Plain Words They Can't Quite Hear

Read the First Amendment again, slowly: "Congress shall make no law… abridging the freedom of speech." Not "Congress shall make no law abridging speech the New York Times approves of." Not "speech unless it's politically inconvenient in an election year." It's categorical in ways that give bureaucrats hives. When old-progressive courts flirted with "balancing" the right away, later courts called the bluff. As Justice Kennedy put it, "If the First Amendment has any force, it prohibits Congress from fining or jailing citizens… for simply engaging in political speech." (Citizens United v. FEC, 558 U.S. 310, 349 (2010)). Note the clause they'd rather forget: "political speech." The kind that threatens incumbents.

Move one amendment down the hall. The Second: "the right of the people to keep and bear Arms, shall not be infringed." Not "the right of state-sanctioned clubs," not "in rural hunting seasons," not "in 1791, and then never again." The Supreme Court finally said the quiet part loud: "The Second Amendment conferred an individual right to keep and bear arms." (District of Columbia v. Heller, 554 U.S. 570, 595 (2008)). When New York tried to make carrying a firearm in public a rare privilege, the Court wrote, "The Second and Fourteenth Amendments protect an individual's right to carry a handgun for self-defense outside the home." (New York State Rifle & Pistol Ass'n v. Bruen, 597 U.S. (2022)). The Founders didn't pen an Easter egg hunt. They wrote a rule.

Yet the modern progressive habit is to shrink rights they don't like and inflate powers they do. The method is and always has been elastic "interpretation," called a "living Constitution" by admirers and "pen-and-phone legislation" by those who can read.

II. The Living Constitution: Taxidermy with a Pulse

"Living Constitution" sounds humane until you watch the autopsy. The core claim is simple: the Constitution evolves as society changes. But the mechanism is telling. Instead of amendment, the democratic, explicit path laid out in Article V, progressives prefer judicial reinterpretation, agency regulation, and catch-all clauses stretched to Olympic dimensions. It's not evolution; it's expropriation.

Start with the Commerce Clause. The text? Congress may "regulate Commerce... among the several States." Sensible. We don't want thirteen, now fifty, trade fiefdoms. But progressives discovered a political Swiss Army knife. In *Wickard v. Filburn* (1942), a farmer growing wheat for his own use could be regulated by Congress because his personal wheat meant he might buy less wheat, which might affect interstate commerce. That's not a chain of reasoning; that's a chain letter. As Justice Thomas would later dryly observe, the clause was never "a general police power of the sort retained by the States." (*United States v. Lopez*, 514 U.S. 549, 584 (1995) (Thomas, J., concurring)). *Lopez* finally set a speed bump: carrying a gun near a school is not commerce. When the line is "things that are not commerce," you know the clause was being used as Silly Putty.

Bureaucracy became the next frontier. Agencies, unmentioned by the Constitution, write rules with the force of law, then interpret their own rules, then enforce them — executive, legislative, and judicial functions in a single fluorescent-lit cubicle. *Chevron* deference, where "reasonable" agency interpretations get judicial blessing, turned into the technocrat's joyride. Even progressives admit it gave unelected administrators a long policy leash. The Court's rollback in cases like *West Virginia v. EPA* (597 U.S. (2022)) revived the "major questions" doctrine: agencies must point to clear congressional authorization before remaking the energy economy. Translation: if you want to refit the national grid, use Congress, not a press conference. As the Court wrote, "A decision of such magnitude and consequence rests with Congress itself, or an agency acting pursuant to a clear delegation from that representative body." That's called democracy, not denial.

Next stop: Substantive Due Process, constitutional Esperanto for policy preferences cloaked in "liberty." The Due Process Clause says no person shall be "deprived of life, liberty, or property, without due process of law." Historically, "due process" meant fair procedure. Progressives rebooted it to mean judges can identify unenumerated rights they deem "fundamental," often by scanning the horizon for "ordered liberty" and "deeply rooted" traditions, except when the tradition is inconvenient. In *Dobbs v. Jackson*

Women's Health Organization (597 U.S. (2022)), the Court finally stiffened its spine: "The Constitution makes no reference to abortion, and no such right is implicitly protected by any constitutional provision." That sentence caused a thousand editorials to detonate, but it's a basic act of honesty: if you want a national abortion rule, pass a law or amend the Constitution. Don't stage-manage a right between commas and penumbras.

III. Penumbras, Emanations, and Other Ghosts

Justice Douglas coined the melodrama in *Griswold v. Connecticut* (1965): "Specific guarantees in the Bill of Rights have penumbras, formed by emanations" that create zones of privacy. That formulation launched jurisprudence by aromatherapy — smell a right and it's yours. Privacy, then autonomy, then the scaffolding for *Roe v. Wade* (1973), which proclaimed a trimester regime not found in text, history, or obstetric textbooks. *Roe's* framework was so unmoored even defenders explained it as necessary policy, not constitutional fidelity. Justice White, dissenting in *Thornburgh v. American College of Obstetricians & Gynecologists* (1986), called *Roe* an "exercise of raw judicial power." He was right. *Dobbs* didn't erase "privacy"; it erased the myth that nine justices are a national ethics committee.

The method replicated elsewhere. Equal Protection, designed to destroy racial caste, got co-opted to supervise every policy disagreement under strict scrutiny if the cause was fashionable enough, except where progressives favored race-based engineering.

Then we're told the Equal Protection Clause means you must treat people differently by race to achieve equality. In *Students for Fair Admissions v. Harvard* (600 U.S. (2023)), the Court returned to first principles: "Eliminating racial discrimination means eliminating all of it." The dissent warned the sky would fall. The sky, stubbornly textualist, refused.

IV. The Free Speech That Isn't Free Enough

Progressives once defended robust free speech. Then they took over institutions and discovered the inconveniences of dissent. Thus the pivot from Skokie to "misinformation," from "I disagree with what you say but will defend your right to say it" to "we need a Disinformation Governance Board." The government leaned on platforms to throttle disfavored views under the talisman of "public health." That's not content moderation; that's state action outsourced. The First Amendment's ban on "abridging the freedom of speech" doesn't come with a footnote: "unless officials feel anxious."

The Court has drawn bright lines. Viewpoint discrimination is the cardinal sin: "The government may not regulate speech based on its substantive content or the message it conveys." (Rosenberger v. Rector & Visitors of Univ. of Va., 515 U.S. 819, 828 (1995)). In 303 Creative LLC v. Elenis (600 U.S. (2023)), the Court affirmed the obvious: the state cannot compel a designer to create speech she does not believe. "The First Amendment's protections belong to all, not just to speakers whose motives the government approves."

When your liberty depends on the censor's mood, you don't have liberty.

V. The Second Amendment: Break-Glass Rights

No right terrifies progressives more than the one that makes the others enforceable. "A well regulated Militia" is their favorite elastic clause, stretched until it snaps. Heller cut through the deliberate fog: "The operative clause's text and history demonstrate that it connotes an individual right to keep and bear arms." The militia clause is a justification, not a leash. Bruen added a test that sent policy shops scrambling: contemporary restrictions must be consistent with "this Nation's historical tradition of firearm regulation." Translation: if you can't find a historical analogue, you can't smuggle a modern ban through a health-and-safety back door. Progressives call that "radical." The Framers would call it Tuesday.

And spare us the "muskets" argument. The First Amendment protects podcasts, not quills; the Fourth protects your iPhone, not a lockbox; the Second covers the contemporary arms that make the right meaningful. The text didn't expire with powdered wigs.

VI. The Administrative Shortcut: When Congress Won't, Agencies Will

You can understand the attraction. Congress is messy; voters are annoying; compromise is hard. Agencies, by contrast, are tireless and unaccountable. So, if you can't get cap-and-trade through the legislature, engineer it via "interpretation." If you can't ban gas

248

stoves by statute, nudge-nudge "efficiency" rules. When challenged, point to Chevron and murmur "expertise." The Court's correction in West Virginia v. EPA restored the most basic of separation-of-powers facts: major national decisions require clear congressional instructions. The Constitution doesn't say "policy by PDF." It says laws are made by the legislature, executed by the executive, and judged by the judiciary.

James Madison was not ambiguous: "The accumulation of all powers, legislative, executive, and judiciary, in the same hands... may justly be pronounced the very definition of tyranny." (The Federalist No. 47). Madison didn't add, "unless the agency has a nice logo."

VII. Federalism Is Not a Talking Point

Progressives admire federalism when Texas does something they like and call it "Jim Crow 2.0" when it doesn't. But the structure—enumerated powers for the federal government, police powers for the states—is not racism; it's architecture. The Tenth Amendment is not a footnote; it says, "The powers not delegated to the United States by the Constitution, nor prohibited by it to the States, are reserved to the States... or to the people." When the Court in NFIB v. Sebelius (567 U.S. 519 (2012)) smacked down the Medicaid expansion as coercive, "a gun to the head," it reminded Washington that "cooperative federalism" becomes extortion when the check is attached to a threat.

Even the Spending Clause has limits, which stunned people who thought money is magic. "In the typical case we look to the States to defend their prerogatives by adopting the simple expedient of not yielding to federal blandishments," wrote Chief Justice Roberts. "But when the State has no real option but to acquiesce... the federal Government has crossed the line." Translation: you can't buy sovereignty with someone else's taxes.

VIII. The Court-Packing Gambit

Which brings us to the power move. If you can't win under the rules, change the refs. Court-packing is not "reform." It is an admission that your agenda loses under neutral principles. Franklin Roosevelt tried it in 1937 with the Judicial Procedures Reform Bill, proposing up to six additional justices. Congress balked because the public smelled the rat. As Justice Ginsburg put it bluntly in 2019: "Nine seems to be a good number. It was a bad idea when President Franklin Roosevelt tried to pack the Court." That wasn't a conservative; that was the progressive icon.

Today's version is dressed in euphemisms: "expand the Court," "balance the Court," "unrig the Court." The marketing pitch claims the Court is out of step with "democracy," which is progressive for "we lost some cases." But the Court's job is to be out of step with temporary majorities when the Constitution commands it. "The very purpose of a Bill of Rights," Justice Jackson wrote, "was to withdraw certain subjects from the vicissitudes of political controversy..." (West Virginia State Board of Education v.

Barnette, 319 U.S. 624, 638 (1943)). In plain English, some things are not up for a vote.

The Framers foresaw the temptation to subvert the judiciary. Hamilton wrote in Federalist 78 that the courts are the "least dangerous" branch because they have "neither FORCE nor WILL, but merely judgment." Court-packing injects "will" right into the bloodstream. If every election resets the size of the Court, constitutional rights become a seasonal item. Today's free speech is tomorrow's "harmful content." Today's federalism is tomorrow's "threat to democracy." What survives is not the Constitution, but the tally.

IX. The Religion Clause: The Freedom That Must Be Tamed

Progressives promise they "love" the First Amendment so much they want to move it across the street. Religion is welcome in private, preferably your attic. But the Free Exercise Clause is not a quiet-hours ordinance. "Congress shall make no law… prohibiting the free exercise" of religion. The modern Court clarified the obvious: the government cannot single out religious exercise for penalties it doesn't impose on secular analogues. In Tandon v. Newsom (593 U.S. (2021)), the Court said restrictions on in-home religious gatherings flunked scrutiny when comparable secular activities faced looser rules. In Kennedy v. Bremerton School District (597 U.S. (2022)), a public school employee's quiet, personal prayer at midfield was protected: "The Constitution and the best of our traditions counsel mutual respect and tolerance, not censorship and suppression, for religious and nonreligious views alike."

The Establishment Clause is not a "no Christians in public" clause. It bars a national church and compulsion, not the whiff of a manger scene. As Justice Gorsuch noted, "Offense... does not equate to coercion." If your liberty depends on other people disappearing their faith, you want dominance, not neutrality.

X. Speech, Guns, Faith, Federalism: A Pattern

The pattern is stark. Where the text constrains progressive goals, the answer is creative reading. Where the structure frustrates the agenda, the answer is administrative workaround. Where the Court resists both, the answer is to "reform" the Court. It's a three-step process for one-step politics.

Step 1: Inflate national power via the Commerce Clause, Spending Clause, and agencies.

Step 2: Deflate individual rights you distrust (speech that endangers your coalition, guns that enable self-defense, religious exercise that resists cultural mandates).

Step 3: When the judiciary restores the text, accuse it of "activism," demand expansion, impose ethics codes crafted by partisans, and threaten jurisdiction stripping.

This is not a conspiracy theory; it's a congressional calendar. Bills to expand the Court have been introduced. "Ethics reform" proposals aimed like sniper fire at disfavored justices appear the moment the Court rules against progressive positions. Editorial boards act as the press office of the legislative branch.

XI. "But Democracy!": The Slogan That Ate the Rulebook

The refrain is that court decisions must conform to "democracy." No, they must conform to the Constitution. That's the deal we made to prevent 51 percent from voting away the rights of the other 49, this year, next year, and in every year we haven't yet ruined. When the Court says Congress cannot delegate sweeping decisions without a clear statement, that's not "anti-democratic." It's constitutional.

It is pro-democratic: it forces elected representatives to take responsibility.

Madison again, Federalist 45: the federal powers are "few and defined," those of the states "numerous and indefinite." That is not an antique slogan. It is the oxygen of self-government in a continental republic. When progressives describe this as "minority rule," what they mean is "rules that prevent a temporary majority from bulldozing constitutional rights." The Bill of Rights is a minority-rule document by design. So is the Senate, so is the Electoral College, so is judicial review. That is not a flaw; it is our firebreak.

XII. The Text and Its Enemies

Here is the heart of it. The Constitution is both a sword and a shield. It limits government and guards the individual. Progressives treat it as a suggestion, a set of aspirations to be harmonized with progressive ethics by judges who "understand the moment." But the Framers did not draft a mood board. They wrote commands. "No law" means no law. "Shall not be infringed" means shall not be infringed. "Reserved to the States" means reserved to the States. When the words do not give you what you want, you have a path: amend. Article V exists. It is hard by design. That is not cruelty; that is wisdom. If you cannot persuade the country to adopt your revolution in writing, you do not get to smuggle it in by footnote.

Consider how the Court has guided the country back to text in recent years:

Free speech: content neutrality and strict scrutiny for compelled speech (303 Creative; Janus v. AFSCME, 585 U.S. (2018): "Compelling individuals to mouth support for views they find objectionable violates that cardinal constitutional command.").

Second Amendment: historical tradition test, recognition of individual rights (Heller; McDonald v. Chicago, 561 U.S. 742 (2010)).

Separation of powers: major questions doctrine (West Virginia v. EPA); limits on recess appointments and agency freelancing (NLRB v. Noel Canning, 573 U.S. 513 (2014)).

Federalism: anti-commandeering and limits on coercive spending (Murphy v. NCAA, 584 U.S. (2018); NFIB v. Sebelius).

The progressive response? Court-packing, jurisdiction stripping, and "ethics" campaigns aimed at delegitimizing the outcomes. They want a Constitution that nods along.

XIII. Originalism Is Not Nostalgia, It's Honesty

Originalism gets caricatured as cosplay, with tri-corner hats and powdered wigs. In reality, it is simple: words mean what they meant when ratified. If you want new meanings, amend. That interpretive discipline is not reactionary; it is democratic. As Justice Scalia put it, "The Constitution is not a living organism. It is a legal document, and it says what it says and doesn't say what it doesn't say." The rule of law resides in meaning, not mood.

Originalism does not freeze society; it frees politics. Do not like the policy? Pass a law. Do not like the balance? Elect different representatives. Want a new right? Convince three-fourths of the states. That is not cruelty; it is consent. The living Constitution, by contrast, is consent on stilts: judges discover what you "really consented to" after the fact.

XIV. The Stakes of Court-Packing

Court-packing is the nuclear option masquerading as home repair. The moment one side expands the Court to tip outcomes, the Court becomes a legislature that the other side must expand later to un-tip them. Game theory predicts the spiral; history confirms it.

The judiciary ceases to be a court and becomes a super-senate with robes. The Constitution becomes a menu. Rights become coupons.

Even those who pine for different outcomes should fear this. The next majority can expand, too. The ratchet is not one way. If you think nine justices are too many to control, wait until there are fifteen, then twenty-one, each added to reverse the last decision like a toddler toggling a light switch. If you think cynicism is high now, imagine telling citizens the meaning of "no law" depends on last November's turnout.

Ginsburg's warning was not etiquette; it was structural: "If anything would make the Court appear partisan, it would be that, one side saying, 'When we are in power, we are going to enlarge the number of judges so we will have more people who will vote the way we want them to.'" She said the quiet part in plain English.

XV. The Liberal Lexicon: How to Hear What Isn't There

A brief glossary of interpretive magic:

"Textualism" means "cruel formalism."

"Democracy" means "policies we like authorized by people we like."

"Norms" are ancient and sacred unless they block our agenda this afternoon.

"Rights" are expanding until they run into your religion, then they shrink.

"Speech" is free until it threatens the palace, then it is "harm."

Watch the wordplay and you can forecast the policy. When they say "balance the Court," they mean "break it." When they say "living Constitution," they mean "judicial legislature." When they say "major questions doctrine endangers governance," they mean "we do not want to pass bills anymore."

XVI. What the Framers Actually Wrote, And Why It Still Works

Hamilton on the judiciary: "No legislative act… contrary to the Constitution, can be valid." (Federalist 78). That is the wellspring of judicial review. Marbury v. Madison (1803) put it in case law: "It is emphatically the province and duty of the Judicial Department to say what the law is." Judicial review is not a trump card for any policy preference; it is a shield for the Constitution against any branch, any party, any era.

Madison on ambition: "Ambition must be made to counteract ambition." (Federalist 51). The answer to faction is structure. You do not save the structure by blowing up the court that enforces it.

The First Amendment's categorical commands, the Second Amendment's unambiguous core, the structural federalism of Articles I and II, and the textual limits on delegation all function as circuit breakers against concentrated power. Progressives call breakers "obstruction." Electricians call them "survival."

XVII. Cases in Point: How "Interpretation" Becomes Policy

Speech and money: the same crowd that insists money is speech when funding public broadcasting says money is corruption when citizens fund political speech. Citizens United corrected that self-dealing: "The First Amendment confirms the freedom to think for ourselves." (558 U.S. at 356). If the government can ration ads, it can ration arguments.

Compelled association: in Janus, the Court held governments cannot force workers to subsidize union speech as the price of public employment. "Forcing free and independent individuals to endorse ideas they find objectionable is always demeaning." (585 U.S. (2018)). Translation: "Shut up and pay" is not a constitutional theory.

Gun control by red tape: post-Bruen, may-issue permit regimes melted into shall-issue in many states, and bureaucrats scrambled to invent "sensitive places" that included, hilariously, most of Earth. Courts struck that down because "sensitive places" historically meant courts, legislatures, and polling places, not "the outdoors."

EPA and Congress: West Virginia v. EPA demolished the dream of transforming the entire power sector by reading a vague phrase ("best system of emission reduction") as carte blanche. If Congress meant cap and trade, Congress could say cap and trade. Removing a few words from context to build a national plan is not "expertise." It is Mad Libs with mandates.

Federal sports betting ban: in Murphy v. NCAA, the Court said the federal government cannot forbid states from legalizing something just because Washington dislikes it. Anti-commandeering is not a fringe idea; it is the guarantee that states are not administrative districts of Washington.

Religion in public: in Carson v. Makin (596 U.S. (2022)), the Court held that if a state funds private schooling, it cannot exclude religious schools just for being religious. Neutrality means neutral, what a concept.

Each of these decisions did not create new rights from incense smoke; they enforced old ones against new encroachments.

XVIII. The Hard Path Is the Only Legitimate One

It is not that progressives cannot have what they want. They can. They have a process: persuade, legislate, amend. The Framers made it hard because they knew something about human nature and power, and because they had read a little bit of history with a musket pointed at their heads. Shortcuts are tempting. They also end democracies.

If your policy cannot survive the light of day in Congress, maybe it does not deserve the shadow of an agency. If your right cannot find a foothold in the text or history, maybe it belongs in a statute, not a syllabus. If your movement cannot win without changing the number of justices, maybe your movement is not a constitutional project. It is an insurgency against the document.

XIX. Closing Argument: Keep the Parchment, Fire the Alchemy

The American experiment does not need alchemists. It needs guardians. The Constitution is not perfect; nothing written by men is. But it is the most successful charter for ordered liberty in human history precisely because it is not whatever we want it to be today. It binds us to a process, to words, to limits, especially when they are inconvenient.

The choice before us is stark. Either the Constitution is law, and we read it as such, or it is costume jewelry, and we wear it when it matches the outfit. If progressives get their court-packing wish, the necklace snaps. Nine is not holy; it is prudent. The text is not scripture; it is law. But law requires faithfulness, not projection.

We can disagree about policy. We can debate abortion, guns, energy, speech, and religion; vote, legislate, and litigate. But when the Constitution speaks, the argument ends. "No law" means no law. "Shall not be infringed" means shall not be infringed. "Few and defined" means few and defined. And "the judicial Power" means judgment, not wind-reading.

If they want a different Constitution, there is a page for that. It is called Article V. Until they turn it, spare us the penumbras, the emanations, the agencies, the ethics theatrics, and the packing schemes. Stop pretending the Framers left blank spaces for your feelings. They left a margin for your amendments.

Inline citations

- Citizens United v. FEC, 558 U.S. 310, 349, 356 (2010).
- District of Columbia v. Heller, 554 U.S. 570, 595 (2008).
- New York State Rifle & Pistol Ass'n v. Bruen, 597 U.S. (2022).
- United States v. Lopez, 514 U.S. 549, 584 (1995) (Thomas, J., concurring).
- West Virginia v. EPA, 597 U.S. (2022).
- Dobbs v. Jackson Women's Health Org., 597 U.S. (2022).
- Griswold v. Connecticut, 381 U.S. 479, 484 (1965).
- Thornburgh v. Am. Coll. of Obstetricians & Gynecologists, 476 U.S. 747, 787 (1986) (White, J., dissenting).
- Students for Fair Admissions v. President and Fellows of Harvard College, 600 U.S. (2023).
- Rosenberger v. Rector & Visitors of Univ. of Va., 515 U.S. 819, 828 (1995).
- 303 Creative LLC v. Elenis, 600 U.S. (2023).
- Janus v. AFSCME, Council 31, 585 U.S. (2018).
- McDonald v. City of Chicago, 561 U.S. 742 (2010).
- NLRB v. Noel Canning, 573 U.S. 513 (2014).
- Murphy v. NCAA, 584 U.S. (2018).
- NFIB v. Sebelius, 567 U.S. 519, 581 (2012).
- West Virginia State Board of Education v. Barnette, 319 U.S. 624, 638 (1943).
- Marbury v. Madison, 5 U.S. (1 Cranch) 137, 177 (1803).
- The Federalist No. 47 (Madison).
- The Federalist No. 51 (Madison).
- The Federalist No. 78 (Hamilton).
- Tandon v. Newsom, 593 U.S. (2021).
- Kennedy v. Bremerton School District, 597 U.S. (2022).
- Carson v. Makin, 596 U.S. (2022).

Footnotes

1. "If the First Amendment has any force…" Citizens United v. FEC, 558 U.S. at 349.

2. "The Second Amendment conferred an individual right…" District of Columbia v. Heller, 554 U.S. at 595.

3. "Protect an individual's right to carry a handgun…" Bruen, 597 U.S. (2022).

4. "Not a general police power…" Lopez, 514 U.S. at 584 (Thomas, J., concurring).

5. "A decision of such magnitude…" West Virginia v. EPA, 597 U.S. (2022).

6. "The Constitution makes no reference to abortion…" Dobbs, 597 U.S. (2022).

7. "Penumbras… emanations," Griswold, 381 U.S. at 484.

8. "Exercise of raw judicial power," Thornburgh, 476 U.S. at 787 (White, J., dissenting).

9. "Eliminating racial discrimination means eliminating all of it." SFFA v. Harvard, 600 U.S. (2023).

10. "The government may not regulate speech…" Rosenberger, 515 U.S. at 828.

11. "Protections belong to all…" 303 Creative, 600 U.S. (2023).

12. "Compelling individuals to mouth support…" Janus, 585 U.S. (2018).

13. "A gun to the head," NFIB, 567 U.S. at 581.

14. Barnette, 319 U.S. at 638.

15. Marbury, 5 U.S. at 177.

16. Madison, Federalist No. 47.

17. Madison, Federalist No. 51.

18. Hamilton, Federalist No. 78.

19. "Mutual respect and tolerance…" Kennedy v. Bremerton, 597 U.S. (2022).

20. "No law… abridging," U.S. Const. amend. I.

21. "Shall not be infringed," U.S. Const. amend. II.

22. "Powers not delegated… reserved," U.S. Const. amend. X.

23. "Best system of emission reduction," Clean Air Act §111, as construed in West Virginia v. EPA.

Chapter 16:

The Great Unbuilding —

How "Defund," "Abolish," and "Reimagine" Turned Cities into Experiments No One Consented To

You can't run a city like a grad-seminar thought experiment and expect anything but smoke alarms and sirens. Yet here we are, picking through the wreckage of slogans that were supposed to "keep us safe" by removing the people whose job is to keep us safe. Defund the police? Abolish ICE? Abolish prisons? Why not abolish locks while we're at it? What harm could possibly come from advertising that rules don't apply and consequences are optional?

Let's be clear: this isn't about demonizing every progressive, many of whom privately admit the obvious. It's about the political class that turned a summer of sloganeering into a policy architecture, and then gaslit you when that architecture collapsed. When the moment demanded tradeoffs, they chose hashtags. How did that go?

Consider the cleanest slogan of 2020: "Defund the police." Asked point-blank what "defunding" really means, Rep. Alexandria Ocasio-Cortez answered, "Defunding police means defunding police. It does not mean budget tricks or funny math." (June 30, 2020) (AOC, 2020). Cori Bush, riding the wave to Congress, proclaimed, "Defund the police has to happen. We need to defund the police and put that money into social safety nets." (July 2020)

(Bush, 2020). Ilhan Omar called the Minneapolis Police Department "rotten to the root" and vowed to "dismantle" it (June 2020) (Omar, 2020). Rashida Tlaib went further after the fatal shooting of Daunte Wright: "No more policing, incarceration, and militarization. It can't be reformed." (Apr. 12, 2021) (Tlaib, 2021).

These aren't parody accounts. These are sitting members of Congress. If these were just overheated tweets, why did city councils, district attorneys, and budget committees translate them into policy?

Minneapolis slashed and "reallocated" millions after council members stood on a stage at Powderhorn Park beneath a giant "Defund Police" banner and pledged to "end policing as we know it." (June 7, 2020) (Minneapolis Council, 2020). Seattle campaigned its way into a City Attorney race where one finalist promised categorical non-prosecution of entire offense categories.[1] Portland's DA publicly declared he would presumptively decline to prosecute a raft of protest-related offenses (Aug. 2020) (Schmidt, 2020). San Francisco elected a DA who treated open-air fentanyl markets as a sociological inevitability until the glass crunching under voters' shoes suggested otherwise. New York City and Los Angeles performed synchronized "cuts," with press-conference math substituting for patrol strength. The result? A spike in disorder, massaged by euphemisms about "lived experience" and "alternative responses," as if rhetoric doubles as ambulances.

Here's a question: if police are the problem, why does crime rise when you remove them? If prisons are "obsolete," why do serial offenders keep proving they're not obsolete? If ICE is the villain, why do the same leaders who refused to cooperate with federal detainers beg for federal funds and logistics when their shelter systems overflow? Policy reality has all the subtlety of a frying pan. You can ignore it, but you can't dodge the swing.

The legal skeleton they pretend isn't there: the police power, not the slogan but the actual governmental function, is as old as the Republic. Courts have repeatedly affirmed that municipalities not only may but must provide for public safety. Now, a caveat the left likes to weaponize: there isn't a constitutional guarantee that police will protect you from every harm. *DeShaney v. Winnebago County* said the Due Process Clause does not impose an affirmative duty to protect individuals from private violence, 489 U.S. 189 (1989) (DeShaney, 1989). But cities still carry statutory duties under state law, charters, and tort frameworks to maintain basic order. They also operate under labor agreements, consent decrees, state-imposed minimums, and political accountability. When you gut the capacity of a core function, the law doesn't step aside to make room for vibes.

Minneapolis learned this the hard way when residents sued to force compliance with the city charter's minimum staffing requirement. In 2022, the Minnesota Supreme Court held that the charter requires employing a minimum number of officers tied to population and that the mayor has a "clear legal duty" to staff to that minimum (*Spann v. Minneapolis City Council*, 979 N.W.2d 729 (Minn. 2022)) (Spann, 2022).[2] Translation: you can tweet "abolish" until your thumbs cramp; the law still expects cops to exist. Minneapolis didn't stumble into a staffing crisis. It was chosen, repackaged as "transformational investment," and then judicially corrected.

Progressive prosecution collided with the basic architecture of criminal law. In New York, bail reforms enacted in 2019–2020 sharply limited judges' discretion to remand for a vast swath of offenses. Repeat offenders gamified "catch and release" (N.Y. Crim. Proc. Law §§ 510.10–.30, as amended 2019–2022) (NYS Bail Reform, 2019–2022).[3] In Philadelphia, DA Larry Krasner's memos deprioritizing "quality of life" and certain gun offenses coincided with historic homicide levels in 2021 and 2022. Correlation isn't causation, but incapacitation can't function when filing decisions are ideologically throttled (Krasner Policies, 2018–2022). In Portland, DA Mike Schmidt announced that his office would presumptively decline to prosecute charges like interfering with a peace officer, disorderly conduct, and other protest-related offenses absent "deliberate property damage, theft, or use of force" (Aug. 2020) (Schmidt, 2020). Result? Shock: when laws become suggestions, suggestions are ignored.

Immigration? The Supremacy Clause hasn't retired. *Arizona v. United States* grounded core immigration authority at the federal level, 567 U.S. 387 (2012) (Arizona v. U.S., 2012). That doesn't mean localities can be dragooned into enforcement. The anti-commandeering doctrine from *Printz v. United States*, 521 U.S. 898 (1997) (Printz, 1997), bars that. But sanctuary policies that block ICE detainers, limit jail cooperation, and bar information-sharing also don't carry divine sanction. 8 U.S.C. § 1373 restricts prohibitions on sharing information about immigration status with federal authorities. Cities walk a legal tightrope when they step from "we won't be your deputies" into "we'll hide the ball." And while the Seventh Circuit cut down the Trump DOJ's grant-conditions gambit in *City of Chicago v. Sessions*, 888 F.3d 272 (7th Cir. 2018) (Sessions, 2018), the core point remains: cooperation is lawful; nullification isn't.[4]

Rhetorical question time: when a city refuses to hold repeat violent offenders pending trial, refuses to cooperate with immigration detainers for individuals charged with serious crimes, and refuses to staff its police force to legal minimums, what do you call that? Governance, or abdication dressed up as compassion?

The budgetary vandalism, measured in numbers and bodies. Minneapolis is the cautionary tale no one wanted and everyone received. After the council's June 2020 pledge to dismantle the MPD, the city "reallocated" millions from recruitment, overtime, and specialized units, and christened the cuts with new programmatic branding (Minneapolis Budget, 2020–21). The department hemorrhaged officers; hundreds of departures and medical leaves dropped sworn staffing far below pre-2020 levels and below the charter minimum until the court stepped in (Spann, 2022). Homicides rose to levels not seen since the 1990s. Neighborhoods that need the most policing got the least. The city later quietly approved retention and hiring bonuses because gravity wins, and "reimagining" doesn't answer 911.

Seattle: the council cut specialty units and the homelessness Navigation Team and antagonized SPD into a wave of retirements and resignations. By 2022–2024, the city was 400-plus officers down (Seattle HR Reports, 2022–2024). City Attorney candidate Nicole Thomas-Kennedy's 2021 campaign tweets called property destruction a "moral imperative" and promised categorical non-prosecution. Voters ultimately installed a more moderate attorney, but the staffing crater remained. You can't deploy a clinician to a violent robbery. If there aren't officers to respond, there isn't safety—only statements.

Portland: The Gun Violence Reduction Team was disbanded in 2020 amid profiling criticism. Homicides then surged to record highs in 2021 and 2022 before the city scrambled to stand up a rebranded Focused Intervention Team—a rose by another name, revived because bullets don't care about branding (Portland Crime Data, 2021–2023). The lesson wasn't subtext; it was neon: you can abolish a team in a press release, but you can't abolish ballistic trajectories.

San Francisco: Chesa Boudin's declination policies on drug dealing and sentencing enhancements played academic theory against sidewalk reality. Open-air fentanyl markets metastasized across the Tenderloin. Voters recalled him in June 2022, not because Fox News told them to, but because their car windows did (Boudin Recall, 2022). Mayor London Breed, who in 2020 flirted with the performative "reform" lexicon, pivoted hard in December 2021: "It's time the reign of criminals who are destroying our city comes to an end" (Dec. 15, 2021) (Breed, 2021). That isn't a right-wing blog post; that's the mayor of San Francisco discovering gravity in public.

Los Angeles: The city council trimmed LAPD in 2020. DA George Gascón issued Day-One directives curbing sentencing enhancements, abandoning some cash bail, and restricting certain prosecutions. After public outcry and spikes in violent crime, his office revised some policies. Venice Beach didn't get "reimagined"; it got victimized. If you tell violent recidivists that consequences are culturally insensitive, expect them to lecture you with a Glock.

Chicago: A city that knows homicide like a tragic relative dabbled in "alternatives to policing" while CPD bled officers and clearance rates cratered. Mayor Lori Lightfoot juggled a federal consent decree and political blowtorches; the revolving-door carjacking crisis wrote its own headlines. Reform is necessary; a hiring famine is self-harm.

New York City: In 2020, the City Council declared a one billion dollar "cut" largely via accounting shifts, while attrition and retirements ate the department's backbone. Shootings surged

270

through 2020–2021, then retreated as staffing stabilized and enforcement returned. The state's bail reforms (effective 2020) limited remand for non-qualifying offenses; amendments in 2020–2023 clawed back some discretion after public backlash (NYS Bail Reform, 2019–2022). Even Mayor Eric Adams, hardly a Trumper, spent political capital begging Albany to let judges consider dangerousness. It is remarkable how law and order matter once you inherit the mess.

Abolish ICE—until the buses arrive. The moral theater of "Abolish ICE" played differently once actual buses rolled up from Texas and Arizona. Cities that passed sanctuary resolutions, barred detainer cooperation, and declared themselves proudly "welcoming" discovered a pesky constraint: real capacity. Humanitarianism without logistics is just chaos with a halo.

Mayors begged for federal funds, emergency waivers, hotel contracts, and National Guard support after refusing to coordinate with ICE to triage criminal detainers from asylum seekers (Sanctuary Ordinances, 2017–2024; 8 U.S.C. § 1357). If abolition is the goal, why hold press conferences demanding federal help? If all enforcement is oppression, why carve out "serious crimes" exceptions in sanctuary policies? Either you believe border and immigration enforcement must exist, or you are comfortable importing cartel business models into municipal budgets.

Let's quote the vanguard. Rep. Ocasio-Cortez: "Abolish ICE… we don't need to be doing any of this at all" (2018) (AOC, 2018).

Sen. Bernie Sanders: "I don't think we need ICE" (2019) (Sanders, 2019). Seattle and other sanctuary city councils restricted cooperation with detainers even as high-profile cases of released offenders committing new crimes triggered lawsuits and public fury (Seattle Resolutions, 2019–2020). The paradox writes itself: if ICE is irredeemable, why do sanctuary policies include lists of exceptions for precisely the criminal categories abolitionists pretend don't exist?

Abolish prisons—but keep the locks on your door. The abolition discourse leapt from academia into municipal policy via prosecutors who treated incapacitation as a class crime. The platform language from activist groups was explicit: prisons are "sites of racialized violence" to be "dismantled." Fine.

Where, exactly, do you place the serial carjacker, the domestic abuser who violates every order, the fentanyl trafficker running a corner like a franchise? "Community-based restorative justice" sounds pastoral until you ask it to stand between a predator and his next victim. Incapacitation is not a vibe; it is a wall.

Courts have recognized public safety as a legitimate government interest in bail and sentencing. Stack v. Boyle described bail's purpose in ensuring appearance; United States v. Salerno upheld preventive detention for dangerous defendants under the Bail Reform Act, 481 U.S. 739 (1987) (Salerno, 1987). Absolutist claims that "jail before trial is unconstitutional" ignore controlling precedent. Pretending the Constitution outlaws incapacitation is like pretending gravity is a microaggression.

"Evidence-based"—without the evidence. Progressive prosecutors wrapped leniency in a lab coat. "Evidence-based," they said, would reduce recidivism. But evidence requires feedback loops. When clearance rates drop because departments are understaffed, and prosecutions fall because DAs refuse to file, your data on "crime" becomes garbage in, victory lap out. If no one is counting, everything looks cured.

Portland again: the decision to end the Gun Violence Reduction Team in 2020 was hailed as an equity win. Homicides surged; by 2022 the city reconstituted a Focused Intervention Team with the same physics—identify shooters, seize guns, incapacitate the small cohort driving violence (Portland FIT, 2021–2023). Minneapolis rediscovered state-federal task forces; after ceremonially rejecting "task force policing" in 2020, the city begged for it by 2022 (MPD-FBI Task Forces, 2022). Rhetorical question: why does the "evidence" always point to defunding before the election and refunding after?

The human cost you can hear at two a.m. This isn't abstract. It is a mom in South Minneapolis who waits forty-five minutes for a squad because a precinct is running skeleton crew. It is the small business owner on Union Square who chains her inventory behind bars inside bars because the city decided theft under nine hundred fifty dollars is basically vibes. It is the bus shelter in the Tenderloin that doubles as an unsupervised injection site. It is the family in Chicago who can recite the dates of each carjacking like you and I list birthdays. It is the immigrant bodega owner who won't call 911 because the last three times no one came.

Even progressive leaders occasionally blurt the truth. London Breed again: "We are not going to just walk by and let somebody use [drugs] in broad daylight" (Dec. 2021) (Breed, 2021). New York Gov. Kathy Hochul in 2022: "We have to restore a sense of security," pushing bail tweaks to allow more discretion (Hochul, 2022). Philadelphia's mayor called for more cops amid homicide spikes. These aren't MAGA hats. They are reluctant arson investigators standing in front of their own matches.

Legal guardrails against magical thinking. A system can be merciful without being suicidal. The Constitution is not a suicide pact, as Justice Jackson said in Terminiello v. Chicago, 337 U.S. 1, 37 (1949) (Jackson, J., dissenting) (Terminiello, 1949). Cities have discretion, yes, but also duties.

Statutes like California's Penal Code did not evaporate because a DA doesn't "feel" like applying them. When prosecutors adopt blanket non-prosecution lists, they flirt with unlawful abdication of statutory responsibilities. While broad discretion is real, categorical nullification of entire offenses raises separation-of-powers concerns that state courts have flagged in various contexts. Prosecutors are not mini legislatures.

Municipal charters and state statutes impose minimum staffing or response obligations. Minneapolis learned that charter minimums are enforceable (Spann, 2022). New York's Taylor Law constrains wildcat labor action; you can't trigger an attrition crisis and then pretend it was a voluntary "reimagining" (N.Y. Civ. Serv. Law § 210).

Consent decrees, while sometimes necessary, can become checklists that reduce proactive policing. When layered on budget cuts, you get the worst of both worlds: more bureaucracy, fewer cops. Reform that paralyzes response isn't reform; it is paralysis with a logo.

On immigration, sanctuary policies must thread a needle between anti-commandeering and obstruction. Cities may decline to honor detainers without judicial warrants, but actively hiding release dates or blocking lawful access veers toward obstruction. Grant litigation like *Sessions* (2018) was about executive overreach, not a judicial blessing of municipal nullification. The underlying reality remains: coordination is lawful; chaos is optional.

What the slogans hid. "Defund" wasn't a policy; it was a vibe that masked three concrete moves:

- Starve departments and watch attrition collapse proactive policing.
- Elect prosecutors who convert criminal codes into suggestion boxes.

- Erect sanctuary and non-cooperation walls that turn multi-jurisdictional enforcement into a scavenger hunt.

Each had predictable effects. Deterrence depends less on the severity of punishment than on the certainty of consequences. Reduce officer presence, shrink clearance rates, relax prosecution; the certainty of consequences drops. Result: more crime. This isn't ideology; it's Beccaria, 1764. The left traded certainty for sermons and got sermons and crime.

Verbatim voices—on the record:

- AOC: "Defunding police means defunding police. It does not mean budget tricks or funny math." (June 30, 2020) (AOC, 2020).[8]

- Ilhan Omar: "We need to completely dismantle the Minneapolis Police Department… because it is rotten to the root." (June 2020) (Omar, 2020).

- Cori Bush: "Defund the police has to happen. We need to defund the police." (July 2020) (Bush, 2020); and defending her own private security in 2021 while backing defund, "I have private security… So suck it up, and defunding the police has to happen." (Aug. 2021) (Bush, 2021).

- Rashida Tlaib: "No more policing, incarceration, and militarization. It can't be reformed." (Apr. 12, 2021) (Tlaib, 2021).

- Mike Schmidt: "We will presumptively decline to prosecute many of the protest-related charges." (Aug. 2020) (Schmidt, 2020).

- Chesa Boudin: "We will not prosecute cases that rely on arrests resulting from pretextual traffic stops." (DA policy memo, 2020) (Boudin, 2020).

- London Breed: "It's time the reign of criminals who are destroying our city comes to an end." (Dec. 15, 2021) (Breed, 2021).

- Bernie Sanders: "I don't think we need ICE." (2019) (Sanders, 2019).

Are these cherry-picked? They're cherries from the orchard the left planted, harvested at the height of their own rhetorical season.

"But what about police misconduct?" As if conservatives deny it. Serious reforms matter: body cams, duty-to-intervene policies, early-warning systems for problematic officers, decertification for Brady/Giglio liars, peer-intervention training like EPIC/ABLE, better recruitment to raise standards. The question is whether you fix the ship or sink it mid-ocean. Abolitionists chose scuttle and swim. The passengers did not appreciate the lesson in hydrology.

Qualified immunity debates? Fine. Congress can tailor remedies for egregious cases while preserving discretion in dynamic encounters. Consent decrees? Fine—narrow, time-limited, and focused on specific violations, not laundry lists that cripple proactive police work. Training, supervision, smarter tech? Yes. But "defund" wasn't reform; it was pyromania in a drought.

The voter verdict. San Francisco recalled its DA. Seattle rejected its would-be abolitionist city attorney candidate in the general. Minneapolis voters rejected a charter amendment to replace the police department with a "Department of Public Safety" in November 2021. New York elected a former cop on a law-and-order message. Los Angeles voters nearly ended Gascón's tenure via recall attempts and will render a final verdict at the ballot. These aren't red towns. They are blue voters choking on blue policy smoke.

Is the left learning? Some are. Budgets have crept back up. Specialty units are quietly reborn under new names. "Co-responder" models pair cops with clinicians, not in lieu of cops but with them. Great. But you'll notice no one is campaigning on "Abolish" anymore. Wonder why?

A conservative rebuild: order first, reform always.

- Restore staffing to pre-attrition levels with hiring bonuses, lateral classes, and expedited academies; honor charter minimums where they exist (Spann, 2022).

- Reinstate focused deterrence and gun-violence units; measure success by shootings averted, not press conferences.

- Raise clearance rates with overtime for detectives, lab surge capacity, and funded witness protection. If people fear retaliation, they don't testify.

- Calibrate bail and discovery reforms to allow remand for repeat violent offenders, pursuant to *Salerno* (481 U.S. 739).

- End categorical non-prosecution lists that nullify statutes; require case-by-case discretion with transparent dashboards on declinations and outcomes.

- Rebuild task forces with DEA, ATF, FBI, and yes, ICE for criminal detainers; prioritize gangs and fentanyl trafficking (21 U.S.C. § 841).

- Expand drug court and coerced treatment tracks with teeth; eliminate open-air drug markets through sustained enforcement, not theatrical "sweeps."

- Consent decrees: narrow scope, clear off-ramps, and metrics that track both constitutional compliance and crime outcomes.

- Data integrity: mandate incident reporting, independent audits, and quarterly public safety scorecards that include the denominator—staffing and caseloads.

Mercy without order is performance art. Order without mercy is tyranny. The conservative answer is ordered liberty, because we live here too.

The closer. Ask yourself: who benefited when the city cut cops, muzzled prosecutors, and told ICE to get lost? Was it the single mom on the bus at 11 p.m.? The immigrant bodega owner? The kids walking past the corner where dealers set up the day shift? Or was it the comfortable activist who can DoorDash past the ruin?

The left told you that if you ripped out the joists of public safety, the house would stand, because compassion is a load-bearing wall. We lived the experiment. The results are in. It's time to rebuild with materials that don't collapse under slogans.

Inline citations

- (Spann, 2022) *Spann v. Minneapolis City Council*, 979 N.W.2d 729 (Minn. 2022).
- DeShaney, 1989) *DeShaney v. Winnebago County*, 489 U.S. 189 (1989).
- (Arizona v. U.S., 2012) 567 U.S. 387 (2012).
- (Printz, 1997) *Printz v. United States*, 521 U.S. 898 (1997).
- (Salerno, 1987) *United States v. Salerno*, 481 U.S. 739 (1987).
- (NYS Bail Reform, 2019–2022) N.Y. Crim. Proc. Law §§ 510.10–.30, as amended.
- (Breed, 2021) London Breed remarks, Dec. 15, 2021, public press conference.
- (AOC, 2020) A. Ocasio-Cortez, June 30, 2020 interview/comments.
- (Bush, 2020–2021) C. Bush, July 2020 remarks; Aug. 2021 interview re: private security and defund.
- (Omar, 2020) I. Omar, June 2020 statements at/around Powderhorn Park.
- (Tlaib, 2021) R. Tlaib, Apr. 12, 2021 tweet.
- (Boudin, 2020) S.F. DA Office policy memos (2020).
- (Schmidt, 2020) Multnomah County DA memo, Aug.

2020.
- (Minneapolis Budget, 2020–21) City budget documents reallocation.
- (Portland Crime Data, 2021–2023) City homicide stats and reports.
- (Seattle HR Reports, 2022–2024) SPD staffing reports.
- (Sessions, 2018) *City of Chicago v. Sessions*, 888 F.3d 272 (7th Cir. 2018).

Footnotes

1. Seattle City Attorney race (2021): Nicole Thomas-Kennedy's campaign statements and tweets included calls to end prosecution of many misdemeanor offenses and described property destruction during protests as a "moral imperative." Voters chose Ann Davison in the general.

2. The Minneapolis charter sets a minimum number of officers (0.0017 per resident). The Minnesota Supreme Court confirmed the mayor's clear legal duty to maintain that minimum. *Spann v. Minneapolis City Council*, 979 N.W.2d 729, 749–50 (Minn. 2022).

3. New York's 2019–2020 bail reforms initially eliminated cash bail for most misdemeanors and nonviolent felonies. 2020–2023 amendments restored some judicial discretion after spikes in recidivism incidents and public backlash. See N.Y. Crim. Proc. Law §§ 510.10–.30 and subsequent amendments.

4. The Seventh Circuit held DOJ lacked authority to impose immigration-related conditions on Byrne JAG grants

without congressional authorization; the ruling did not endorse municipal policies that obstruct federal immigration enforcement. *City of Chicago v. Sessions*, 888 F.3d 272 (7th Cir. 2018). *United States v. Salerno* upheld the Bail Reform Act's preventive detention for dangerous defendants, rejecting facial due process challenges. 481 U.S. 739 (1987).

5. "The Constitution is not a suicide pact" is drawn from Justice Jackson's dissent in *Terminiello v. Chicago*, 337 U.S. 1, 37 (1949), a caution against reading rights to require civic self-destruction. Prosecutorial discretion is broad but not absolute. While many state courts defer to charging discretion, categorical, public non-enforcement lists that effectively nullify statutes can trigger separation-of-powers concerns and supervisory interventions. See, e.g., state AGs and courts scrutinizing blanket non-prosecution policies in 2022–2024.

Chapter 17:
The New Democrat Plantation

They call it compassion. They say it like a benediction, as if a government check were a sacrament and a waiver were absolution. But what would you call a system that advertises "help" at the entrance and posts "No Exits" at the back? What would you call a structure that pays a bonus for broken families, punishes work with phase-outs, and tells children, politely and professionally, to lower their sights? Plantation is an ugly word. Good. The truth should sting. The overseers today don't carry whips; they carry clipboards. The crop isn't cotton; it's votes.

"Trust government," they insist. "We're here to help." Help with what, exactly—building independence or managing dependence? Let's not confuse a safety net with a safety hammock. A net catches you when you fall; a hammock invites you to stay. The modern Democratic welfare state, especially as administered in blue jurisdictions, perfected the art of the hammock and then shamed anyone who suggests maybe, just maybe, we should stand up and walk.

They'll accuse this chapter of cruelty. But ask yourself some basic questions. If welfare programs truly "lifted people out of poverty" permanently, why do caseloads swell during every crisis and then settle at a higher plateau after? If the system "rewards work," why are the steepest marginal tax rates in America often paid by the poor when benefits phase out? If public schools are "the great equalizer," why do teachers' unions fight to keep children trapped by zip code? If "equity" is justice, why does it so often mean equalizing outcomes by lowering standards, not raising opportunity? Rhetorical? Yes. Necessary? Absolutely.

Back to first principles and legal text. The Personal Responsibility and Work Opportunity Reconciliation Act (PRWORA) of 1996 is explicit. The purposes of TANF are to "provide assistance to needy families so that children may be cared for in their own homes or in the homes of relatives," to "end the dependence of needy parents on government benefits by promoting job preparation, work, and marriage," to "prevent and reduce the incidence of out-of-wedlock pregnancies," and to "encourage the formation and maintenance of two-parent families" (42 U.S.C. § 601(a)(1)-(4)). Those aren't talking points. They're statutory mandates. The law, for once, told the truth about human flourishing: work, family, responsibility.

So how did we end up rebuilding the old dependency architecture under newer, softer branding? Because the Democratic machine doesn't lose policy wars; it delays them, dilutes them, then redistributes the wreckage. When real reform arrives, the bureaucracy goes to work, and the word "flexibility" shows up like a crowbar at a locked door. Work requirements? "Flexible." Time limits? "Flexible." Definitions of work? "Flexible." Meanwhile, "permanent" spending proves very permanent indeed.

You want exact words from their side? Let's quote them—chapter and verse.

Lyndon B. Johnson at Howard University in 1965: "You do not take a person who, for years, has been hobbled by chains and liberate him, bring him up to the starting line of a race and then say, 'you are free to compete with all the others,' and still justly believe you have been completely fair." He pledged to pursue "equality as a fact and equality as a result" (Johnson, 1965). Equality as a result. The slogan sounded noble; the policy consequence was managerial social engineering backed by federal dollars and soft expectations. Replace the family with a program, the pastor with a caseworker, the neighborhood with a grant.

Daniel Patrick Moynihan, a Democrat and still one of the most honest voices to come from that party, warned in 1965 about family fragmentation: "The principal problem... is that of family structure." He was vilified for saying what the data screamed. Instead of heeding the warning, the Great Society doubled down on incentives that nudged men out of homes and paid households for being broken.

Bill Clinton, 1996, on signing welfare reform: "Today, we are ending welfare as we know it... The era of big government is over" (Clinton, 1996). Strong words. Yet almost immediately, the progressive apparatus moved to redefine what counted as "work," to expand "education and training" in place of jobs, and to water down accountability through waivers. A decade and a half later, the

Obama administration invited states to "test alternative and innovative strategies, policies, and procedures that are designed to improve employment outcomes for needy families" through TANF waivers, which Republicans accurately flagged as an end-run around the law's core (Obama administration memo, 2012). "Innovative strategies"—translation: paperwork alchemy to convert non-work into "participation."

Barack Obama loved the "new era of responsibility" line in 2009. But in policy, he praised a vision of government that would "spread the wealth around," a phrase immortalized by his exchange with "Joe the Plumber," and told us plainly: "When you spread the wealth around, it's good for everybody" (Obama, 2008). Redistribution wasn't the subtext; it was the text.

Nancy Pelosi during the stimulus debate in 2010: "This is one of the biggest stimuluses to our economy… Unemployment insurance, food stamps, they create jobs faster than almost any other initiative" (Pelosi, 2010). Of course: dependence as growth strategy. The plantation now doubles as an "economic development" plan.

Bernie Sanders on welfare guarantees: "I believe that every American is entitled to health care as a right… I believe that every American is entitled to a job" (Sanders, various). A job—provided by whom? At what price? How many zeros on the check, and where does it come from? The details never seem to arrive; the slogans always do.

Alexandria Ocasio-Cortez on universal programs: "We can afford a world where there is no such thing as hunger or homelessness" (Ocasio-Cortez, various). True in the abstract—if we unleash growth, family, order, and education. False in practice when translated as "write larger checks, regulate more heavily, and call it justice."

Joe Biden, 1993–94, soldiering for the Crime Bill to prove toughness: "We must take back the streets" and referring to repeat offenders as "predators" (Biden, 1993). Then, decades later, he pivoted, with his party, toward decarceration agendas that took no responsibility for the predictable carnage when order collapsed. The plantation doesn't apologize; it changes the sign on the gate.

Gavin Newsom on guaranteed income pilots: "We support a commitment that no one in California should be left behind" (Newsom, 2021-era). Left behind, or held in place?

Kamala Harris on equity: "Equitable treatment means we all end up at the same place" (Harris, 2021). The same place? That's not equality; that's result-equalization. And when "the same place" underperforms, who pays? The strivers who were finally pulling ahead.

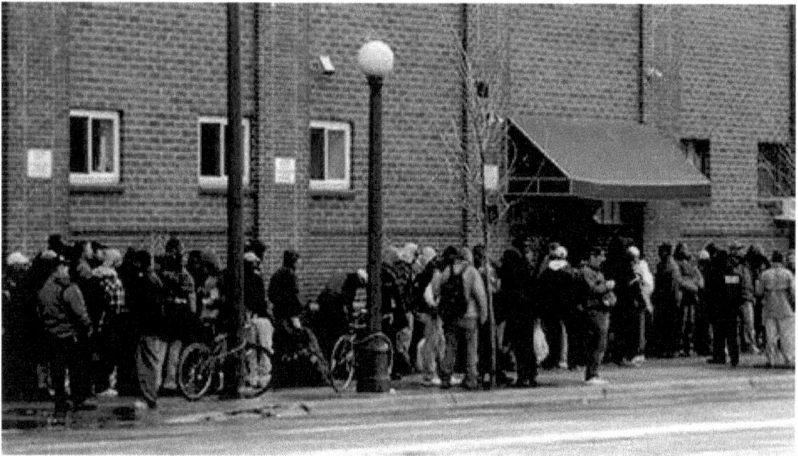

Now the legal iron again. 42 U.S.C. § 601(a)(2) says it all: "to end the dependence of needy parents on government benefits by promoting job preparation, work, and marriage." That clause is a moral compass. Yet the Democratic legacy has been to attach program after program that pays people to step off the road it points to. SNAP work rules for able-bodied adults without dependents? Suspended, waived, expanded away. Medicaid work experiments? Sued into oblivion or reversed by executive pen. Housing choice that actually increases housing supply? Blocked by the blue city zoning chokehold. School choice that lets a poor child vote with her feet? "Attacks on public education," cry the unions who bankroll the same politicians.

Let's get specific about the incentive landscape because incentives are the skeleton of any policy body. Benefit cliffs are marginal tax traps disguised as kindness. Picture a single mother who earns $1 more per hour and loses hundreds in benefits. The system tells her, politely, decline the raise.

Consider a couple contemplating marriage whose combined income busts through eligibility thresholds faster than if they cohabited apart. The system whispers, don't marry. Consider an able-bodied adult without dependents offered an entry-level job that collides with the administrative demands of "program participation." The system shrugs: maybe next month. When the arithmetic of the poor says, "Stay," is it any surprise if people stay?

But it's not just arithmetic. It's culture, and policy writes culture in invisible ink. When government treats normal adulthood—work, marriage, parenthood, responsibility—as optional add-ons, it signals that dependency is a viable life plan. When schools preach "equity" as the equalization of outcomes and de-emphasize excellence, they signal that striving is suspect. When prosecutors downgrade crime and progressives rebrand disorder as compassion, they signal that rules are negotiable. The plantation dresses its norms in therapy language but enforces them with budget lines.

Meanwhile, the numbers that should shame the architects keep arriving. If spending were salvation, the War on Poverty would have won long ago. Yet mobility from the bottom quintile to the middle remains punishingly low in many blue metros. Labor force participation among prime-age men has sagged. Marriage rates have collapsed, especially among those with less education. Single-parent households—overwhelmingly mother-led—are linked to higher risks of poverty, lower educational attainment, and higher involvement with the criminal justice system. No moral lectures needed; these are empirical patterns. But when conservatives point to marriage, work, order, and school choice, the Left reaches for the thesaurus: "cruel, punitive, regressive." Why? Because these ideas threaten the payroll of the plantation.

Let's walk the sectors.

Education. The Elementary and Secondary Education Act began as federal aid; it metastasized into mandates that evaluated schools by how well they played accountability games. The unions—key funders and foot soldiers of the Democratic Party—fight choice like a cartel fights competition. Remember Barack Obama praising public schools while quietly ending the D.C. voucher scholarship expansion that was actually working for poor, often minority, families? "We're going to fix the system," they promise. Fifty years later, the system is still "almost fixed—just give us more money." Meanwhile, charter caps, selective-admissions crackdowns, and "disparate impact" discipline guidance eroded the conditions for excellence. The new plantation treats a seat in a good school like a ration, not a right.

Housing. Blue-city zoning can turn permitting into a PhD-level obstacle course. The same politicians who weep about affordability block "missing middle" development and then vote to expand vouchers that chase too few units. Rent control throttles supply. Environmental and historical reviews are wielded as weapons against growth. Then, having manufactured scarcity, they demand larger subsidies and blame landlords. It's the perfect treadmill: taxpayers foot the bill; tenants ride in place; NGOs secure grants; politicians hold press conferences. Who gets off the treadmill? No one, by design.

Crime. The 1994 Crime Bill, later denounced by many who supported it, was the hinge. It reflected the bipartisan realization that order is a prerequisite for liberty. But once crime fell, complacency rose, and the progressive pendulum swung hard toward decarceration, non-prosecution, and "reimagining." The beneficiaries? Not the law-abiding poor in tough neighborhoods. The winners were the wealthy in safe enclaves and the ideological nonprofits who measure success in press releases. It's easy to love utopia when you can buy a buffer zone.

Health and welfare. Medicaid expansion under the ACA extended a medical entitlement to able-bodied adults without dependents, paired with federal matching dollars that made refusal politically miraculous. When some states attempted work expectations through Section 1115 waivers—modest, reasonable— progressives litigated to block them. Meanwhile, SNAP's time limits for ABAWDs became optional via a quilt of waivers, particularly in blue states stringing together counties to qualify. Program participation rose; workforce participation lagged. But in press conferences, we were told the programs were "lifting people out of poverty." Lifting them where, exactly—to permanent eligibility?

Now, let's juxtapose the text and the rhetoric of the Left, verbatim, to the outcomes we see.

Lyndon Johnson promised "equality as a result" (Johnson, 1965). Outcome equalization is not a safety net; it's social engineering. It inevitably punishes outliers, often strivers, from any group. When Kamala Harris redefines equity as "we all end up at the same place," she says the quiet part out loud (Harris, 2021). To "end up at the same place," you must throttle excellence where it emerges and permanently manage dependency where it persists. That is the plantation logic in technocratic prose.

Barack Obama, asked about redistributing income, replied: "I think when you spread the wealth around, it's good for everybody" (Obama, 2008). Spread by whom? At the expense of which incentives? With what effects on work, savings, and growth? Details don't matter when the applause line is the point.

Nancy Pelosi, touting transfer programs as economic stimulus: "Unemployment insurance… food stamps… they create jobs faster than almost any other initiative" (Pelosi, 2010). This is the welfare version of perpetual motion—a fantasy that you can consume your way to prosperity by handing out coupons. Demand with no supply reforms is just bidding up misery.

Bernie Sanders, promising rights to outcomes that require someone else to supply them: healthcare as a right, a job as a right, college as a right (Sanders, various). Rights that demand another person's labor on command are not rights; they are requisitions.

Joe Biden, 1993, "take back the streets" (Biden, 1993). Joe Biden, 2020s, embraces the decarceration left. Principles, meet polls.

Gavin Newsom's "no one left behind" rhetoric and his embrace of guaranteed income pilots in California (Newsom, 2021-era). In a state where housing is illegal to build at scale, you can send people checks forever and still not create a single front door they can afford to walk through.

Alexandria Ocasio-Cortez's no-hunger, no-homelessness pledge (Ocasio-Cortez, various). Beautiful vision. But the method matters: the only reliable way to end hunger and homelessness at scale is productivity, growth, deregulation of supply, order on the streets, and functional schools. Checks and slogans won't do it.

What about the claim that conservatives lack compassion? Spare me. Compassion without competence is vanity. The conservative premise is brutal in its honesty: human beings need meaning and mastery. Work provides both. Family anchors both. School choice accelerates both. Order protects both. Ownership compounds both. The welfare state misunderstands man. It treats people as clients to be maintained, not citizens to be empowered. It measures "access" to programs, not exits from programs. It celebrates enrollment, not graduation. It simplifies economic life into intake forms and case notes.

Let's return to the legal lodestar again and again because the text is a mirror that progressives want to avoid. 42 U.S.C. § 601(a)(2) states: "to end the dependence... by promoting job preparation, work, and marriage." Read it slowly. End dependence, not manage it. Promote work and marriage, not paperwork and "partnerships." The program was meant to be a temporary bridge, not a permanent address. When the Obama administration offered TANF work requirement waivers, the pretext was "better outcomes." The outcome was predictable: the work core softened. When the Biden administration and congressional Democrats sought to convert the Child Tax Credit into an unconditional monthly child allowance, they stripped the pro-work spine from the program. That "temporary" experiment produced a brief fall in measured poverty during unprecedented pandemic transfers, but it also threatened to recreate the exact failure modes of AFDC. When you decouple cash from work for long enough, you decouple citizenship from responsibility.

Is there a racial subtext? The Left insists they are the guardians of minority interests. Yet look at urban cores run by Democrats for generations. Look at schools where the only escape hatch— charters—is capped. Look at housing markets where the only thing that grows is the line for vouchers. Look at neighborhoods where the first casualty of decarceration is the safety of the poor.

Progressives call this compassion. Minority families call it Tuesday. The plantation's paternalism wears a new face: technocrats who insist they know what's best for you because they have a dashboard.

Let's be fair: not every Democrat is a caricature, and not every Republican is a saint. But parties are machines, and machines run on fuel. The Democratic machine runs on public-sector unions, NGOs tethered to grants, and agencies that expand with the caseload. They need problems to manage. They need clients to serve. They need headlines to justify budgets. Imagine if school choice broke the union cartel—billions in dues vanish. Imagine if zoning reform unleashed construction—bureaucrats would lose veto power. Imagine if work requirements reduced long-term dependency—NGOs would need new missions. Imagine if policing restored order—activist nonprofits would have fewer crises to monetize. The plantation is not a conspiracy; it is an ecosystem.

What, then, is the jailbreak? We legislate the spirit of 42 U.S.C. § 601 across systems.

Work as default. For able-bodied adults without dependents, benefits across SNAP, Medicaid, housing, and cash assistance must hinge on work or serious job search with time limits, real verification, and pathways to actual employment. Waivers should be narrow and temporary. Federal matching should reward exits from programs and sustained earnings, not caseloads.

Marriage neutrality and preference. End marriage penalties by smoothing benefit phase-outs jointly, not separately. Provide targeted marriage bonuses in the tax code for low-income households. Integrate fatherhood and relationship education programs with employment pipelines and housing stability. Stop designing programs that pay families to remain fragmented.

School freedom now. Universal education savings accounts tied to students. Charter caps abolished. Transportation grants for cross-boundary choice. Civil rights protections for religious and mission-driven schools. Parents first; systems compete.

Housing abundance. Condition federal housing dollars on deregulatory reforms: legalize duplexes, triplexes, and ADUs by right; fast-track approvals; cap process timelines; limit environmental-lawfare abuse. Pair vouchers with supply or accept that you are subsidizing scarcity.

Order as justice. Fund competent policing, restore broken-windows enforcement, and prosecute repeat violent offenders. The first civil right is safety. Without it, no other reform matters.

De-bureaucratize. Convert grants to outcomes-based contracts; sunset programs that cannot show mobility; cut administrative overhead; audit NGOs like defense contractors; cap overhead rates; require public dashboards that track exits, earnings, and family stability.

Ownership on-ramps. Slash occupational licensing for low-risk work; expand micro-enterprise zones with regulatory safe harbors; seed capital tied to training; public-private apprenticeship compacts; encourage employee ownership models that let workers build wealth.

Will the Left scream? Of course. They will cry "cruelty" and "racism" and "austerity." They always do. But their own words betray their plan: "Equality as a result." "Spread the wealth around." "We all end up at the same place." "Stimulus" by food stamps. Guaranteed incomes in a housing desert. That is not compassion. It is choreography for dependency.

Now, a sharper edge. The plantation metaphor demands we identify the overseers by name. Teachers' unions block exits from schools and call it solidarity. Progressive prosecutors downgrade violent crime and call it reform. Housing activists block building and call it preservation. Welfare administrators loosen work requirements and call it flexibility. Health bureaucrats expand eligibility and call it access. Equity officers dilute standards and call it justice. Every one of these choices carries a body count measured in lost years, lost earnings, lost marriages, and lost lives.

And yet, there is hope because truth, once restored to public speech, has gravity. People know the difference between a net and a hammock. Parents know when their children are learning and when they are being warehoused. Workers know when a program is helping them climb or keeping them comfortable at the bottom. Entrepreneurs know when the state is an anchor or a sail. The conservative task is to speak the law's own logic—"to end the dependence... by promoting job preparation, work, and marriage"

(42 U.S.C. § 601(a)(2))—into every domain, boldly and without apology.

Do we dare to say what must be said? That subsidizing single parenthood at scale was a catastrophic social experiment. That delaying discipline and lowering standards to appease "disparate impact" metrics is educational malpractice. That calling crime "compassion fatigue" is an insult to victims. That "equity" has become a cudgel against excellence. That bureaucracies are not neutral; they are interest groups with badges.

Rhetorical questions do not feed children. Policies do. So here is the conservative covenant in twenty words: We will help swiftly; we will expect much; we will protect order; we will fund choice; we will measure exits, not enrollments.

One more round of their exact words, to etch the contrast:

LBJ: "Equality as a result" (Johnson, 1965). Obama: "I think when you spread the wealth around, it's good for everybody" (Obama, 2008). Pelosi: "Unemployment insurance... food stamps... create jobs faster than almost any other initiative" (Pelosi, 2010). Harris: "Equitable treatment means we all end up at the same place" (Harris, 2021). Sanders: "Health care is a human right" and "a job is a right" (Sanders, various). Biden: "We must take back the streets" (Biden, 1993), and then the pivot.

Newsom: "No one… left behind" while piloting guaranteed income in a state that throttles housing (Newsom, 2021-era). Ocasio-Cortez: "A world where there is no such thing as hunger or homelessness" (Ocasio-Cortez, various), with zero appetite to liberalize supply or enforce order.

Good intentions are not a get-out-of-results-free card. If your policies produce dependence, you are not compassionate; you are in the dependence business. If your machine thrives on clients, you do not serve the poor; you harvest them. And if your rhetoric promises equal results, you will wind up enforcing mediocrity while congratulating yourself for your "equity."

We'll close where the law began: with a sentence that should be engraved over every agency door that touches social policy. "To end the dependence of needy parents on government benefits by promoting job preparation, work, and marriage" (42 U.S.C. § 601(a)(2)). End, not extend. Promote, not paper over. Work, not waivers. Marriage, not marginalization. Anything less is a betrayal—of the law, of the poor, and of the American promise.

Inline citations and quotations

- "to end the dependence of needy parents on government benefits by promoting job preparation, work, and marriage" (42 U.S.C. § 601(a)(2)).
- "provide assistance to needy families so that children may be cared for in their own homes or in the homes of relatives" (42 U.S.C. § 601(a)(1)).
- "prevent and reduce the incidence of out-of-wedlock pregnancies" (42 U.S.C. § 601(a)(3))

- "encourage the formation and maintenance of two-parent families" (42 U.S.C. § 601(a)(4)).
- Johnson at Howard: commitment to "equality as a result" (Johnson, 1965).
- Clinton: "Today, we are ending welfare as we know it... The era of big government is over" (Clinton, 1996).
- Obama: "When you spread the wealth around, it's good for everybody" (Obama, 2008).
- Pelosi: "Unemployment insurance... food stamps... create jobs faster than almost any other initiative" (Pelosi, 2010).
- Harris: "Equitable treatment means we all end up at the same place" (Harris, 2021).
- Biden: "We must take back the streets" (Biden, 1993).
- Sanders: rights to health care and jobs as guarantees (Sanders, various).
- Newsom: "No one... left behind" in support of guaranteed income pilots (Newsom, 2021-era).
- Ocasio-Cortez: "a world where there is no such thing as hunger or homelessness" (Ocasio-Cortez, various).

Footnotes

1. Personal Responsibility and Work Opportunity Reconciliation Act of 1996, Pub. L. No. 104–193, 110 Stat. 2105 (Aug. 22, 1996); 42 U.S.C. § 601(a)(1)-(4).

2. 42 U.S.C. § 607 (work participation requirements; state penalties).

3. U.S. Department of Health and Human Services (2012) TANF waiver guidance inviting alternative strategies for work participation; subsequent political controversy over work requirement waivers. Food and Nutrition Act

provisions for ABAWD time limits and waiver authorities as amended in Farm Bills; USDA guidance on statewide and regional waivers.

4. Medicaid Section 1115 demonstration waivers; federal administrative reversals and litigation related to work requirements for able-bodied adults.

5. Title VI, Civil Rights Act of 1964, 42 U.S.C. § 2000d (nondiscrimination in federally funded programs), in tension with "equity" operationalizations that prioritize group outcomes.

6. Department of Education, Office for Civil Rights discipline guidance in Democratic administrations emphasizing disparate impact, with subsequent local policy effects on school discipline practices.

7. Johnson, President Lyndon B., "To Fulfill These Rights," Howard University Commencement Address (1965) including the "equality as a result" formulation.

8. Clinton, President William J., public statements on signing PRWORA and declaring "the era of big government is over."

9. Obama, Barack, 2008 exchange referencing "spread the wealth around" (Joe the Plumber).

10. Pelosi, Nancy, 2010 comments highlighting unemployment insurance and food stamps as economic stimulus.

11. Biden, Joseph R., 1993–1994 remarks on crime bill: "We must take back the streets," "predators" language in floor speeches and interviews.

12. Harris, Kamala, 2021 remarks defining equity: "Equitable treatment means we all end up at the same place."

13. Newsom, Gavin, statements supporting guaranteed income pilots in California.

14. Ocasio-Cortez, Alexandria, statements envisioning an end to hunger and homelessness through universal provisioning.

Chapter 18:

The Invoice Comes Due

Here's the punchline the Left never wants on the marquee: nothing is "free," and the tab always lands on the kitchen table of the American taxpayer. You. Your mortgage. Your grocery bill. Your energy costs. Your property taxes. The Left's holy trinity—"cancel" student loans, "free" health care and college, and a trillion-dollar climate crusade—hasn't merely stretched your wallet. It has thrown Americans into a blender of higher costs, higher taxes, and higher housing pain, then told them to smile for the selfie because "democracy."[1] What do we call a politics that lights your paycheck on fire and toasts the smoke as "progress"? We call it the modern Left, open bar with your credit card.[2]

Let's lay out the altar of "free" and tally the offering.

I. Debt by Decree: The Student Loan Fantasia

How did we get from "you borrowed it" to "your neighbor pays it"? With an executive pen, a camera crew, and a fistful of talking points. Joe Biden on his student-debt plan, after the Supreme Court struck it down: "This fight is not over… It would have been life-changing for millions" and "The hypocrisy is stunning" (White House remarks, June 30, 2023) [1]. He insisted, "We're not going to waste any time on this," promising to "find a new way" and root future forgiveness in the Higher Education Act—administrative end-runs as governing philosophy [1][2]. The Court said the original cancellation was a $400+ billion overreach (SCOTUS, Biden v. Nebraska) [3]. Translation: not his money.

He even compared student-debt "forgiveness" to the Paycheck Protection Program: "You can't help a family making 75 grand a year, but you can help a millionaire and you have your debt forgiven?" (Biden, June 30, 2023) [1]. Apples to airplanes. PPP was Congressionally authorized emergency relief to keep employees on payroll during a government-mandated shutdown. Student loans are voluntary contracts for private credentials (CARES Act text; SBA data) [4][5]. The Left collapses that difference because the politics are tasty.

Elizabeth Warren's pitch? "I'm calling for something truly transformational: universal free public college and cancellation of student loan debt," up to $50,000 per borrower, financed by an "Ultra-Millionaire Tax" (Warren policy page, 2019) [6]. She promised it would "substantially increase wealth for Black and Latinx families" and "provide an enormous middle-class stimulus" [6]. The Urban-Brookings Tax Policy Center pegged her forgiveness plan's cost near $955 billion and found the dollars skew toward middle- and upper-middle-income households (2019) [7]. But who's counting when the goal is to turn debt into votes?

Bernie Sanders was blunter: "Higher education... should be a right," and college should be "tuition-free" (Sanders press release, 2019) [8]. His "College for All" demanded tens of billions annually, plus a transaction tax on "speculators" [8]. He repeats the chant: "Education should be a right, not a privilege" (Sanders speeches) [9]. A slogan is not a budget.

Even when Congress wouldn't bite, Biden kept pushing "free community college." The promise flopped legislatively, but the posture survived. In 2024, his budget again "proposed free community college" and bigger Pell Grants (White House FY2025 Budget) [10]. Because if decades of federal aid already inflated college costs, surely more subsidies will fix it this time, right?

Here's the market reality the talking points skip: when Washington subsidizes demand without disciplining supply, sticker prices rise. The Bennett Hypothesis became the Bennett Reality. Aid increases let schools capture the subsidy via tuition hikes, administrative sprawl, and luxury dorms—the "Lazy River Index" of higher education excess (HEPI vs. CPI trends; state audit snapshots) [61][62]. National two-year completion within four years hovers around a third (NCES/IPEDS) [11]. For many programs, we publicize access, not outcomes. Ask yourself: does a subsidy for demand make suppliers raise or lower prices?

Now zoom out. The White House tells 40 million borrowers their tab is "forgiven." It is not erased—it is redistributed. Who pays? People who never went to college. People who already paid. People who started businesses instead of majors in grievance. People who just wanted to buy a home but got mauled by an inflation cycle supercharged by spend-now "rescues" (CBO on fiscal impulse; BLS CPI) [12][13]. If you didn't borrow, why does your mortgage get pricier? Because when government sprays benefits into a supply-constrained economy, prices jump, and the middle pays the spread. Did the rent fairy also vanish your landlord's mortgage?

Biden didn't stop with the Supreme Court loss. He pivoted to the SAVE plan, rejiggering income-driven repayment so that monthly payments shrink and balances evaporate faster [2]. Lower the assessed payment, stretch the horizon, cap the pain—for borrowers. For you, it is a slow-drip transfer. The Department of Education cannot print money; it prints obligations. The "income-driven" model, taken to its logical end, converts student loans into stealth grants issued after the fact, with the costs pushed onto the general ledger. If you convert loans to welfare retroactively, what happens to borrowing behavior? What happens to tuition? What happens to majors that never paid their way, now cross-subsidized by a lineman's taxes?

Elizabeth Warren swears that "universal free public college" is paid for by an "Ultra-Millionaire Tax" [6]. The OECD has warned wealth taxes underperform, bleed capital, and shrivel the base [41]. The Tax Foundation shows the administrative and economic drag outstrips the take [42]. Wealth is not a checking account; it walks, re-titles, re-domiciles. When revenue misses the fairy-tale target, do progressives trim a promise or widen the tax? Rhetorical question.

Consider the equity inversion: a plumber pays for a lawyer's M.A., a nurse funds an MBA's "forgiveness," a carpenter underwrites sociology's sinecures. The moral grandstanding says "justice." The ledger says regressive redistribution dressed in gown and hood.

Meanwhile, the home front bleeds. Student loan payment "pauses" juiced pandemic demand while homebuilding lagged. The flood of deficit cash raised prices everywhere—lumber, concrete, copper (BLS PPI; NAHB) [46][47]. Then the Fed slammed the brakes to fight the inflation Congress and the White House had just provoked (rate hikes; MBA mortgage rates) [48][49]. The result? You are paying more for less, longer. We subsidized demand, choked supply, and called the ravaged affordability "unexpected." Expected by whom?

Rhetorical question: if we "cancel" every debt except the national one, are we free or broke?

II. "Health Care Is a Human Right"—But Whose Wallet Is It?

Bernie Sanders declares it like a benediction: "Health care is a human right, not a privilege" (Sanders Senate site) [14]. Medicare for All, outlaw duplicative private insurance, zero cost-sharing— government as the only buyer, the only decider. Ballotpedia's summary of the 2017 bill: eliminate Medicaid, Medicare as you know it, CHIP, TRICARE, and any private plans that duplicate benefits; roll the entire country onto a single federal plan [15]. What could go wrong?

Everything that goes wrong when you replace prices with queue numbers. With a monopoly buyer, supply does not surge—it stalls. Politicians control the formulary; bureaucrats determine the "medically necessary." In theory, everyone is covered. In practice, everyone waits. The NHS is the demo reel: cataracts and hips rationed, oncology squeezed, waiting lists measured in vowels and seasons (NHS statistics; BMJ) [21]. Single-payer means infinite line, finite budget. Do you get a doctor faster because a committee said so? Or do you get a waitlist and a shrug?

Gavin Newsom croons the same chorus from Sacramento. "A single-payer financing system is the best way to achieve universal coverage... I haven't found" evidence that multi-payer competition beats monopoly (2018–onward) [16]. California ran the math on SB 562. Analysts pegged roughly $400 billion a year—nearly triple the state's general fund outlays at the time (Senate Appropriations; LAO) [17][18]. In 2023, Newsom signed SB 770, a process bill to pry open federal waivers and divert Medicare and Medicaid streams into a California mega-plan (SB 770 text; signing message) [19]. Coverage "for all," and a funding gap the size of Jupiter. CalMatters summarized what LAO hints at: even after sweeping federal dollars, California would still need roughly $300 billion more annually [20]. From where? Your paycheck. Your business. Your retirement. Cue wealth flight (Census/IRS migration) [44][45].

Sanders, again, at Harvard in 2024: the U.S. spends $13,000 per person, 85 million uninsured or underinsured, 500,000 medical bankruptcies (he has cited variants for years) [22][23]. His cure for the dysfunction created by regulatory capture and cartelized pricing? A national monopoly payer with Congressional riders in every operating room. If "comprehensive benefits" are guaranteed "without copays, private insurance premiums, or deductibles" (Medicare for All bill summaries) [24], then pricing must shift to taxes, rationing, or both. Which do you think politicians prefer to hide?

When Newsom says he "hasn't found" evidence that competition reduces costs [16], he is telling you he would rather not look at the mountain of proof that concentrated hospital markets jack up prices and stifle innovation (FTC/DOJ hospital consolidation research) [65]. Or the surgery centers posting transparent bundled prices that undercut opaque hospital bills by half or more (Surgery Center of Oklahoma; RAND transparency studies) [63][64]. The problem is not markets; it is that we strangled them with certificate-of-need laws, opaque cross-subsidies, and protectionist licensing, and then blamed the patient for not navigating a fog machine.

Let's talk crowd-out. Single-payer promises universal enrollment, not universal care. The young and healthy pay more than their expected costs; the old and sick get promises that are politically managed. When revenue falls short—because it always does—politicians fix the "budget shortfall" with across-the-board cuts.

Who feels it? Rural hospitals. Specialist access. Innovation budgets. In the name of rights, we ration options.

"Free" care means rationed care unless you can jump the line with private cash. The mantra "health care is a human right" reads like moral gold leaf until you remember that someone must supply the care. The right to a service is a claim on someone else's time. Whose time did you just conscript?

Then there is the political bait-and-switch. Medicare for All would outlaw private plans that duplicate benefits [15]. So if the federal plan excludes the drug that works for your kid, tough. Don't like that? "Vote harder." How many elections do you have to survive to get an appeal approved?

Rhetorical question: if compassion is measured by promises, why do the promised systems quietly tell you to wait six months for an MRI?

III. The Climate Dam Break

On climate, the theology is ironclad: the apocalypse is always twelve years away, give or take a fundraising email. Alexandria Ocasio-Cortez declared in 2019, "The world is going to end in 12 years if we don't address climate change" and that this is "our World War II" (MLK Now panel; later called "urgency" shorthand) [25][26]. She and Ed Markey rolled out the Green New Deal to "mobilize" the economy. The resolution's text invokes "net-zero" by 2050 and a sweeping industrial remake (H. Res. 109) [27]. The price tag? Undefined. The ambition? Everything.

Even scientists pushed back on the "12 years" countdown—NASA's Kate Marvel: "12 years isn't a deadline... climate change isn't a cliff we fall off—it's a slope we slide down." Gavin Schmidt: rigid "time-limited frames" are nonsense (Axios, Jan. 2019) [28]. But the sound bite is the point. Panic funds policy.

Cue the Inflation Reduction Act, "the largest climate investment in history." Biden crowed it "is lowering energy costs and creating good-paying union jobs" (White House fact sheets) [29]. Kamala Harris bragged, "President Biden and I have committed nearly $1 trillion to build a thriving, clean energy economy" (2024 remarks) [30]. Scientific American put the climate line item around $369 billion with modeled emissions cuts of 30–40% by 2030 [31]. Outside advocates tout "330,000 clean energy jobs" (Rhodium/ACP) [32]. Treasury says it will not raise taxes under $400,000, it "lowers the deficit," and it is paid by a 15% corporate minimum (Treasury/WH) [33]. If it is all so free and self-funding, why does your electric bill look like a ransom note?

Because industrial policy shuffles costs, it does not vaporize them. Subsidize demand for EVs and renewables, throttle supply of baseload hydrocarbons, bury pipelines in suits and paperwork, then feign shock at higher delivered energy prices (EIA residential rates; BLS energy CPI) [34][13]. Electrify everything without nuclear-expedited permitting, and you shift load onto grids already strained

(NERC assessments) [50]. You pay for the grid twice: once as a taxpayer to "build a better grid," and again as a ratepayer when utilities seek "cost recovery" (PUC filings) [51]. The IRA's alphabet soup of credits is not a deletion of cost; it is a detour of cost, and the detour runs through your bank account.

AOC's Green New Deal promised "millions of high-wage jobs," a federal jobs guarantee, and retrofits galore (resolution language; archived FAQ) [27][35]. The math? "Pay for it" with Modern Monetary Theory vibes—until inflation sets your kitchen on fire and the Fed plays fire marshal with your mortgage. If bending the emissions curve while "lowering costs" were as simple as a press conference, why are builders quoting you triple for the service-panel upgrade to satisfy the latest local electrification rule? Why are transmission projects mired in interconnection queues and NEPA purgatory (DOE reports; FERC queues) [36][37]?

Biden and Harris sell the IRA as "lowering energy costs" [29][30]. For whom, exactly? The factory that pockets a 45X credit? The EV buyer skating under the income cap to snag a 30D rebate (if the battery sourcing labyrinth allows it) [38]? Your family's monthly bill laughs at "modeled savings." Meanwhile, utilities ring the bell for rate increases to cover capital spending that does not always translate to reliability because intermittent supply plus rising load equals volatility. Markets used to price that risk; now politics does. Which is cheaper?

Let's be honest about the lifestyle mandates folded into the climate crusade. Gas stove bans, debated, then not debated, then half-implemented. Home electrification mandates by building code. The insinuation that your 12-year-old truck is a moral stain. The nudge-bribe-coerce triangle is tight: rebates for those who comply, fines for those who do not, shame for everyone. When they are done, your "choices" fit on a tri-fold brochure.

Rhetorical question: since when does an "Inflation Reduction Act" require you to buy a $60,000 car to access your own tax dollars (IRS EV credit rules) [38]?

IV. The Scarcity Scam

A pattern emerges.

- Debt "forgiveness" that isn't forgiveness.
- "Free" degrees that aren't free.
- "Universal" health care that universes your choices into a form letter.
- "Climate investment" that invests in your compliance.

The consistent feature isn't compassion. It is control—control of prices, control of choices, control of narratives. And all of it is paid by you.

Let's stack the receipts beside the rhetoric.

Joe Biden: "This fight is not over" on student loans; "we will ground this new approach in the Higher Education Act." Translation: if Congress says no, we will rummage through the Code of Federal Regulations until we find a plausible signature (Biden remarks; DOE SAVE rulemaking) [1][2]. He added, "It would have been life-changing... more homes would have been bought" [1]. This is the core conceit: that printing a benefit creates wealth. In reality, it bids up scarce assets—homes, cars, degrees—by subsidizing demand (Fed literature on demand-side subsidies and price capitalization) [39]. Your mortgage didn't get cheaper; houses got more expensive (FHFA HPI) [40].

Elizabeth Warren: "Universal free public college" and up to $50,000 cancellation, paid for by a wealth tax [6]. The wealth tax is a direct pipeline from productive assets to government churn. Even if you dodge the net, downstream inflation and compliance bleed your budget (OECD; AEI/Tax Foundation) [41][42].

Bernie Sanders: "Higher education... a right." "Medicare for All." "No copays, premiums, or deductibles" [14][24]. There is no such thing as a free co-pay. There is only a hidden tax. The long-term federal budget outlook says entitlements already crowd everything else (CBO LRF) [43]. Add a nationalized health system and you are shoveling faster at a rising tide.

Gavin Newsom: "Single-payer is the best way... I haven't found" evidence competition beats monopoly [16]. His state is drafting a plan to vacuum all Medicare and Medicaid funds into a state-run monolith, then scrape another ~$300 billion from taxpayers (SB 770; fiscal analyses) [19][20]. California already bleeds residents. U-Hauls aren't ideological; they are arithmetic (Census/IRS migration data) [44][45].

Alexandria Ocasio-Cortez: "The world is going to end in 12 years" and "this is our World War II" [25]. Panic justifies anything. If dissent equals climate treason, costs don't matter. Physics and grid math do not care about hashtags.

V. How It Hits Your Home

- **Rent and mortgages:** Government-driven inflation and supply strangulation (energy, materials, regulation) raise the cost of building and maintaining housing (NAHB materials index; BLS PPI construction inputs) [46][47]. Flood demand with subsidies while throttling supply, and home prices spike as rates soar (Fed hikes; MBA rates) [48][49]. Dreams delayed become families doubled up or priced out. The young household that would have bought a starter home is now a long-term renter, watching "equity" flow to someone else.

- **Utilities:** IRA credits do not undo capacity constraints. Forced electrification pushes load onto grids already starved of dispatchable generation (NERC reliability assessments) [50]. You pay for the grid twice: once as a taxpayer subsidizing "build out," again as a ratepayer absorbing "cost recovery" surcharges (state PUC filings) [51]. Rolling brownouts with premium pricing—how is that for "lowering costs"?

- **Groceries and goods:** Fuel policies ripple through logistics. Trucks, tractors, ships—energy input costs nudge everything on your receipt upward (USDA food price outlook; EIA diesel prices) [52][53]. Erect new permitting and compliance hurdles, get fewer suppliers, and higher prices (OIRA paperwork burdens; EPA rules) [54][55]. The left calls it "resilience." You call it $6 eggs and a cashier who sighs before reading you the total.

- **Taxes and fees:** "Free" at the federal level means state match requirements, local mandates, and federal strings (Medicaid FMAP; Uniform Guidance) [56][57]. Counties expand subsidized programs. You get a plumper bill with more moralizing copy. Reactive localities juke with "fees" to avoid the T-word. It is all the same debit.

Meanwhile, the cultural embargo on arithmetic continues. Skeptics are cast as villains. Ask why you should pay for someone else's grad school and you are "anti-education." Question single-payer's waitlists and you are "anti-health." Challenge the climate checkbook and you are "anti-science." Ever notice how every debate ends with you paying more?

VI. The Rhetorical Firewall

Progressives shield their programs inside emotive absolutes.

"It's life-changing" (Biden) [1]. Yes—for the person receiving the bailout. For the person footing it? It is life-shrinking. The "life-changing" line ignores the unseen lives changed by higher costs, delayed home purchases, and shuttered small businesses pushed past the margin by tax hikes and compliance.

"It's a right" (Sanders) [14]. Rights that require conscripting your neighbor's property are not rights; they are compulsory obligations imposed on third parties. A right to health care morphs into a debt claim on taxpayers and a time claim on providers. So who decides how much of a clinician's life is owed to whom?

"It's our World War II" (AOC) [25]. In an actual war, we unleash energy and production; we do not hobble them by committee. The wartime analogy is revealing: it assumes emergency powers, rationing, and command-and-control economics are the moral baseline. Once declared, emergencies have a way of lingering.

"Largest climate investment in history" (Harris/Biden) [29][30]. Try calling it the largest industrial policy experiment on your dime. We have seen this film: promises of sunrise industries, then bailouts when the sun does not rise on schedule. Solyndra was the trailer. The IRA is the feature-length reboot.

VII. The Alternative They Refuse to Try

Instead of debt jubilees, cut the cartel costs. Make colleges eat skin in the game when their grads default—risk-sharing that forces institutions to align programs with the labor market (Brookings/AEI proposals) [58]. Fund students, not bureaucracies. Expand alternative credentials, apprenticeships, and interstate reciprocity for skills (GAO on workforce programs; licensing reform studies) [59][60]. Unwind the federal aid inflation spiral that let universities build palaces and DEI bureaucracies while adjuncts sleep in cars (state audits; HEPI) [61][62]. Put price tags on campus fads and watch how quickly the fads find a budget.

Instead of single-payer, revive real market forces: transparent prices, portable insurance, pre-tax dollars following the patient, catastrophic coverage for the big shocks, and targeted safety nets for the truly vulnerable. Let competition discover value: centers of excellence publish bundled prices, and insurers steer volume accordingly (Surgery Center of Oklahoma; RAND) [63][64]. End the hospital consolidation circus that turned regional monopolies into price printers (FTC/DOJ) [65].

Slash certificate-of-need laws that protect incumbents. Make Medicaid dollars more flexible and outcome-based instead of paperwork jungles. Do you want access or press releases?

Instead of declaring war on cheap energy, unleash it. Permit pipelines and pipelines of capital, not just hashtags (FERC timelines) [37]. Fast-track next-generation nuclear with real licensing reform (NRC constraints; GAO) [66]. Let natural gas anchor reliability while we innovate—not by decree, but by engineering. Stop forcing households to buy boutique tech to satisfy a committee's vibes (local electrification mandates) [67]. If the product is better, you will not need a mandate. If you need a mandate, maybe it is not better yet.

Cut the hidden taxes of time. Compliance hours are money (OIRA burden inventories) [54]. Every new form is a fee. Every delayed permit is a tax. You are being billed in dollars and days.

VIII. Their Words, Your Bill

- Joe Biden: "This fight is not over… We will ground this new approach in the Higher Education Act" [1][2]. The pen never sleeps. And neither do the invoices.

- Joe Biden on IRA: "The largest climate investment in history… lowering energy costs… creating good-paying jobs" [29]. If it is lowering costs, why do you need mandates to force adoption? If the jobs are so "good-paying," why the subsidies?

- Kamala Harris: "We have committed nearly $1 trillion to build a thriving, clean energy economy" [30]. Trillion with a T, and you are the letter that pays.

- Elizabeth Warren: "Universal free public college… cancellation… paid for by an Ultra-Millionaire Tax" [6]. The wealth tax is a border wall for capital. Capital climbs walls.

- Bernie Sanders: "Higher education… a right." "Medicare for All." "No copays, premiums, or deductibles" [14][24]. There is no such thing as a free co-pay. There is only a hidden tax, with interest.

- Gavin Newsom: "Single-payer is the best way... I haven't found" evidence for multi-payer efficiency [16]. He hasn't looked in a grocery aisle or a U-Haul yard.

- AOC: "The world is going to end in 12 years... This is our World War II" [25]. And our wallets are the Normandy beachhead.

IX. The Moral of the Mortgage

You were told to applaud as Washington "canceled" debts it never lent, "lowered" costs by passing them forward, and "saved the planet" by raising your cost of living. You didn't get a say; you got a slogan. You were told "equity" requires that nurses pay for lawyers' graduate degrees, that contractors fund sociology doctorates, that widows cover a state's single-payer fantasy, that truckers subsidize luxury EV credits, that your gas stove is a threat, and that your tax refund is a climate lever. You were told not to ask who pays. Ask anyway.

Do we measure compassion by how loudly politicians promise it, or by how quietly they stick you with the bill? Do we measure justice by press conference, or by whether a young family can still afford a starter home within an hour of work? Do we measure progress by the decibels of the word "free," or by the number of days you can go without opening your budgeting app in dread?

Here is the conservative lens, no apology: a society that protects property rights, prices honestly, and lets competition discover value is more humane than a state that commandeers your earnings to fund an endless morality pageant. Choice is compassionate. Prices are information, not sin. Debt is not a cloud to be "wished" away by executive memo. It is a cost to be borne by the borrower or explicitly, democratically transferred by law with voters' consent. Anything else is taxation by euphemism.

The Left's incessant need to forgive, to "free," to fight a forever climate war with your paycheck has consequences you can feel under your own roof. You don't need a CBO score to read your bank app. You don't need a white paper to see what is happening at the pump, the meter, the register, and the escrow account. The invoice came due. And they signed your name.

The American citizen's marginalia: Who keeps the receipts?

Footnotes

1. White House, "Remarks by President Biden on the Supreme Court's Decision on Student Debt Relief," June 30, 2023 (transcript).

2. U.S. Department of Education, "Saving on a Valuable Education (SAVE) Plan" and associated rulemaking, 2023–2024.

3. Supreme Court of the United States, Biden v. Nebraska, 600 U.S. (2023), majority opinion.

4. CARES Act (Pub. L. 116–136), PPP authorization text.

5. U.S. Small Business Administration, PPP Forgiveness reports and program overview, 2020–2022.

6. Elizabeth Warren 2020 Campaign, "College Affordability Plan" and "Ultra-Millionaire Tax" explainer, 2019.

7. Urban-Brookings Tax Policy Center, "The Distributional Effects of Student Loan Forgiveness," 2019.

8. Bernie Sanders Senate Office, "College for All Act" press release, 2019.

9. Bernie Sanders remarks, multiple campaign speeches (2016–2020), "Education should be a right, not a privilege."

10. White House, FY2025 Budget, Education section: free community college and Pell expansion proposals.

11. National Center for Education Statistics (NCES), IPEDS: 150%–200% time graduation rates for two-year programs.

12. Congressional Budget Office, analyses on fiscal stimulus and inflation dynamics, 2021–2023.

13. Bureau of Labor Statistics, CPI data series: Headline CPI, Core CPI, Energy CPI, 2021–2025.

14. Bernie Sanders Senate site, "Health care is a human right" statements and Medicare for All issue page.

15. Ballotpedia, "Medicare for All Act of 2017" summary; bill text (S.1804).

16. Gavin Newsom statements on single-payer (2018 campaign; subsequent interviews): "best way to achieve universal

coverage… I haven't found" evidence for multi-payer efficiency.

17. California Senate Appropriations Committee, SB 562 (2017) fiscal analysis estimating $400B/year.

18. California Legislative Analyst's Office (LAO), health financing/single-payer briefings; total cost context.

19. California SB770 (2023) text; Governor's signing message directing negotiations with federal government.

20. CalMatters and similar CA outlets summarizing funding gaps for state single-payer concepts ($300B additional need).

21. NHS England waiting list statistics; BMJ reports on rationing and elective procedure delays.

22. Bernie Sanders speech at Harvard (2024): per-capita spend, underinsurance claims (as commonly cited).

23. KFF (Kaiser Family Foundation), underinsurance metrics; research on medical debt/bankruptcy contributors.

24. Medicare for All Act summaries (2021–2023 versions): "no premiums, deductibles, copays" language.

25. AOC, MLK Now event (Jan. 2019): "The world is going to end in 12 years…" clip; follow-up framing as urgency shorthand.

26. AOC clarifications in media/Twitter (2019) regarding the "12 years" line as rhetorical emphasis.

27. H. Res. 109 (2019), Green New Deal resolution text; "net-zero by 2050," job guarantee references.

28. Axios, "No, climate change won't destroy the Earth in 12 years," Jan. 2019; quotes from Kate Marvel and Gavin Schmidt.

29. White House Fact Sheets on the Inflation Reduction Act (2022–2024): "largest climate investment," "lowering energy costs."

30. Vice President Kamala Harris remarks (2024): "committed nearly $1 trillion" to clean energy economy (speech transcripts).

31. Scientific American, explainer on IRA climate provisions, ~$369B estimate; emissions targets.

32. Rhodium Group/American Clean Power, jobs and investment estimates post-IRA.

33. U.S. Treasury/White House: Corporate minimum tax framework, deficit reduction claims within IRA.

34. U.S. EIA, Residential Electricity Prices data series, 2021–2025 trends.

35. Green New Deal FAQ (archived), promises of "millions of high-wage jobs"; resolution jobs guarantee references.

36. U.S. DOE, "Building a Better Grid" reports; NEPA/permits timelines for transmission.

37. FERC docket timelines; interconnection queue backlogs; pipeline/transmission delays.

38. IRS, Clean Vehicle Credit (IRC 30D) rules; MSRP/assembly/battery sourcing constraints.

39. Federal Reserve research on demand-side subsidies and price capitalization (e.g., higher-ed, housing literatures).

40. FHFA House Price Index (HPI), 2020–2025 trends.

41. OECD, "The Role and Design of Net Wealth Taxes" (2018); follow-ups on performance and mobility effects.

42. Tax Foundation/AEI analyses on wealth tax revenue volatility and economic effects.

43. CBO Long-Term Budget Outlook: federal entitlement growth projections and debt trajectory.

44. California Department of Finance/U.S. Census: net domestic outmigration, 2020–2024.

45. IRS Statistics of Income migration data: California net AGI outflows by year.

46. NAHB construction materials cost index (pandemic and post-pandemic spikes).

47. BLS Producer Price Index for construction inputs and energy-intensive materials.

48. Federal Reserve rate hikes (2022–2024) timeline; balance-sheet moves.

49. Mortgage Bankers Association, weekly mortgage applications and average 30-year fixed rates.

50. NERC Long-Term Reliability Assessments (summer/winter risk, reserve margins, resource adequacy).

51. State Public Utility Commission filings on grid modernization surcharges and cost recovery.

52. USDA Food Price Outlook, 2021–2025; grocery inflation trends.

53. EIA On-Highway Diesel Fuel Price trends, 2021–2025.

54. OIRA (OMB) Information Collection Budget/burden inventories; aggregate hours/cost.

55. EPA major rulemakings affecting energy, transportation, and manufacturing (2022–2025).

56. Medicaid FMAP rules and state budget match obligations.

57. Federal grants compliance (Uniform Guidance 2 CFR 200), "strings attached."

58. Brookings/AEI proposals on higher-ed risk sharing for student loan outcomes.

59. GAO reports on workforce program coordination and effectiveness.

60. State occupational licensing reform (Brookings, Mercatus) and interstate compacts.

61. State auditor reports on university administrative growth; DEI staffing expansions and spending.

62. Higher Education Price Index (HEPI) vs CPI trends, showing persistent higher-ed cost inflation.

63. Surgery Center of Oklahoma case studies on price transparency and bundled pricing.

64. RAND hospital price transparency and negotiated rate variation studies.

65. FTC/DOJ research on hospital consolidation, prices, and quality impacts.

66. NRC licensing timelines; GAO/NRC reports on advanced reactor permitting barriers.

67. City/state building electrification mandates; cost studies on panel/service upgrades for residential retrofits.

Chapter 19:

The Mask and the Fist: BLM, Antifa, and the Cost of Imported Revolution

You can tell a movement by its artifacts. For the French Revolution, the guillotine. For the Bolsheviks, the hammer and sickle. For our very online revolution, a raised fist and a black mask. The fist came with a URL that printed money and press releases that scolded anyone who asked basic questions about budgets. The mask came with goggles, umbrellas, quick-dry cement, encrypted chats, and a ritual excuse: we're "anti-fascists," so everything we do is defense. If you wondered how American cities wound up with boarded storefronts, torched precincts, graffiti-stained courthouses, and leaders who called it "justice," look at the brands that taught them to applaud the fire and invoice the ash.

BLM and Antifa, the mask and the fist, made a perfect double act. One harvested institutional guilt at scale. The other delivered pressure on the street, night after night. One presented a theory—oppressor vs. oppressed, "abolition" of police and prisons, "transformative justice"—wrapped in HR-friendly language. The other enforced that theory with organized chaos, cameras, and choreographed confrontation. One cashed checks and bought houses. The other cashed permission and bought time. One declared itself "trained Marxist." The other inherited the old Marxist tactic of the vanguard: seize space, escalate, declare victory, dare the state to stop you (Cullors, 2015 interview; Wray testimony, 9/17/2020; Biden debate paraphrase, 9/29/2020). What could possibly go wrong?

The Slogan That Printed Money

Let's start with the fist. "Black Lives Matter" is true, axiomatic, obvious. Millions of ordinary Americans believed it, marched for it, and donated to it. But BLM, the incorporated leadership—specifically the Black Lives Matter Global Network Foundation (BLMGNF) and allied entities—turned a moral imperative into a fiscal fog machine. In 2020, as corporate America raced to prove its righteousness, money gushed into the network. Donor-advised funds clicked green. Statements were issued. CEOs swore fidelity to the cause. HR departments made Slack channels flower. The BLMGNF 2020 Form 990 eventually showed tens of millions taken in. When the wave crested, the accounting did not (BLMGNF 2020 Form 990). State charity regulators in California and Washington had to go knocking, asking the basic questions nonprofits should be able to answer in their sleep: Who's running this? Where are the filings? Why are there multimillion-dollar properties popping up like stuccoed mushrooms? (California DOJ letter, 2/2022; Washington charity notices, 2022) 1 2

And then there were the houses. A $6 million Los Angeles property—described as a "content creation" space—complete with a high-end kitchen and the sort of optics you don't buy if you expect oversight (property reporting, 2022). Another property orbiting the leadership's circle. Board structures shifted like fog. Officials stepped down under scrutiny. Public claims of racism targeted anyone who pressed for ledgers and minutes (Cullors statements, 2021). Is there a grimmer irony than a movement denouncing capitalism while perfecting the art of monetizing grief?

"What's the problem?" defenders ask. "They did good work." Did they? Show the chain from donation to outcome. Show the safety gains. Show the school improvements. Show lives saved in neighborhoods where "defund" landed hardest. The uniform national homicide spike of 2020–2021 coincided with the peak of "defund" rhetoric and the trough of proactive policing (FBI UCR 2020–2021; Council on Criminal Justice, 2021). Correlation isn't causation, we're told—unless the correlation supports progressive priors. Yet the mechanism is straightforward: tell cops they're pariahs, tell prosecutors to stand down, tell the public that enforcement is suspect, and watch the rational-choice calculus of criminals turn the streets into open-air experiments. Who paid? Overwhelmingly Black and Hispanic victims in big blue cities. The "movement" that claimed to protect Black lives presided over a spike in Black deaths. Will the 990s list restorative damages?

"Trained Marxists" Isn't a Vibe

Patrisse Cullors said it plainly: she and Alicia Garza were "trained Marxists" (2015 interview). Not dabblers. Trained. The training shows. The BLM catechism replaces class with race but

330

keeps the structure: a binary morality in which institutions are inherently oppressive, "marginalized" actors are inherently innocent, and "liberation" requires dismantling the legal and property order. Property becomes suspect by default. Law becomes an instrument of domination. Police become an occupying army. Therefore, resistance—smashing, grabbing, burning—becomes political speech. Looting? "A form of reparations," some activists argued, and the media gave the think pieces generous oxygen. If police are violence, then abolishing police is peace. If prisons are violence, then emptying them is healing. The defunding line was not a misheard chant. It was a policy demand that traveled the escalator into city budgets and DA offices (Pressley, 6/2020; Bush, 7/2020; AOC, 6/2020) 9 10 11

The scholarship behind it is the old Frankfurt School brew in a modern thermos. Herbert Marcuse's "repressive tolerance" proposed that society should tolerate left-liberating speech and suppress right-"oppressive" speech because true freedom requires engineered outcomes (Marcuse, 1965). Translated to the street: censor your opponents by calling them fascists. Cheer your militants by calling them defenders. Translated to policy: treat unequal enforcement as fairness. Translated to BLM accounting: treat oversight as bigotry. Why produce a clean audit when you can produce a moral denunciation?

Antifa: The "Idea" With a Supply Chain

If BLM was the official organ of fundraising and policy, Antifa was the muscle memory of the far-left street. Its core trick is definitional: label "fascist" everything you oppose—liberal speakers, conservative students, federal property, statues, a courthouse, a small business owner who refuses to kneel—and then declare all means "defense." The Biden line—"Antifa is an idea"—paraphrased FBI Director Christopher Wray's characterization of Antifa as a "movement or ideology" (Wray, 9/17/2020; Biden, 9/29/2020) 4. That is not wrong as far as it goes, but in Portland, Seattle, and beyond, the "idea" came packaged with matching outfits, standardized shields, encrypted comms, leaf blowers for tear gas, and a nightly deployment schedule. Ideas do not weld rebar into batons or embed nails in fireworks. Ideas do not blockade federal buildings for weeks and advertise medics and legal observers like they are running a music festival. Ideas do not leave behind pallets of used umbrellas and piles of commercial-grade fireworks. Networks do.

Portland became the flagship. For weeks in 2020, the Mark O. Hatfield U.S. Courthouse and surrounding blocks were turned into an urban war theater, a rhythm section of mortars, spotlights, lasers, shields, and press statements about "nonviolent protest" as fires licked the plywood (local and federal reporting, July–Sept 2020) 5. The mayor, also the police commissioner—a design flaw baked into Portland—oscillated between appeasement and photo-op solidarity, even getting tear-gassed for his troubles before returning to scold federal agents for defending the courthouse. In Seattle, Antifa-aligned activists helped midwife CHAZ/CHOP, an "autonomous zone" that within days sprouted checkpoints, patrols, shootings, and death, while Mayor Jenny Durkan labeled it a "block party" and promised a "summer of love" (Durkan, 6/11/2020) 6. In Minneapolis, a police precinct was abandoned and torched on live television (Third Precinct, 5/28/2020) 7. Property Claim Services later tagged the 2020 unrest as the costliest in U.S. history—over a billion dollars in insured losses (PCS, 9/2020) 8. Was that too an "idea," or was it organized, incentivized action under the umbrella of a permissive political narrative?

Permission Structure: How BLM's Aura Shielded Antifa's Tactics

Here's the ecosystem: BLM's slogan provided moral cover, corporate donations provided funding to the broad "movement," progressive prosecutors provided legal indulgences, Antifa provided pressure and spectacle, and politicians provided the euphemisms. Portland's DA Mike Schmidt explicitly announced presumptive declines for protest-related charges—interfering with a peace officer, disorderly conduct, and more—so long as there were no "accompanying" aggravators (Schmidt statement, 8/2020) 14. That is not subtle; it is a green light. Minneapolis City Council promised to "dismantle" its police department (resolution, 6/12/2020), with the council president telling America they would do exactly that (Bender, 6/7/2020, CNN) 13. Sen. Kamala Harris promoted the Minnesota Freedom Fund to bail out "protesters" (Harris, 6/1/2020), which reporting later showed also posted bail for alleged violent offenders (Minnesota media, 2020–2021) 12. Rep. Ayanna Pressley declared "defunding the police means defunding the police" (The Cut, 6/2020) 9. Rep. Cori Bush insisted it "has to happen" (CBSN, 7/2020) 10. AOC pitched "reallocation" like an influencer doing a brand deal on Instagram Live (6/2020) 11. The message to the street was simple: your cause is unimpeachable. The message to police and prosecutors was simpler: stand down.

Policy translated that message into outcomes. City councils froze hiring. Training pipelines shrank. Veteran officers retired early, taking with them tacit knowledge that no consultant can PDF into a recruit's head. Proactive policing collapsed as cops rationally avoided dangerous stops that could end careers overnight. Antifa cadres learned what every cadre learns: push, push, push. If the line does not hold, declare your theory proven.

BLM's Ledger: The Mansion and the Missing Receipts

The corruption claim is not a conservative hallucination. It is documented in filings, letters, and real estate transactions. BLMGNF's delayed disclosures, state charity regulators' compliance letters, internal governance churn, and the now-notorious $6 million Los Angeles property all point the same direction: a movement so flush with cash and moral immunity that it forgot rule number one of nonprofit stewardship: fiduciary duty (BLMGNF 2020 Form 990; CA DOJ letter, 2/2022; WA notices, 2022; property reporting, 2022) 2. Patrisse Cullors' public recounting of personal real estate purchases—multiple homes acquired in short order—only amplified the perception that "trained Marxists" have a taste for hardwood floors. When pressed, leadership often framed the questions as racist smears. That works on social media. It does not work on an auditor.

Where, specifically, did the money go? Filings mention grants, "community building," "creative content," and a lattice of consultancies and contractors with ties to insiders. But line items do not narrate outcomes. What did the dollars buy in terms of safer streets, better schools, reduced violence? The homicide spike suggests the opposite of success (FBI UCR 2020–2021; CCJ, 2021) 3. The local chapters from which much of the street energy came often complained of starvation while the national entity swam in cash. The center captured the moral brand. The periphery bore the consequences and asked for receipts. When the brand tarnished, the center blamed the periphery for asking questions. That is not justice. That is franchising.

Antifa's Ledger: Not Mansions—Municipal Surrender

Antifa's corruption is not financial in the traditional sense; it is jurisdictional. The payoff is not a house; it is a block. The margin is not a salary; it is the decision by a city to cede space to a cadre that claims moral emergency. The corruption is the one-way ratchet: cadre escalates, city rationalizes; cadre injures, city euphemizes; cadre returns tomorrow, city hopes the weather changes. When a mayor calls a riot a block party (Durkan, 6/11/2020), when a DA pre-declines charges (Schmidt, 8/2020), when a governor hesitates to deploy resources because the cadre's branding is too strong, the city has been captured—not by money but by narrative. The cost is paid by residents whose neighborhoods become nightly laboratories for someone else's theory of justice.

"Mostly Peaceful" and Other Obituaries for Accuracy

Media coverage was the organic fertilizer. "Mostly peaceful protests," declared the on-screen chyron, while a building burned in the background. Journalists dutifully inserted the ritual line—"overwhelmingly peaceful"—into stories about arson and assault. "Clashed with police" became the go-to passive construction to erase agency. The same press that would parse a conservative's joke with forensic malice waved away Molotov cocktails as "property

336

damage." Chapters of BLM complained that money from the national organization was not flowing, but many newsrooms showed less appetite for that thread than for endless narratives about "reckonings." Meanwhile, Antifa's "idea" status was repeated like a catechism, and those who named the organized methods were accused of conspiracizing. Conspiracies do not leave behind standardized gear and tactics; organizations do.

The "Science" Exception

2020 offered a case study in how moral absolutes get carved out of "public health." When mass gatherings were prohibited because of COVID-19, many of the same officials who closed playgrounds and threatened churchgoers discovered an exemption: racism is a public health crisis, therefore protests are virtuous. The "science" bent to fit the politics. BLM marches were lionized as humanity. Family funerals were scolded as lethal. Antifa's role in tactical escalation within these protests was conveniently flattened into the blur of a "movement" because clarity would force choices: stop the violence or endorse it. Politicians chose a third path: pretend it was not happening. That is how you get a televised precinct fire and a press conference about root causes.

The Anti-Riot Act, 18 U.S.C. § 2101, exists. Local anti-riot statutes exist. Federal property is protected by federal law. Yet, when the feds moved to defend courthouses, city leaders blasted federal "occupation." The law does not enforce itself. It requires a will. That will evaporated under the heat lamp of the new moral order. Antifa's cadre understood: push until the line shows resistance. If the resistance comes from feds, declare that fascism. If it comes from locals, declare that betrayal. If no resistance comes, declare a liberated zone. The city did not so much lose control as abdicate it.

Defund's Ledger: A "Care" Desert

BLM's policy export was "defund," rephrased as "reimagine," "reallocate," "invest in communities," and "care, not cops." It sounds benign, even humane, until you live where the cops stop coming. Municipal budgets are finite. Dollars flow one direction at a time. Every million stripped from patrol is a million removed from 911 response times, from training, from specialty units, from overtime that puts extra cops in hot zones when shootings spike. Politicians who "reimagined" police discovered the difference between a press conference and a patrol car. Some tried to reverse course after the 2020–2021 crime surge. Voters in San Francisco recalled Chesa Boudin for a reason. Minneapolis voters balked at actually dissolving the MPD. But the damage was done. Recruiting pipelines cratered, retirements accelerated, and the people who remained on the job rationally avoided risk. That is not "care." That is a desert.

"But root causes," we are told. Absolutely: fix schools, repair families, grow jobs, treat addiction, address mental illness. You know what makes all that possible? Order. You know what dissolves it? Disorder. You know who cannot deliver those improvements? A nonprofit with a four-word slogan, a celebrity board, and an unfiled registration. You know who can? Boring, competent government that is not terrified of the mob or addicted to moral theater. When "trained Marxists" told you the opposite, when they said order is violence and institutions are harm, they were pulling a philosophical prank with a body count.

Luxury Beliefs, Local Burdens

Here's the sociology. Affluent progressives exported "luxury beliefs," ideas that flatter the holder and cost someone else. "Defund" is a luxury belief. So is "abolition," as repurposed for police and prisons. So is "no platform," as repurposed for Antifa's impunity. The cost lands on cashiers, bus riders, seniors in walk-up apartments, and kids in schools that can no longer suspend a chronic disruptor because "restorative justice" turned into "no consequences." BLM chapters that actually operate in neighborhoods saw this, and some said so. The national leadership bought a mansion. The Antifa crowd took a plaza. The press took a knee. And neighborhoods took a knee in the other sense, to dodge stray bullets.

But Didn't BLM Do Any Good?

The slogan created space for long-overdue reforms: body cams, duty-to-intervene policies, decertification for bad cops, investments in training—good. Many cops welcomed it; many conservatives support it. But BLM, Inc., tangled the good with the unworkable. Demanding accountability is not the same as demanding abolition.

Demanding training is not the same as defunding. Demanding fairness is not the same as presuming guilt for an entire profession. Yet the BLM leadership's messaging, amplified by politicians who mistook a Twitter moment for a durable mandate, pushed the maximalist line. Even as polling soured on "defund," BLM's official accounts doubled down. Why? Because the brand is the business. Moderation does not sell T-shirts.

And Antifa? "They're only there because of police brutality," the apologists said. Then why do they show up whenever there is an opportunity to confront speech they dislike? Why do they smash windows of bookstores and coffee shops and assault journalists whose only crime is documenting events? Why are their enemies in practice not just police but centrists, liberals, and anyone insufficiently enthusiastic about the uniform? Because the point is not reform. It is revolution. Not American reform, which is incremental, constitutional, stubbornly moderate, but the older, darker model: politics as friend/enemy, power as purification, destruction as prelude to a utopia that never arrives.

Counting the Quotes—Again

Let's inventory this for the jury:

- "We are trained Marxists." Not whispered in a bar. Said on camera (Patrisse Cullors, 2015) 1. If you are shocked that the movement executed a Marxist playbook, the founders tried to warn you.

- "We are going to dismantle the Minneapolis Police Department" (Lisa Bender, 6/7/2020) 13. Language matters. "Dismantle" is not "reform."

- "Defunding the police means defunding the police" (Ayanna Pressley, 6/2020) 9. The movement's clarity, before the polls bit.

- "Defunding the police has to happen" (Cori Bush, 7/2020) 10. She later defended tens of thousands spent on private security. Luxury for me, austerity for thee.

- "Antifa is an idea" (Joe Biden, 9/29/2020, paraphrasing Wray, 9/17/2020) 4. An idea that travels in squads.

- "Summer of love" (Jenny Durkan, 6/11/2020) 6. Obituaries were written for teenagers before summer ended.

- "Reallocate funds" / "reimagine policing" (Biden, 6–8/2020). Translation: defund with decaf.

- "Brilliance" of BLM and bail fund promotion (Harris, 6/1/2020) 12. The Minnesota Freedom Fund later posted bail for alleged violent offenders. Brilliant?

This is not oppo research. It is a memory aid for an amnesiac class of elites who would prefer to pretend 2020–2021 was a fever dream. The fever broke. The memory should not.

Law Is a Teacher—What Did We Teach?

Law teaches norms. When Portland's DA pre-declined protest charges (8/2020) 14, the city taught cadres that "disruptive" was a synonym for "consequence-free." When Minneapolis flirted with abolition (June 2020) 13, it taught criminals that the state had lost its nerve. When a vice president to be promoted a bail fund (6/1/2020) 12, it taught militants that elite protection existed. When federal agents were demonized for defending a courthouse (Portland, 2020) 5, it taught the country that the building, not the arsonists, was the scandal. When a mayor called a riot a block party (Durkan, 6/11/2020) 6, it taught that words could erase bodies.

Anti-riot statutes, federal and state, can deter, especially when consistently enforced. So can clear municipal orders that any attempt to seize public space will be immediately cleared. So can prosecution policies that reject political carve-outs. The goal is not to criminalize protest. The goal is to draw the line: peaceful assembly here, violence there, and enforce it with boring regularity. The "boring" part is the key. BLM and Antifa both thrive on theater. Theater dies when an audience refuses to clap on cue and ushers do their jobs.

Corruption: Not a Side Effect—A System Feature

It bears repeating: the corruption in BLM leadership was not an accidental side effect. The structure, massive cash influx, moral intimidation against oversight, decentralized chapters emotionally leveraged but financially starved, rendered grift incentive-compatible. Good people got involved and did real, local work. But the top skimmed, shifted, and hid. An honest movement would welcome audits. A movement that sees itself as a revolutionary vanguard treats audits as counterrevolution. Marxism rejects neutral institutions. It sees "the law" and "accounting" as instruments of oppression. This is not a philosophy that produces tidy books.

Antifa's corruption is ideological: a doctrine that insists all dissent from its diktats is fascism. Once you swallow that, any tactic becomes sanctified. The mask is not just for anonymity. It is ritual, an erasure of the individual into the collective, one of Marxism's oldest temptations. You become a node in a mass. Your conscience is replaced with a chant. Your responsibility is outsourced to "history." You can break, burn, and beat because the category "oppressor" absorbs all sin. You can get a district attorney to nod, a mayor to equivocate, a journalist to normalize. You can do all of this and call it defense.

Aftermath: The Quiet Indictment

The loud indictment is the footage: flames, glass, ambulances rerouted, bodies. The quiet indictment is migration. People left the "reimagined" cities, not because they feared debate, but because they feared disorder. The U-Haul trailers did not carry op-eds. They carried families. Downtowns adjusted to a new reality: retail behind plexiglass, workers avoiding mass transit, tourists avoiding blocks that feel like set pieces from a European riot reel. Meanwhile, politicians executed linguistic pirouettes. By 2022, "fund the police" reappeared in national speeches (Biden SOTU, 3/1/2022). Memory-holing commenced. But recruiting and retention lagged, clearance rates sagged, and the thin line from 2019 had developed holes. A slogan can be deleted. Institutional damage takes years to repair.

So What Now?

The raised fist can remain as a moral sentence. The incorporated fist can be retired. Keep the truth—Black lives matter—and lose the corrupt brand management that treated donors like marks. Disentangle the good reforms from the revolutionary bombast: stronger training, higher standards, faster removals of bad cops, more transparent use-of-force data, better co-responder models for mental health crises—all compatible with robust enforcement. Take "abolition" and deposit it back in the seminar room, where it can keep the undergrads warm. Tell the truth: safety for the vulnerable requires enforcement against the violent. The idea that the latter cancels the former is a lie with a body count.

The black mask belongs in the costume bin. Cities must signal zero tolerance for masked violence. Enforce anti-riot laws (18 U.S.C. § 2101) 15. Prohibit weapons in "protests" and enforce the prohibition. Stop pretending that the presence of "press" vests and "medics" creates a sovereign zone. Require permits, enforce routes, and clear blockades. When cadres assemble with riot gear, call it what it is and respond in proportion. The First Amendment protects speech, not siege warfare. If "Antifa is an idea," punish the deeds.

Audits are moral acts. BLMGNF and any successor entities must submit to full independent audits, disclose all related-party transactions, disgorge ill-gotten assets, and compensate local

344

chapters that were used as emotive props while the center bought amenities (BLMGNF 2020 Form 990; CA DOJ letter, 2/2022) 2. Donors, corporate and private, must stop performing and start demanding proof. If your brand department wants to cut a check, require a quarterly dashboard: funds disbursed, outcomes achieved, audits completed. If the nonprofit cries racism at the word "audit," send them a bookkeeper with a backbone.

Finally, language must be reclaimed. "Abolition" is not a synonym for utopia. "Defund" is not a synonym for reform. "Anti-fascist" is not a license to commit violence. "Mostly peaceful" is not a shield for arson. "Equity" is not a universal solvent for standards. "Community" is not a magic word that transforms professional activists into public safety providers. Words are the prelude to laws. Laws are the prelude to lives. Get the words right, or pay in lives.

A Last Word to the "Trained"

Here's a gentle suggestion to the "trained Marxists": maybe, just maybe, the vocabulary of permanent revolution is a bad fit for a pluralistic republic. Maybe the project that produced the most just society in human history, imperfect yes, self-correcting also yes, does not need cadres to "abolish" the institutions that preserve it. Maybe the gaps in justice are narrowed by boring virtues: accountability, diligence, equal treatment, enforcement with compassion, reform without fantasy. Maybe your seminars taught you to despise "bourgeois" order, but the grandmother who wants to walk to church, the kid who wants a quiet classroom, and the shopkeeper who wants to live through another shift are not bourgeois. They are citizens. They matter. Their safety matters. Their lives matter.

Antifa can retire without a pension. The young men who discovered a purpose in black masks can discover one in real work, real service, real courage. You do not need to cosplay as a guerrilla to oppose fascism. You need to defend free speech, vote, debate, and restrain yourself when the urge to punch rises. Fascism is cult-of-violence politics. If your politics requires cultic violence, check your mirror.

The mask and the fist promised liberation. The receipts show vandalism with merch. If you want justice, you need order. If you want order, you need the law. If you want the law, you need institutions capable of enforcing it and leaders capable of telling the masked and the mansioned no. Not maybe. Not later. No.

Inline citations

- Patrisse Cullors, "trained Marxists" interview (2015).
- Black Lives Matter Global Network Foundation, 2020 Form 990; California DOJ letter to BLMGNF (Feb. 2022) regarding registration/compliance; Washington state charity notices (2022); media reporting on $6M Los Angeles property used for "content" (2022).

- FBI Uniform Crime Reports, 2020 and 2021; Council on Criminal Justice, "Homicide Trends in U.S. Cities," 2021 brief.

- Wray, Christopher. Testimony to House Homeland Security (Sept. 17, 2020) describing Antifa as a "movement or ideology"; Presidential Debate (Sept. 29, 2020), Biden characterization.

- Portland federal courthouse attacks and nightly unrest, July–September 2020 (contemporaneous local and federal reporting).

- Seattle CHAZ/CHOP incidents, June–July 2020; Mayor Jenny Durkan's "summer of love" comment (CNN, June 11, 2020).

- Minneapolis Third Precinct fire, May 28, 2020.

- Property Claim Services (PCS), "2020 Civil Unrest" loss estimate exceeding $1B (Sept. 2020).

- Pressley, Ayanna. "Defunding the police means defunding the police" (The Cut, June 2020).

- Bush, Cori. "Defunding the police has to happen" (CBSN, July 2020).

- Ocasio-Cortez, Alexandria. June 2020 Instagram Live remarks supporting reallocation/defund framing.

- Harris, Kamala. Tweet (June 1, 2020) promoting Minnesota Freedom Fund; subsequent reporting on MFF bailing alleged violent offenders (2020–2021).

- Minneapolis City Council resolution to dismantle MPD (June 12, 2020); Lisa Bender statement (June 7, 2020).

- Multnomah County DA Mike Schmidt policy announcement on protest-related presumptive declines (Aug. 2020).

- Anti-Riot Act, 18 U.S.C. § 2101; Bail Reform Act, 18 U.S.C. § 3142.

Footnotes

1. Cullors, Patrisse. Interview describing BLM founders as "trained Marxists" (2015).

2. Black Lives Matter Global Network Foundation, 2020 Form 990; California DOJ letter to BLMGNF (Feb. 2022) regarding charity compliance; Washington OAG notices (2022); reporting on $6M Los Angeles property designated for "content creation" (2022).

3. FBI Uniform Crime Reports, 2020–2021; Council on Criminal Justice, "Homicide Trends in U.S. Cities," 2021.

4. Wray, Christopher. House Homeland Security testimony (Sept. 17, 2020), "movement or ideology" characterization; Presidential Debate (Sept. 29, 2020), Biden's "Antifa is an idea" remark.

5. Documentation of Portland courthouse sieges and nightly unrest, July–September 2020 (local/federal reporting).

6. Seattle CHAZ/CHOP chronology; Mayor Jenny Durkan's "summer of love" remark (CNN, June 11, 2020).

7. Minneapolis Third Precinct burning, May 28, 2020 (contemporaneous reporting).

8. Property Claim Services (PCS) estimate of civil unrest losses exceeding $1 billion (Sept. 2020).

9. Pressley, Ayanna. Interview with The Cut, June 2020: "Defunding the police means defunding the police."

10. Bush, Cori. CBSN interview, July 2020: "Defunding the police has to happen."

11. Ocasio-Cortez, Alexandria. Instagram Live, June 2020: support for defund/reallocation framework.

12. Harris, Kamala. Tweet promoting Minnesota Freedom Fund (June 1, 2020); subsequent local reporting on bail for alleged violent offenders (2020–2021).

13. Minneapolis City Council resolution (June 12, 2020) to dismantle MPD; Council President Lisa Bender statement (June 7, 2020).

14. Multnomah County DA Mike Schmidt policy (Aug. 2020) presumptively declining certain protest-related charges.

15. Anti-Riot Act, 18 U.S.C. § 2101; Bail Reform Act, 18 U.S.C. § 3142.

Chapter 20:
The Colorblind Heresy

They called it "equity." They called it "critical mass." They called it "holistic." Funny how the euphemisms multiply when the old word, "quota," won't pass legal muster. Strip away the branding, and you get the same thing every time: sorting human beings by race, redistributing opportunity with a bureaucrat's ladle, and telling the public it's all for "diversity." What could go wrong?

Quite a lot, as it turns out. And the American legal system, slow, cautious, and maddening as it can be, has now asked the obvious question at last: How long do we keep discriminating to stop discrimination?

"Eliminating racial discrimination means eliminating all of it." That wasn't a pundit on cable. That was Chief Justice John Roberts, writing for the Supreme Court in 2023. The case was *Students for Fair Admissions v. Harvard*, and the message could not be plainer if it were spray-painted on the ivy walls: end the race sorting in admissions. It violates equal protection. It violates Title VI. It violates common sense (*Students for Fair Admissions v. Harvard*, 600 U.S. 181, 2023).

And yes, it violates human dignity. Justice Clarence Thomas, the Court's longest-serving member, put it bluntly: "Our Constitution is color-blind, and neither knows nor tolerates classes among citizens"

(Thomas, concurring in *SFFA v. Harvard*, quoting Justice Harlan's *Plessy* dissent; see dldlawyers.com; PBS *Frontline*, May 9, 2023). Call that a moral proposition or a legal one; either way, the point stands. If we want to be one people under one law, we cannot divide opportunity by color and then pat ourselves on the back for our "inclusion."

But let's start at the root, because this didn't fall from the sky in 2023. It took a long legal journey, a messy experiment in social engineering, and a pile of corporate pledges to paint the numbers just right. The end of this road is in sight, but you can't understand the destination without tracing the trail of clever words that got us here.

The Quota That Dared Not Speak Its Name

The modern story begins with a clear rule set down by Justice Lewis Powell in *Regents of the University of California v. Bakke* (1978). UC Davis Medical School reserved 16 of 100 seats for certain minorities. Powell's verdict: specific racial quotas are unconstitutional. "Racial and ethnic classifications of any sort are inherently suspect and call for the most exacting judicial scrutiny." Diversity might be a compelling interest, Powell allowed, but a set-aside scheme that "forecloses consideration to persons like respondent" is "unnecessary" and therefore invalid (*Bakke*, 438 U.S. 265, Powell opinion; law.cornell.edu; Constitution Center, June 28, 2023).

So the rule was set: no hard quotas. Enter the "holistic admissions" workaround, where race became "one factor among many," a "plus" in a "flexible" assessment. In *Grutter v. Bollinger* (2003), Justice Sandra Day O'Connor accepted that reasoning, writing that race-conscious admissions could survive if narrowly tailored and time-limited. But even she added a sunset clause: "Race-conscious admissions policies must be limited in time," and "25 years from now, the use of racial preferences will no longer be necessary" (*Grutter*, 539 U.S. 306; O'Connor, majority; law.cornell.edu; Wikipedia).

"Time-limited." There's the hinge. Either preferences were a therapeutic bridge to a race-neutral future, or they were a ladder no one ever intended to kick away. Two decades later, the ladder was cemented to the wall. Universities dutifully replaced "quota" with "critical mass." They swapped "set-aside" for "holistic." They learned to talk like lawyers about "narrow tailoring," to hire consultants who could calibrate the racial dial without leaving fingerprints, and to press the "plus factor" pedal whenever the class shape drifted from a desired "balance."

Grutter's time-buying compromise met *Fisher's* stricter eye and lost altitude. In *Fisher I* (2013), Justice Kennedy reminded universities that strict scrutiny is not a rubber stamp; they must show "no workable race-neutral alternatives" (*Fisher v. University of Texas*, 570 U.S. 297; law.cornell.edu; SCOTUS blog, June 24, 2013). *Fisher II* (2016) upheld UT's plan on a narrow record but warned the burden remains: universities must "engage in constant deliberation and continued reflection" and prove necessity "with clarity" (*Fisher II*, 579 U.S. 365; Opencasebook).

If that sounds like the Court was putting schools on probation, that's because it was. In 2023, probation ended. The Court in *SFFA* said the quiet part out loud: there's no coherent, measurable, end-dated objective here, and the actual operation of these programs treats race as a negative for disfavored applicants (600 U.S. 181; Stanford Law, Dec. 12, 2023; *Harvard Crimson*, June 30, 2023). How do we know? Because the data—dragged blinking into open court—showed it.

The Data They Didn't Want to Talk About

Holistic? Or just a halo for old-fashioned balancing? The Harvard record was ugly. Asian American applicants, outperforming on academics and extracurriculars, were consistently tagged with lower "personal ratings." Harvard denied animus. The numbers denied Harvard. SFFA's expert, Dr. Peter Arcidiacono, showed systemic impacts; internal Harvard research had flagged "negative effects" for Asians as far back as 2012–2013 (*Harvard Magazine*, Jan–Feb 2019; *Cornell L. Rev. Online*, Nov. 17, 2018). If you need a euphemism for this, here's one: "plus factor." If you need a plain-English term, try this: penalty.

Even Harvard's own promotional gloss couldn't hide the result. When a process yields "personal" scores that mysteriously sag for one group, academics and activities being equal, maybe the process is the problem. The Court thought so. "Courts may not license separating students on the basis of race without an exceedingly persuasive justification," and "Eliminating racial discrimination means eliminating all of it" (*SFFA* majority; Stanford Law FAQ, 2023).

The "personal rating" saga wasn't a one-off glitch; it was a window into the mechanics of "holistic" sorting. Subjective factors—leadership, grit, "likability"—become spigots to fine-tune the racial mix without admitting that's the goal. We're told this is nuanced and enlightened. Would we tolerate it if the dials turned the other way? Would we praise "holistic" evaluations that habitually down-scored whites or Blacks on "personality" to hit an aesthetic target? Of course not. So why is the trick acceptable when the losers are Asian American kids with sky-high SATs and violin cases?

You can call it "contextual evaluation" if that helps you sleep. But if the context is a pie chart in a back office showing last year's class distribution with red arrows on groups the dean wants "more of" or "less of," the label is beside the point. The practice is racial balancing. *Bakke* said "no." *Grutter* said "maybe, for a little while." *Fisher* said "prove it." *SFFA* said "time's up."

The Law Never Blessed Racial Balancing — It Warned Against It

Even before *SFFA*, the Court sent flares. In *Ricci v. DeStefano* (2009), New Haven scrapped firefighter promotion exam results because few Black candidates passed at the top. The city feared a disparate-impact lawsuit. The Court ruled for the firefighters who earned promotion: you can't "engage in intentional discrimination" to avoid a feared disparate-impact suit unless you have a "strong basis in evidence" that you'd lose that suit. New Haven did not (*Ricci*, 557 U.S. 557; law.cornell.edu). That's another way of saying you can't adjust standards based on race simply because the outcomes aren't demographically tidy.

Title VII says what it says. The EEOC, now at long last, has said the quiet, obvious thing out loud in 2025 guidance: unlawful DEI includes "using 'quotas' or other 'balancing' of the workforce on the basis of race, sex," and "using protected characteristics as factors in hiring, firing, promotion, compensation, or recruiting." Also unlawful: excluding people from opportunities based on protected traits, segregating ERGs, or giving preferences based on race or sex (EEOC/DOJ tech assistance, Mar. 19, 2025: JD Supra; Fisher Phillips; Elias Law Group). That's not radical; it's the Civil Rights Act applied evenly. If the rule cuts both ways, it's a rule, not a carveout.

As for education, the legal architecture finally matched the constitutional text. *Bakke* rejected quotas and introduced the diversity-as-interest idea. *Grutter* accepted that interest under strict scrutiny but tagged it with a generational fuse, O'Connor's 25-year hope. *Fisher* insisted on evidence and real alternatives. *SFFA* closed the loop: admissions programs that sort by race violate the Equal Protection Clause and Title VI; their goals are unmeasurable, their endpoints nonexistent, and their mechanisms inherently treat race as a negative for some (*SFFA*, 600 U.S. 181; Stanford Law FAQ, 2023).

The Corporate Quota — Now in Pinstripes

Universities weren't alone. Corporate America sprinted into quotas in everything but name. Goldman Sachs announced in 2020 it "won't take a company public unless it has at least one diverse board member," later upping that to two, including at least one woman (Forbes, Jan. 23, 2020; SHRM, Dec. 8, 2023; *Business Insider*, Dec. 12, 2024). By 2025, after legal icebergs rose in the channel, Goldman "ended [its] formal board diversity policy," citing "legal developments" (FA-Mag/Bloomberg, Feb. 11, 2025). Translation: conditions have changed; the fig leaf fell off.

Nasdaq tried a similar nudge-turned-necessity, adopting a "have, or explain why you do not have, at least two diverse directors" rule. The SEC approved it in 2021, with commissioners calling it "a positive first step" and saying investors demand such data (SEC.gov statement, Aug. 6, 2021). Then the Fifth Circuit vacated it in 2024. The SEC had exceeded its authority, and the "major questions" doctrine said no, not without a clear congressional mandate (White & Case, Dec. 13, 2024; Ogletree Deakins, Dec. 30, 2024). Quotas by proxy are still quotas.

California went for the blunt instrument. AB 979 required California-headquartered public companies to reserve board seats for defined "underrepresented communities." Courts at both state and federal levels struck it down as unconstitutional race-based quotas (Harvard Law Forum, Apr. 23, 2022; Ballotpedia; Akin Gump, May 24, 2023). You can rebrand a quota as a "goal," but the Constitution, and judges who can read, will still notice when seats are "reserved."

Meanwhile, the real-world consequences of coercive "representation" bubbled into scandal. Wells Fargo mandated that "at least half" of interview candidates for $100,000-plus roles be "diverse." Reports emerged—credible ones—that managers conducted "fake" interviews for roles already filled to satisfy the numbers. The bank paused and "revised" the policy amid SEC and DOJ scrutiny. Shareholder suits survived motions. By 2025, they reached settlement in principle while still denying wrongdoing (*Business Insider*, June 7, 2022; *Courthouse News*, July 29, 2024; *Yahoo/Charlotte Observer*, Sept. 18, 2025; *BankingDive*, Sept. 17, 2025). Say it with me: when you force numbers, people game metrics. What's more corrosive to "inclusion" than staging sham interviews for candidates who never had a shot?

Notice the pattern. Soft law morphs into hard edges. "Goals" become gates. "Signals" become screening criteria. And when courts finally notice, companies scurry to "reassess." The cynic calls that compliance theater. The realist calls it an overdue return to the law.

The Federal "Equity" Push — And Its Endgame

The political class did its best to keep the race lever bolted to the policy dashboard. The Biden White House announced "Advancing Equity" across agencies via EO 13985 and EO 14091: "affirmatively advancing equity" is "the responsibility of the whole of our Government," a "comprehensive approach" across procurement, grants, and workforce (White House archives, "Advancing Equity" page).

After *SFFA*, President Biden condemned the Court, declaring he "strongly, strongly disagrees," calling the majority a break from "decades of precedent," and insisting colleges "should not abandon their commitment" to "diverse backgrounds." He quoted the opinion's carve-out about discussing race in essays (White House remarks, June 29, 2023; PBS *NewsHour*, June 29, 2023). He also tossed a grenade at the Court as "not a normal court" (*Roll Call*, June 29, 2023).

Rhetorical questions time: if a program can't survive strict scrutiny, is it "decades of precedent" or decades of evasions? If "equity" means permanent racial preferences with no meaningful endpoint, what is that if not a rolling quota? And when the head of state tells institutions to find a way around the law via essay workarounds, is that leadership or subversion? If a governor told agencies to ignore a Supreme Court ruling on gun rights, would the press call that "resilience" or "resistance"?

The federal "equity" push extends beyond admissions. Agency grant programs rolled out "priority" points for "underserved" categories. Procurement offices floated "supplier diversity" targets. Federal contractors built "representation goals." All were couched in the language of "inclusive growth." None of that immunizes policies from Title VI or Title VII scrutiny. The more these "equity" programs translate into preferences by protected traits, the more they invite the very lawsuits the administration's lawyers will be forced to defend.

And there's the irony: the government that should model fidelity to equal protection is busy exploring workarounds that private litigants then challenge—and win.

The Argument They Can't Win: Standards Don't Have a Race

Defenders of overt racial preferences insist this isn't about lowering standards. "Many people wrongly believe that affirmative action allows unqualified students… to be admitted ahead of qualified students," President Biden said. "This is not how college admissions work" (White House, June 29, 2023).

Really? Then why the frantic admissions engineering? Why the "personal rating" discounting of Asian applicants with stronger academic profiles? Why the "critical mass" fixation? If the process doesn't change outcomes, why fight so hard to preserve it?

If you fix your eyes on "representation," you will warp metrics. That's not slander; that's arithmetic. When some groups have dramatically different average preparation due to K–12 failures and family breakdown, the only way to equalize outcomes at a fixed seat count is to tilt the scale. The scale tilts by soft variables: essays, personality, "lived experience," and "leadership," with all the subjectivity in the world to backfill a pre-decided racial mix. Call it a "plus factor," and the public relations team can breathe easier. But on the ground, someone with objectively stronger preparation gets edged out because the admissions office is chasing a photograph for the brochure.

Justice Thomas diagnosed the poison decades ago. These policies stigmatize beneficiaries and punish disfavored groups, "demeaning to the individual" and "pernicious" in effect (Thomas in *Grutter*; echoed in *SFFA* concurrence; PBS; dldlawyers.com). Think about that. You tell every Black and Hispanic high-achiever she might be "a plus," not the product of excellence. You tell every Asian American kid he'll need to compete with one arm tied behind his back on "personality." Then you call that "anti-racist." How is that not the textbook definition of racism—judging, preferring, and penalizing by race?

And in employment? Ask New Haven's firefighters. They passed the test. The city threw it out. The Court said no. Before you "balance" by race, you need a "strong basis in evidence" of a Title VII disparate-impact violation you would actually lose (*Ricci*, 557 U.S. 557). Benchmarks matter. Standards matter. Standards do not have a race.

Here's the practical corollary: lower the bar to meet a representation target, and you lower trust in the credential for everyone. That's not a smear; it's how markets and reputations work. When a law school announces that "diversity" is a "compelling interest" worth bending selection criteria over, employers will quietly adjust their expectations about the meaning of that degree. Ask yourself: is that fair to the strivers of every color who excelled under pressure? Or is it a tax on their achievements, imposed in the name of optics?

The Pipeline vs. Parity Problem

There is an honorable and urgent project buried under the wreckage of racial preferences: widen the pipeline. But the preference regime flipped means and end. Instead of fixing preparation—where disparities originate—it outsourced equality to admissions committees and HR departments. Those offices cannot fix family structure, primary education quality, neighborhood safety, nutrition, or early literacy. So they do what they can: tweak, tilt, and massage. They fire the starter pistol and then hand out head starts based on demographics, not on demonstrated need or individual hardship.

A better path exists, and it does not require a single checkbox for race:

• Replace legacy preferences with class-based boosts focused on family income, parental education, and wealth. If equity is the goal, why are we rewarding the children of alumni? End that relic and watch the pipeline diversify overnight—on merit, not melanin.

• Supercharge community college transfer agreements with elite universities. Guarantee admission for top performers from every county and district. You want geographic and economic diversity? That's how you get it.

• Expand early college high schools and dual-enrollment programs in high-poverty areas. Let 16-year-olds earn 30–60 college credits before they ever see an Ivy brochure. Preparation beats preference.

• Fund high-dosage tutoring in K–8 reading and math, not performative workshops. It's not sexy, but it works. It closes gaps where they begin.

• Adopt test-optional policies with rigor, not as an excuse to hide the ball. If you drop standardized tests, fortify objective measures elsewhere, such as graded writing samples, proctored assessments, or blind auditions for specific skills. The goal is to de-bias inputs without blinding yourself.

• In hiring, cut degree inflation. Use validated, job-relevant tests, work-sample trials, and blind screeners for early rounds. If you want fairer outcomes, tie selection to the job, not to proxies like "cultural fit" that can mask bias either way.

Notice what all of these have in common: they are race-neutral in rule and race-savvy in impact. They target the cause (preparation and access), not the effect (headcount parity). They lift dignity because they treat people as individuals with stories, not as dataset entries with collectible traits.

The AI Fig Leaf: Automate Bias, Audit the PR

In the hiring world, New York City tried something new: regulate the machines. Local Law 144 says that if you use an Automated Employment Decision Tool, you need a "bias audit" and public disclosure, with penalties for noncompliance (NYC DCWP, Local Law 144; rules.cityofnewyork.us; Deloitte overview; Holistic AI and Fairly AI summaries). Note what this does and doesn't do. It doesn't legalize quotas. It doesn't bless "balancing." It forces transparency around selection-rate ratios by race and sex. That's fine—sunlight is good—but if anyone thinks it greenlights the old DEI alchemy, think again. The EEOC's 2025 guidance just stated that using protected traits to drive outcomes is still illegal. You can audit your model for disparate impact, but you can't add a race variable and pretend it's "fairness correction."

The deeper point is that when institutions chase statistical parity without fixing pipelines, they will be tempted again to bend standards or game processes. The Wells Fargo debacle showed what happens when policy meets pressure and reality: faux interviews. In universities, "personality" fudge. In boards, reserved seats. In admissions essays, "the regime we hold unlawful today" recreated through the backdoor the Court warned against (SFFA, 600 U.S. at 2176). Every time the numbers lag the target, the system looks for a lever. The more hidden the lever, the more corrosive the trust.

The University "Commitment" and the Corporate Retreat

Universities rushed out statements promising they "follow the law," but also that they "prize diversity as a driver of excellence." Cornell stated it was "committed to merit-based decisions... [we] do not admit or evaluate... based on race... Finally: Cornell follows the law" (Cornell Statements, Feb. 21, 2025). Meanwhile, its diversity portal celebrates a "commitment to diverse candidate pools," "Belonging at Cornell," and a tapestry of DEI initiatives (diversity.cornell.edu; hr.cornell.edu). Which is it? If it's merit and law, fine. If it's coded preferences rerouted through "holistic" noise, the courts just took away the map. Honesty demands they say plainly: race is out; hardship is in; excellence remains the bar.

In the C-suite, winds are shifting. Fortune 500s are retooling or downgrading DEI marketing. McDonald's dropped "representation goals" verbiage and supplier DEI pledges. Walmart narrowed "DEI" language to "belonging." Meta and Amazon pulled back public DEI claims. Goldman eliminated its IPO board diversity mandate (Purpose Brand, Mar. 26, 2025; FA-Mag/Bloomberg, Feb. 11, 2025). Not because the case for inclusion evaporated, but because the coercive architecture built on protected traits is legally radioactive. Investors read court opinions too. General counsels prefer compliance to crusades.

Does that mean the inclusion project must end? No. It means it must grow up. Mentorship is legal. Outreach is legal. Apprenticeships, internships, skills training, objective selection, and transparency are legal. What's not legal is pre-deciding winners and losers by skin tone and calling the paperwork "holistic."

The Human Cost of Euphemisms

Let's talk about the human beings trapped under the euphemisms. Picture a 17-year-old girl from a struggling Detroit neighborhood, first in her family to finish high school. She grinds, she excels, and she wins the state science fair. She gets into Michigan on raw merit. Then the discourse tells her: you're here because of "holistic" admissions. How does that feel? Do you think she wants her achievements recoded as a "plus factor"?

Flip the script. Picture a Vietnamese-American boy in Houston. His parents run a nail salon six days a week. He tutors himself on YouTube, perfects calculus using second-hand textbooks, and builds an app in his bedroom that actually works. He applies to Harvard. He gets waitlisted and then rejected. He learns later that his "personal rating" sagged compared to peers with lower objective scores (Harvard Magazine, 2019; Cornell L. Rev. Online, 2018). What should he think about the fairness of the process that judged his "likability"?

Both kids are casualties of the same creed: the belief that justice can be measured in demographic ratios and achieved by quiet tilts at the point of selection. It's not justice. It's social engineering with a smiley-face sticker.

The Rhetorical Cross-Examination

• If "diversity" is a compelling interest, isn't equal treatment a compelling principle? Which one survives when the two conflict?

• If the supposed benefits of preferences require secrecy and euphemism—"holistic," "plus factor," "critical mass"—why can't they be defended in the daylight of measurable ends?

• If preferences "help" minorities, why do they so often plant stigma? Why do the beneficiaries themselves—Justice Thomas among them—report the "presumption… you didn't deserve to be there on merit" (PBS Frontline, May 9, 2023)?

• If the goal is opportunity, why not target actual disadvantage without deputizing skin color as a proxy?

• If equal protection is "living," why does it freeze a regime of racial sorting into perpetuity, with no end point and no standard for "mission accomplished"?

• If corporate "goals" are harmless, why did Goldman drop its IPO mandate after "legal developments" (FA-Mag/Bloomberg, Feb. 11, 2025)? If "have or explain" is a gentle nudge, why did the Fifth Circuit strike down Nasdaq's rule (White & Case, Dec. 13, 2024)?

• If "diverse slate" policies are noble, why did they produce sham interviews at Wells Fargo and lawsuits in tow (Business Insider, June 7, 2022; BankingDive, Sept. 17, 2025)?

A Conservative Lens: Colorblind Law, Color-Brave Effort

So let's say out loud what polite society whispers. Affirmative action by race was, is, and will remain a racist policy. Not because it hates anyone, but because it treats human beings first as racial categories and only second as individuals. It invites stigma, resentment, cynicism, and mutual suspicion. It tempts managers and deans to "balance" by skin color and call it virtue. It swallows excellence with euphemism and spits out a line-up photo for the annual report.

"Courts may not license separating students on the basis of race without an exceedingly persuasive justification... Eliminating racial discrimination means eliminating all of it" (SFFA, Roberts; Stanford Law FAQ). That's the legal bottom line. Here's the moral one: the only sustainable path is colorblind law coupled with color-brave effort—effort aimed at the causes of unequal preparation and opportunity, not at massaging outcomes after the fact.

If you want more Black doctors and Latino engineers, don't gut admissions metrics. Fix K–12 reading, restore order in classrooms, invest in parental empowerment, and set high standards early. If you want broader access to elite institutions, widen the pipeline: fund early college, apprenticeships, and honors programs in non-elite schools. End legacy preferences that entrench privilege. Recruit by

ZIP code and high-poverty school rank. Supercharge community college transfer lanes. If you want fair hiring, end credentialism, test what matters, and audit for job-related validity, then stand your ground when the numbers aren't cosmetically symmetrical.

And for heaven's sake, stop telling young Americans their worth is a color swatch. The great civil rights promise was not equality of outcomes but equality before the law. We fulfill it not by lowering the bar or splitting the country's soul into racial ledgers, but by offering every person a fair chance to clear the bar, and by raising more people to the strength required to do it.

Case Studies: The Evidence Pile

• Universities and quotas:

- UC Davis's 16-seat set-aside—struck down (Bakke, 438 U.S. 265; law.cornell.edu).

- "Critical mass" tolerated but time-limited in *Grutter*, with O'Connor's 25-year hope (Grutter, 539 U.S. 306; Wikipedia; law.cornell.edu).

- *Fisher I* and *II*: strict scrutiny is real; race-neutral alternatives required if workable (law.cornell.edu; SCOTUSblog; Opencasebook).

- *SFFA v. Harvard/UNC*: preferences unconstitutional; vague goals, negative use of race, no endpoints (600 U.S. 181; Stanford Law FAQ; Harvard Crimson).

• Disparate impact vs. disparate treatment:

- *Ricci v. DeStefano*: New Haven couldn't discard results without a "strong basis in evidence" of disparate-impact liability (557 U.S. 557; law.cornell.edu).

- **Corporate DEI quotas:**

- Nasdaq "have or explain" board rule approved (SEC, Aug. 6, 2021) and then vacated by the Fifth Circuit (White & Case, Dec. 13, 2024; Ogletree, Dec. 30, 2024).

- California AB 979 board quotas struck down in state and federal courts (Harvard Law Forum, Apr. 23, 2022; Akin Gump, May 24, 2023; Ballotpedia).

- Goldman's IPO board mandate announced (Forbes, Jan. 23, 2020; SHRM, Dec. 8, 2023), later abandoned (FA-Mag/Bloomberg, Feb. 11, 2025).

- Wells Fargo's "diverse slate" scandal: pause, revisions, investigations, litigation, settlement in principle (Business Insider, June 7, 2022; Courthouse News, July 29, 2024; BankingDive, Sept. 17, 2025; Yahoo/Charlotte Observer, Sept. 18, 2025).

- **Government equity push vs. legal limits:**
- Biden EO 13985/14091: "affirmatively advancing equity" is government-wide policy (White House archives).

- Biden remarks opposing the *SFFA* decision, urging colleges not to abandon diversity and to use essays (White House; PBS; Roll Call).

- **Compliance perimeter tightening:**

- EEOC/DOJ 2025 guidance: quotas and use of protected traits in employment decisions are unlawful; applies equally to all groups (JD Supra; Fisher Phillips; Elias Law Group).

- **Hiring tech guardrails:**

- NYC Local Law 144: AI hiring bias audits, disclosure, notice (NYC DCWP; rules.cityofnewyork.us; Deloitte; Holistic AI; Fairly AI). Transparency, not a license to discriminate.

A Practical Charter: How to Do Diversity Without Discrimination

Enough diagnosis. Here's the prescription—lawful, principled, and effective:

1. **Admissions without race sorting**

   • Replace racial "plus factors" with adversity indices that measure economic hardship, school context, family education, foster care history, homelessness, neighborhood poverty rate, violent-crime exposure, and first-generation status.

   • Cap legacy and donor preferences at zero. Publish the numbers you save.

• Guarantee admission for top students from every public high school within the state system (the "Top X%" model), then support them with robust bridge programs.

• Use structured, double-blind scoring for essays and recommendations where feasible. Train readers to evidentiary standards and audit for consistency.

2. **Hiring without head counting**

• Define job-critical competencies. Use validated work-sample tests and structured interviews scored with rubrics.

• Use blind résumé screens for first-pass reviews. Redact names, addresses, and graduation years to reduce bias both ways.

• Swap degree requirements for skills proofs such as certifications, portfolios, or apprenticeships. Partner with community colleges and bootcamps for talent pipelines.

• Ban "diverse slate" quotas. Instead, require "broad sourcing"—postings in multiple channels, including HBCU/HSI career centers, veterans' networks, and disability organizations. Measure outreach, not outcomes.

3. **Culture without coercion**

• Open ERGs to allies; bar exclusion by protected traits. Focus programming on mentorship and career skills, not political litmus tests.

• Train on civility, conflict resolution, and feedback, not on ideological catechisms. Measure training by behavior change (for example, 360 feedback), not attendance stickers.

4. **Accountability without race math**

• Publish anonymized selection-process metrics and validity studies. If a step predicts success, keep it. If not, fix it. That's equity by design, not by decree.

The Moral Core: Dignity Is Not a Demographic

Is there a society on earth that got freer and fairer by telling citizens their essential identity is their race? The American promise was different. It asked a harder thing: build a republic where the law sees individuals, not categories; where solidarity grows from choice, not blood; where we confront the past without reproducing its sins in reverse.

Affirmative action by race was born of a grief that demanded action. But compassion without principle curdles into condescension. Preference is the counterfeit coin of fairness: it looks like justice at a glance, but it buys resentment at full price. If we're serious about opportunity, we must be serious about neutrality in the rules and seriousness in the remedies—starting early, building competence, and rewarding excellence.

"Equal protection of the laws" was never a suggestion. It was a promise. The Court has renewed the note. Now it's our turn to pay it forward without the fine print.

Footnotes

1. Regents of the University of California v. Bakke, 438 U.S. 265 (1978). See law.cornell.edu; "When the Supreme Court First Ruled on Affirmative Action," Constitution Center (June 28, 2023).

2. Grutter v. Bollinger, 539 U.S. 306 (2003). Majority opinion of Justice O'Connor ("race-conscious admissions policies must be limited in time"); law.cornell.edu; Wikipedia.

3. Fisher v. University of Texas at Austin, 570 U.S. 297 (2013) (Fisher I) and 579 U.S. 365 (2016) (Fisher II). See law.cornell.edu; SCOTUS blog (June 24, 2013); Opencase book (Fisher II summaries).

4. Students for Fair Admissions v. Harvard, 600 U.S. 181 (2023). Majority by Roberts; concurrences by Thomas and Gorsuch; dissents by Sotomayor and Jackson. See Stanford Law Center FAQ (Dec. 12, 2023); Harvard Crimson (June 30, 2023); Wikipedia.

5. Evidence regarding Harvard's "personal rating" and Asian-American penalty: Harvard Magazine (Jan–Feb 2019); Cornell Law Review Online (Nov. 17, 2018).

6. Ricci v. DeStefano, 557 U.S. 557 (2009). Majority by Kennedy; "strong basis in evidence" standard. See law.cornell.edu; Wikipedia.

7. Nasdaq board diversity rule: SEC approval (Aug. 6, 2021) (SEC.gov statement); later vacated by the Fifth Circuit en banc (Dec. 11, 2024). See White & Case (Dec. 13, 2024); Ogletree Deakins (Dec. 30, 2024).

8. California AB 979 board quotas struck down: Harvard Law School Forum on Corporate Governance (Apr. 23, 2022); Ballotpedia summary; Akin Gump (May 24, 2023).

9. Goldman Sachs IPO diversity policy announced and later abandoned: Forbes (Jan. 23, 2020); SHRM (Dec. 8, 2023); Business Insider (Dec. 12, 2024); FA-Mag/Bloomberg (Feb. 11, 2025).

10. Wells Fargo "diverse slate" controversy: Business Insider (June 7, 2022); Courthouse News (July 29, 2024); Yahoo/Charlotte Observer (Sept. 18, 2025); BankingDive (Sept. 17, 2025).

11. Biden administration "equity" executive orders: White House archives, "Advancing Equity and Racial Justice Through the Federal Government" (EO 13985; EO 14091). Biden remarks on SFFA decision: White House transcript (June 29, 2023); PBS NewsHour (June 29, 2023). "Not a Normal Court": Roll Call (June 29, 2023).

12. EEOC/DOJ 2025 DEI guidance: JD Supra (Mar. 26, 2025); Fisher Phillips (Mar. 21, 2025); Elias Law Group (Mar. 19, 2025).

13. NYC Local Law 144 on Automated Employment Decision Tools: NYC DCWP site (nyc.gov); rules.cityofnewyork.us; Deloitte overview; HolisticAI (Jan. 15, 2024); Fairly AI (Apr. 1, 2025).

14. Cornell statements following federal guidance: "Cornell's Guiding Principles" (Feb. 21, 2025); diversity.cornell.edu; hr.cornell.edu.

Inline Citations

• (Bakke, 438 U.S. 265; law.cornell.edu)

• (Grutter, 539 U.S. 306; O'Connor: "25 years")

• (Fisher I, 570 U.S. 297; Fisher II, 579 U.S. 365; SCOTUSblog; Opencasebook)

• (SFFA v. Harvard, 600 U.S. 181; Stanford Law FAQ, 2023)

• (Harvard Magazine, 2019; Cornell L. Rev. Online, 2018)

• (Ricci, 557 U.S. 557; law.cornell.edu)

• (SEC approval of Nasdaq rule, Aug. 6, 2021; SEC.gov)

• (Fifth Circuit vacatur, Dec. 11, 2024; White & Case; Ogletree)

• (AB 979 rulings; Harvard Law Forum; Akin Gump; Ballotpedia)

• (Goldman IPO policy and reversal; Forbes; FA-Mag/Bloomberg)

• (Wells Fargo "fake interviews"; Business Insider; Courthouse News; BankingDive)

• (Biden EO 13985/14091; White House archives)

• (Biden remarks; White House; PBS; Roll Call)

• (EEOC/DOJ guidance; JD Supra; Fisher Phillips; Elias Law Group)

• (NYC Local Law 144; NYC DCWP; Deloitte; HolisticAI; Fairly AI)

• (Cornell statements; diversity.cornell.edu; hr.cornell.edu.)

Chapter 21:
The Year They Tried to Edit the Past

You can always tell when a narrative is losing its grip: it starts moving the goalposts. One day the consensus sits there like bedrock—complex, often tragic, always human—and the next day a flurry of op-eds and glossy "projects" arrive to declare that we have been wrong all along. America's essence? Not liberty wrestling with its contradictions, but slavery as the operating system, the bootloader, the BIOS. How convenient. How reductive. How false.

Is this about denying horror? No. It is about resisting a slick, moralized rewrite, one that trades honest history for a political cudgel. Because when a movement insists that history must be retranslated so it always convicts the present enemy, it is not doing history. It is running a prosecution.

The latest prosecution's Exhibit A is the claim that America was "founded" on slavery, full stop, period, case closed. You have seen the headlines. You have heard the talking points. "The year 1619 is our true founding," we are told, because the arrival of a handful of enslaved Africans at Point Comfort is said to define the entire national project. If that is true, then what do you make of the Pilgrims' compacts, the sermons of New England, the pamphlets of the Founders, the debates of abolitionists, and the constitutional machinery that split apart and reassembled at horrendous cost in a Civil War? Epiphenomena? Rhetorical garnish?

Ask yourself: when history becomes an argument that never risks counterevidence, is it still history, or just a sermon with footnotes?

The ideology of rewritten history—yes, rewritten—is not really about past events. It is about present power. That is why the same voices say slavery in America was exclusively a race story, uniquely American, uniquely white against black, even though the record is painfully, globally, insistently complicated. Do such complexities absolve anyone? Of course not. But flattening them does not absolve ignorance either. It fertilizes it.

Let us reset the terms like adults. It is possible, indeed necessary, to hold two truths: slavery in America was a moral catastrophe and a civic contradiction of our founding ideals; and slavery as a human institution is older than America, broader than race, and entangled across peoples, continents, and colors, including whites and blacks, sellers and buyers, captors and captives, Christians and Muslims, monarchies and republics. You can honor the particular horror experienced by enslaved Africans and their descendants while also acknowledging that the Atlantic world was not a cartoon with one villain in one color. Is that too much nuance for the activists who insist history should feel like a courtroom closing argument?

Consider the habit. The political left advances sweeping claims such as "America was built on slavery," "capitalism equals exploitation," and "whiteness explains all outcomes," and then annexes historical memory to serve today's crusade. Any dissent is branded denial. Any complexity is "whataboutism." Any historian who asks for accuracy is held suspect. Is that scholarship, or a sacrament?

The 1619 Thesis and Its Afterlives

The most famous contemporary example, though hardly the only one, is the 1619 Project, launched with a flourish and a curriculum rollout. Its flagship essay asserted that the American Revolution was fought "in large part" to protect slavery (NYT Magazine, 2019). This, we are told, is the keystone. Really? The Revolution—the sprawling political, economic, and spiritual drama that ran from tax policy to sovereignty to common-law rights to evangelical awakenings—happened because George III threatened Virginia planters' slaveholdings? That is the story?

Historians across the spectrum raised their hands. Gordon S. Wood, among the most respected scholars of the Founding, called that claim "wrong in so many ways" (Wood, interview, 2019). James McPherson, dean of Civil War historians, said he saw "no evidence" that preserving slavery motivated the Revolution (McPherson, 2019). Even some friendly readers urged correction. And after months of pressure, the Project quietly edited lines about "true founding" and hedged its revolutionary thesis online (NYT updates, 2020). You did not imagine that. It happened. The edits came without a clear admission of error, only a recalibration in the margins. What do you call a revision that pretends it was always there?

We could stop there, but the point is not to pile on one publication. It is to expose the method: take a part for the whole, claim inevitability where there was conflict, erase counterevidence, and dignify power with inevitability. The method confuses moral clarity with historical simplicity. But the truth, frequently unpleasant, is that America's story is a war of ideas inside a society, not a talking point against it.

Was slavery central to parts of the economy? Yes. Was it interwoven with politics, law, and culture? Obviously. But the Founding also birthed the conceptual vocabulary—natural rights, universal equality in principle—that abolitionists later weaponized against the institution. That is not propaganda; it is the same historical logic abolitionists themselves used. William Lloyd Garrison thundered with the Declaration in one hand and the Constitution in the other, calling the latter "a covenant with death," even as others like Frederick Douglass argued the Constitution, rightly read, was "a glorious liberty document." Two abolitionists, two readings, one shared conviction: the founding principles could be turned against slavery. If slavery was the point of America, then why did the logic of the Founding generate the movement that destroyed it?

Who Rewrote Whom?

Let us ask a few discomfiting questions. If slavery in America is uniquely and exclusively racial, how do you account for:

• White indentured servants in colonial America whose contracts sometimes collapsed into de facto slavery. Chattel? No. Lifelong? Rare. But brutal? Often. The system exploited the poor across lines of origin and language (Morgan, *American Slavery, American Freedom*).

• European captives enslaved in North Africa by the Barbary states—up to a million between the 16th and 19th centuries by some estimates—men and women seized in raids, chained to oars, ransomed by charity, erased by modern memory because their suffering does not fit the schema (Davis, *Christian Slaves, Muslim Masters*).

• Native slavery networks in the Southeast, where tribes trafficked war captives before and during European colonization, integrating them into local economies (Gallay, *The Indian Slave Trade*).

• Free black slaveholders in parts of the antebellum South—yes, a minority, yes, often complex family entanglements, and yes, sometimes entrepreneurial ownership indistinguishable from white planters (Koger, *Black Slaveowners*; Berlin, *Slaves Without Masters*).

Do these facts mean race did not matter? Of course race mattered, enormously. The American slave system hardened into a race-based caste, with law and custom aligning to mark blackness as bondage and whiteness as the citizen norm. But does the centrality of race in American slavery erase the broader human habit of enslaving the vulnerable? It cannot. The truth is both/and, not either/or. And what the left's revisionist zeal often refuses is precisely that both/and. Why? Because both/and complicates the indictment. Both/and admits that evil can be human, not just white. Both/and puts the story back into history and takes it out of the pamphlet.

"But recognizing complexity undermines moral clarity," they protest.

No, it strengthens it. If you only hate slavery when it is politically convenient, you don't hate slavery. You hate your opponents. That's not ethics. That's partisanship with an IKEA halo.

The "1619" claim about capitalism

Let's examine another fashionable thesis: "American capitalism was built on slavery; its efficiency, accounting, and dynamism come from the plantation" [NYT Magazine, 2019]. It's a provocative thought. It's also empirically shaky. Yes, cotton mattered. Yes, credit networks touched London, New York, and New Orleans. Yes, plantation ledgers were meticulous. But careful economic historians have dismantled the idea that plantation accounting birthed modern capitalism or that slavery's profits were sufficient to explain the Industrial Revolution's vast lift [Olmstead & Rhode; Hoppit; Deirdre McCloskey; Eric Hilt].

Was cotton important? Absolutely. Was it the essence of capitalism? That's like saying Roman aqueducts invented modern sanitation. It's clever. It's not correct.

Why press the point? Because the narrative's purpose is not to clarify. It is to taint. If capitalism equals slavery, then all the fruits of the modern market—the medicines, the food abundance, the ordinary prosperity—are morally compromised, and the only righteous path is to discard the whole arrangement. "See?" they say. "The ledger books were soaked in blood."

Indeed, sin stains history. But if the standard is stainlessness, welcome to nihilism. The right standard is repentance and reform, not myth and erasure.

Was America founded in 1619?

Let's be plain. A polity can have many origins: a cultural beginning, a legal founding, a moral awakening. The claim that 1619 is our "true founding" takes a tragic arrival by force and makes it the city's cornerstone by fiat. Not by law, not by declaration, not by covenant—by assertion.

The Founders—flawed, divided, contradictory—signed a document in 1776 that announced a universal proposition that later generations forced into actual universality. That struggle is our moral biography, not an embarrassing footnote to a true story that starts on a ship's deck.

"But the Founders were hypocrites," the retort goes.

Hypocrites? Often. Human? Always. The existence of hypocrisy doesn't impeach the truth of a principle; it proves the need for it. Would you prefer that they had declared inequality as a principle so their practice could be pure? "We hold these truths to be self-evident, that all men are created unequal." Would that satisfy the critics' craving for consistency?

The Founders wrote a check they could not cash. Their children bled to honor it. That is not cynicism's punchline. That is the Republic's price.

Whites in bondage, blacks with power, the universal in the particular

Let's confront more uncomfortable evidence the new narratives would prefer to erase.

1. **White bondage in early America.** The colonies were filled with indentured laborers, many from Britain and Ireland, who sold years of their lives for passage and hope. Some died under conditions indistinguishable from enslavement's brutality: starved, beaten, extended contracts for "infractions." No, this was not chattel slavery defined by race, inheritable in the maternal line. The law drew a line. But on the dock or in the field, lines blur. That ugliness—exploitation of the poor regardless of color—undercuts the popular claim that whiteness always equaled power. Sometimes whiteness equaled disposable.

2. **The Barbary memory hole.** From the 1500s into the 1800s, North African corsairs hunted the Mediterranean, Ireland's coast, even Iceland, dragging off villagers to markets in Algiers, Tunis, and Tripoli. Estimates vary; the human wreckage does not [Davis]. American sailors, post-independence, faced the same predation. Our early Navy fought to secure freedom of commerce and free captives [Lambert, *The Barbary Wars*]. If America is uniquely the oppressor, why does our earliest foreign war read like a liberation mission?

3. **Black slaveholding.** It sounds like a trap set by trolls, but the record stands. In places like New Orleans, Charleston, and parts of Louisiana, free people of color owned property, businesses, and yes, slaves. Sometimes as family arrangements to protect kin from white law; sometimes as commercial ownership. The "free colored" class in New Orleans, often of mixed heritage, formed a distinct community with economic leverage [Hirsch & Logsdon, *Creole New Orleans*]. Reality resists slogans. Does this excuse anything? No. It shows that power and exploitation are not racially monopolized.

Say it plainly: slavery in the Atlantic world became deeply racialized, and the American version hardened into a uniquely virulent caste system that marked blackness as bondage. But that truth coexists with a broader human culpability.

The activists who insist we pick a single pole—"only racism explains slavery," "only capitalism explains slavery," "America is only its worst sin"—are asking us to replace history with a catechism.

What gets lost when we make sin the skeleton key? The agency of the enslaved, whose rebellions, flight, literacy, and faith changed the country. The economic contradictions inside planters' lives. The northern complicities—the mills, the ships, the insurance tables. The southern dissenters—from evangelicals who saw brotherhood in Christ to political minorities who risked reputation to challenge the code. All of this makes a people, wrestling.

Don't we teach that? Or do we teach that one side was stone and the other side clay, and that only today's enlightened class has the correct goggles?

When newsrooms become pulpit

Turn to the media. Set aside the PR veneer and read the pieces. "America Wasn't a Democracy Until Black Americans Made It One," declared one marquee essay [NYT Magazine, 2019]. Really? The franchise expanded by blood and amendment, yes. Black Americans led moral revivals, yes. But to deny that republican government existed until one heroic chapter is to write out the very institutions that made reform possible.

The claim is moving. It is also nonsensical. Democracy is not a switch that flips from 0 to 1. It is a regime that grows—or withers—

by consent, institutions, and reform. Rhetoric that declares "none of it counted until us" isn't history. It's ownership.

Another refrain: "Police derive from slave patrols." In the South, some policing functions did overlap with slave patrols—true. In the North, municipal policing evolved from night watch systems and bourgeois anxieties about disorder, also true. So which generalization wins? None. Specific histories differ by region. That's how history works—carefully.

Yet one oversimplified story is exported into school curricula to deliver a moral: everything you trust is corruption's child. Is that moral empowering, or convenient for a politics that wants to burn down institutions to rebuild them in its image?

A historian's ethic: humility before the dead

Let me say what the activists will not: the dead do not owe us their purity. We owe them our honesty. We owe it to the enslaved to tell their story with the particularity and dignity their lives deserve— names, places, choices, tragedies, triumphs—not as props in a morality play designed for today's caucus.

We owe it to the Founders to judge them against the standards they proclaimed as well as those they failed, and we owe it to ourselves to see the bravery in their revolt and the cowardice in their compromises—both at once.

We owe it to the black and white and native and immigrant dead to tell the truth even when it does not flatter our faction.

Does that require stepping on toes? Good. History that cannot bruise is propaganda. But propaganda that refuses counterevidence is not a bruise—it's a blindfold.

The fallacy of a single founding sin

Let's return to the thesis that America's true founding is slavery. The claim succeeds rhetorically because it feels like moral X-ray vision: "We found the skeleton key." But single-cause narratives misfire. The British Empire, a slaveholding and slave-trading power, also birthed abolitionist thought in its churches and courts. The same Atlantic that carried human cargo carried Wilberforce's speeches.

Is Britain founded on slavery or on parliamentary liberty? Is it both? Of course. So is America. To explain us by only our worst is an act of reduction, not of justice.

The United States signed a Constitution that included foul compromises—three-fifths for representation, a fugitive slave clause, a twenty-year trade reprieve. And yet, the Constitution also created the matrix of federal power through which slavery was curbed, challenged, and finally crushed. The same instrument that permitted also contained the seeds to destroy.

Does that cognitive dissonance give you a headache? Good. History causes headaches. It's how you know you're not dreaming.

"But why insist that whites were also slaves?" the critics ask. Because it's true, and truth matters. Because acknowledging the

Barbary horrors and European indenture doesn't minimize the black American tragedy; it situates it in the human condition and complicates the impulse to racialize evil as if it belongs to one skin. If we cannot bear to admit that cruelty is portable, we will never understand how to stop it when the colors change.

"And why insist that some blacks owned slaves?" Again, because it's true. Because it demonstrates how power operates in every human network and shows that the moral imperative is to build institutions that constrain power, not to invert hierarchies and pretend justice is achieved.

Bad faith, good faith, and the inheritance we keep

The left asks us to believe that good faith is naivety—that to have any pride in the American project is to close your eyes to chains. On the contrary, good faith is to look at the chains and still decide to keep the promise. If your solution is to declare the promise fraudulent, you will never recognize its fulfillment when you see it.

America is not a lie. America is a pledge—and we have enforced it unevenly, cruelly, nobly, bloodily. The moral drama of this country is not exposure ("gotcha!") but covenant ("try again"). Who taught that? The very movements the left claims as exclusive ancestors: abolitionists, civil rights preachers, immigrant patriots. You do not march across a bridge singing *We Shall Overcome* if you believe the house is evil to the studs. You march because the house is yours.

Rhetorical questions the activists won't answer

• If the Revolution was to preserve slavery, why did the British offer freedom to slaves who fled to their lines, yet American abolitionist momentum surged after independence?

• If capitalism equals slavery, what do you do with the countries that abolished slavery and then saw markets and middle classes expand?

• If the Founders' ideals are voided by their failures, why do modern activists lean on those very ideals—rights, equality, due process—to advance their cause?

• If whiteness is permanent guilt, how did white abolitionists choose to spend their lives and fortunes, and why did thousands of white soldiers die to obliterate slavery?

• If history is a moral math problem where the sum must be condemnation, what is the point of studying anything beyond confirmation?

A conservative lens: what it preserves and why it fights

Conservatism is not a defense of every ancestor's action. It is a defense of the patrimony—the practices and principles that, despite sin, generate reform without revolution and justice without utopia. It says institutions beat sentiments, law beats slogans, and liberty's guardrails beat centralized salvation. It says, "Do not smash the mechanism that made your progress possible." It says, "Remember, because amnesia destroys."

The left's historical program is amnesia in a noble costume. It deletes context, demonizes the mixed, and replaces the messy commons with a purified myth that always incriminates the same villain. That's not a curriculum. That's a grudge.

A humane patriotism names names, dates dates, quotes quotes, and confesses sins. But it refuses to shrink the republic to a single crime. It rejects the piety that mistakes power for righteousness and novelty for truth. It tells the whole story: the ships and the sermons, the lash and the law, the auction and the amendment, the overseer and the orator, the rebel and the reformer. It refuses to forget anyone.

Case studies the pamphleteers omit

• **New England gradual emancipation.** Massachusetts effectively ended slavery by judicial decision in 1783 under its new constitution's equality clause (*Commonwealth v. Jennison*). Vermont abolished it in 1777. Pennsylvania began gradual emancipation in 1780. If America's soul was slavery, why did some American polities—early, imperfectly—move to uproot it before Britain ended slavery in the empire (1833)? The nation's story is not North-angel versus South-devil, but it does reveal that the revolutionary talk of rights traveled into courtrooms and legislatures.

• **Black self-assertion within the Founding frame.** Benjamin Banneker's letter to Thomas Jefferson called America to account on its own terms, wielding the Declaration like a mirror. Frederick Douglass's famous 1852 oration, after its scalding indictment, still held out the Constitution as redeemable. "Interpreted as it ought to be interpreted, the Constitution is a glorious liberty document," he declared [Douglass, 1852]. Why would he say that if the founding charter were merely a slaver's covenant?

• **The global context.** The transatlantic trade was the largest forced migration in history. It was also one branch of a global tree of bondage. African polities participated, Arab traders operated, European markets financed, and American plantations consumed. Morally, each link is guilty. Historically, each link is causal. Reduce any link and the chain is weaker—but do not pretend there was only one link.

"Reframing" versus refracting

The left speaks of "reframing" history, as if the facts sit still and only the camera moves. The honest historian does not reframe so much as refract—turn the prism and see new colors without pretending the old ones never existed. Reframing, in practice, too often means cropping out the parts that make your argument harder. Refracting means you keep them, and you work.

What would refracting look like here? It would mean:

• Teaching slavery's centrality in the South's economy and politics while also showing the fissures, resistances, and moral debates within the South.

- Teaching the North's complicity—textiles, shipping, finance—so that moral superiority is tempered by accounting ledgers.

- Teaching black agency not merely as victimhood but as institution-building: churches, schools, newspapers, mutual aid, regiments, businesses.

- Teaching that whites suffered and were enslaved in other contexts, not to diminish black suffering but to universalize the warning that any system can brutalize, and law must be vigilant.

- Teaching that some black Americans owned slaves and that human beings inhabit roles—master, victim, buyer, seller—not by race alone but by power and circumstance.

- Teaching that the Founding invented the very grammar of dissent that abolition and civil rights used—deliberately, powerfully, successfully.

"Respectfully combative" is not a contradiction

Respect tells the truth: the lash tore flesh, families shattered, labor extracted, lives stunted, souls scarred. Combative tells the truth too: you cannot turn that truth into a cudgel to smash the very stage where free citizens argue about their inheritance. You cannot cartoon the dead and call it virtue. You cannot parody the past to prosecute the present and call it education. You must do the work—dates, documents, cross-examination, debate.

The ending the revisionists offer is sour: "America is a crime scene." The ending the honest historian offers is hard: "America is a promise kept imperfectly by sinners who fought each other and themselves."

Which ending produces citizens? Which produces clients? Which produces reformers? Which produces inquisitors?

Let me be snarky for just a moment, since snark seems to be the lingua franca of the very outlets driving the rewrite. If everything noble is "whitewashing" and everything ignoble is "speaking truth," then why bother with archives? Just hand out your press releases and call them primary sources. If the Revolution was a planter's tantrum, the Constitution a slaver's spreadsheet, the Civil War a misunderstanding, Reconstruction a footnote, and the civil rights movement a marketing campaign, then what, precisely, has the left inherited from America that it wishes to preserve? The post office?

The courage to keep the whole

The task is not to blink. It is to see in stereo, to look at the whip and the words, the ship and the sermon, the market and the manumission, and to tell the story that holds them without flinching or flattening. That's grown-up history. That's the kind of memory a free people can survive.

We can honor the enslaved by telling their truth and still refuse a political rebrand that makes their suffering the single gear in a machine that runs for centuries. We can honor the Founders by confessing their failures and still refuse to declare their ideals invalid. We can honor black achievement by recognizing agency and complexity, not reducing it to a subplot in someone else's morality play.

America is not 1619 or 1776. America is the argument between them and the blood that settled some parts of it. If you must choose one year, pick neither. Choose the years where the principles marched into the street and met the people who believed them.

And if, after all this, the activists insist that to question is to betray, to complicate is to deny, to contextualize is to erase, ask one last question. What are they so afraid of?

Extended case files, inconvenient facts

Let's drill deeper, because the archive keeps receipts whether or not newsroom catechisms prefer them.

• **Haiti and the reverberation paradox.** Revolutionary France declared the Rights of Man while clinging to Caribbean plantations. The Haitian Revolution (1791–1804) exploded that hypocrisy, creating the first Black republic and terrifying planters across the Americas. Southern elites in the U.S. doubled down on slave codes to prevent "another Haiti," while abolitionists pointed to Haiti as a moral reckoning. Which side "owns" the lesson? Neither. The point is that principles and interests collide, and events ricochet. History is pinball, not chess by masterminds.

• **The Somerset decision (1772) in Britain.** A British court effectively declared slavery unsupported by English common law in England proper, which energized abolitionists and emboldened enslaved people to claim freedom on English soil. Yet Britain's empire continued profiting from slavery overseas until 1833. So was Britain "founded on slavery" or "founded on liberty"? Both impulses ran in tandem, like ours. Single-axis storytelling fails this test.

• **Founding-era antislavery societies.** By the mid-1780s, northern states housed antislavery societies—Philadelphia's led by Quakers and Benjamin Franklin, who petitioned Congress against the slave trade in 1790. Congress brushed it aside, but the petition itself reveals something the "founding-for-slavery" thesis cannot swallow: antislavery activism was native to the early Republic's political bloodstream. If the body's "true heart" was slavery, why did antibodies appear so quickly?

• **Internal slave trade and northern complicity.** After 1808, when the Constitution's reprieve on banning the transatlantic trade expired, Congress outlawed importation. The domestic trade then grew, trafficking enslaved people from the Upper South to the Cotton Kingdom. Northern banks financed, insurers underwrote, and textile mills spun the cotton. Moral superiority in the North coexisted with profits from Southern sin—precisely the sort of messy ledger honest history records and polemic prefers to redact.

- **Free black communities' complexity.** In cities like Philadelphia, free black churches (for example, Richard Allen's Mother Bethel AME) organized mutual aid, education, and abolitionist activism. These communities also navigated color hierarchies and class divisions—lighter-skinned elites, artisan classes, laborers—mirroring human dynamics found everywhere. The left's "oppressor/oppressed" binary hides that interior complexity behind a moral mural.

- **The African supply side.** African polities and merchant networks captured and sold rival peoples to European traders. This truth enrages ideologues who crave a one-directional guilt flow. Should it? No. It enlarges culpability, and thus the responsibility to build systems that prevent such predation anywhere. It also explains why abolition required a global legal architecture, not just American penitence.

- **Manumission waves and backlash.** Post-Revolutionary Virginia saw a significant uptick in private manumissions, inspired by evangelical revivals and republican ideals. Then came backlash—tighter laws, fear of insurrection. Progress zigzags. The arc of history doesn't "bend" on its own; people pull, and others push back. When pundits speak as if inevitability ran the show, they erase the courage that made each step.

• **The Missouri Compromise and sectional conscience.** When Missouri petitioned for statehood as a slave state (1819), a ferocious national debate erupted. The compromise (1820) admitted Missouri as slave, Maine as free, and marked a line for future territories. If slavery was the country's "essence," why did compromise require such contortions? Essences don't bargain; interests do, under a constitutional framework that magnified the moral stakes.

• **The abolitionist press and gag rules.** Abolitionists flooded Congress with petitions; the House responded with gag rules (1836–1844) to table antislavery petitions automatically. John Quincy Adams fought them with procedural brilliance, waving the First Amendment like a sword. That spectacle—citizens petitioning, representatives suppressing, an ex-president resisting—undermines the idea that American institutions were uniform engines of oppression. They were venues of contest, often ugly, sometimes glorious.

• **The Civil War's moral arithmetic.** Yes, the war was about slavery's expansion and the South's determination to protect human property; yes, Lincoln led with Union to hold border states. But the Emancipation Proclamation turned the war's moral axis, and black soldiers in Union blue fought for freedom with rifles and hymns. White soldiers died by the tens of thousands to crush a slaveholders' rebellion. How does a "founded on slavery" nation spend such blood to end it? Because the country was more than its sin. It was also its cure.

The Barbary reminder, again, with faces

It's one thing to cite the Barbary slave trade abstractly; it's another to picture it. Imagine a Cornish fishing village in 1625: sails on the horizon, smoke in the churchyard, families dragged at blade-point to boats, then to markets where the price of a man is matched against the price of timber. Imagine an American merchant crew in the 1790s, shackled in Algiers, writing letters begging for ransom while diplomats negotiate tribute. These are not "gotchas." They are witnesses. They testify that enslavement is a human tactic, not a racial monopoly [Davis, 2003; Lambert, 2005]. If we cannot hold those faces beside the faces in Charleston's market, we are not doing history. We are doing team sports.

The "capitalism is cotton" canard—receipts, part II

The "New History of Capitalism" argues that whip-driven efficiency "improved" output and that modern management flows from the plantation ledger. It sounds chilling, and that chill is the point. But when scholars pulled the data, the story wobbled. The famous "picking records" proving accelerating productivity under torture turned out ambiguous once you control for seed varieties, weather, selection bias, and record-keeping quirks [Olmstead & Rhode, 2010]. Meanwhile, the extraordinary escape velocity of 19th-century growth tracks inventions in energy, metallurgy, transportation, and institutions in places without plantation agriculture. Did cotton matter? Yes. Did it "found" capitalism? No more than guano founded modern agriculture because fertilizer matters.

Ask a blunt question: If capitalism equals slavery, why did capitalism also generate abolitionist civil society—voluntary associations, newspapers, and fundraising networks—that agitated to end slavery? Why did maritime insurance markets that touched slave voyages also underwrite the ships that carried missionaries and reformers? Systems are not moral agents; people are. Capitalism is a tool. It can carry sin or repentance, sometimes both, in the same ledger.

Media quotations and selective memory

Listen to the cadence: "In order to understand the brutality of American capitalism, you have to start on the plantation" [NYT Magazine, 2019]. Must you? Or might you start in medieval guild halls, Dutch joint-stock companies, Scottish moral philosophy, English courts, and American tinkers? The line is memorable. That's why it's written—to stick. But memorability is not the same as accuracy.

As Gordon Wood put it, reducing the Revolution to planter panic "misrepresents the complexity of motivations" [Wood, 2019]. James McPherson, asked whether the Revolution was about preserving slavery, replied, "I don't think so. I see no evidence for that" [McPherson, 2019]. The supposed "reframe" collapses under expert weight, so the frame is resized, the caption tweaked, and the print hung back on the wall with a new placard [NYT updates, 2020]. Museum curators of morality.

Progressive moral claims are often built on noble intentions but drafted with prosecutorial rhetoric. "America wasn't a democracy until Black Americans made it one" [NYT Magazine, 2019]. Honor the truth inside that line: Black Americans did more than their share to deepen American democracy. But the sentence as written erases the reality of institutions, elections, town halls, and courts that existed and evolved. It's not necessary to diminish the past to elevate the heroism. Doing so backfires; it breeds cynicism, not citizenship.

Pedagogy or polemic?

A civics worth having teaches students that America has a tragic contradiction at its center—freedom proclaimed, bondage practiced—and then asks them to trace how the contradiction narrowed by law, arms, and conscience. It doesn't insist the contradiction is the essence. Why? Because if the essence is sin, then reform is preposterous and irony is destiny. If the essence is a promise, then reform is duty. Which lesson creates adults?

Context is not exoneration

Let's inoculate against a dishonest rebuttal: to insist on context is not to excuse evil. It is to put evil where it lived, so we can recognize the masks it wears elsewhere and later. When we acknowledge that Africans enslaved Africans, that Arabs enslaved Europeans, that Europeans enslaved Africans, and that Americans enslaved Africans and also killed each other to end it, we do not score points for "our side." We expand the circle of vigilance.

Next time it will be different badges, different slogans, maybe even different victims. But the pattern? The pattern is the same: power meets opportunity, and law either stops it or becomes its tool.

The Founders, read without sentimentality

Washington freed the people he enslaved in his will and struggled with the institution in private; Jefferson wrote universal equality and lived a contradiction that gnaws at his name; Adams rejected slavery and mocked Southern pretensions; Madison split hairs and stitched compromises. None of them absolved by achievement, none of them canceled by sin. They were the men on the ground at history's shear line, and they left us words and mechanisms that their grandsons wielded to wreck bondage.

If your politics requires you to despise them without remainder, your politics is a jealous god. If your politics forbids you from criticizing them, your politics is idolatry. A grown nation can do neither worship nor torching. It can read, argue, amend, and move.

Black Americans, read with full agency

Enslaved people stole literacy in secret schools, founded churches under brush arbors, preserved marriages despite auction blocks, served as scouts and soldiers, negotiated for wages, testified in courts, pooled coins to buy freedom, and told their stories in narratives that changed minds. They were not extras in someone else's epic; they were the authors of chapters without which the book falls apart.

They also—some of them, in free communities—owned property, ran shops, published papers, and, in rarer cases, owned other human beings. Acknowledging that last fact does not sully the heroism; it underlines the thesis of human frailty. Power tempts. That is why we build constitutions.

After emancipation came Black Reconstruction—governance, schools, businesses—followed by Redemption and Jim Crow's steel curtain. Then came the long Black freedom struggle: the NAACP's court cases, the Montgomery bus boycott, sit-ins, Freedom Rides, Birmingham's fire hoses, Selma's bridge.

None of that happened because someone reframed the past. It happened because citizens forced the frame to match the text—law to match principle. They appealed to 1776, 1868, and 1870, not to 1619. That appeal wasn't naïve. It was strategically and morally brilliant.

The curriculum of citizenship

What should we teach? That a free people can carry a grievous sin and still create the very tools that uproot it. That the same presses that printed slave notices also printed abolitionist broadsides. That the same Congress that passed the Fugitive Slave Act also created the amendment process and, under the pressure of war and conscience, passed the Thirteenth, Fourteenth, and Fifteenth Amendments.

That the story of America is not a masquerade with a single face but a procession of faces arguing in a common square.

Teach the timeline without the teleprompter:

• 1619: A ship unloads captive Africans at Point Comfort. Not a founding, but a wound.

• 1776: A declaration of universal equality, signed by men, some of whom owned people. Hypocrisy? Yes. Also a fuse lit under the institution.

• 1787–88: A Constitution with compromises and constraints, giving a framework capable of evolution.

• 1808: The legal transatlantic trade ends in the U.S.; the domestic trade fattens. Progress and perversity in one date.

• 1830s–50s: Abolitionist fire and sectional crisis. Citizens turn principle into agitation.

• 1861–65: War, death, emancipation. The nation kills its sin at bayonet point, then tries to rebuild the sinner.

• 1865–77: Reconstruction—brief, bright, besieged.

• 1890–1950s: Jim Crow's long night; migration, organization, cultural brilliance.

• 1954–1965: Brown, Montgomery, Civil Rights and Voting Rights Acts. The promise tightens its grip on reality.

Where does "true founding" fit here? Everywhere and nowhere. The true founding is the relentless return to the creed through catastrophe. A nation is not a year; it is a vow with timestamps.

Snark break, respectfully applied

If the editorial boards that sermonize about "our true founding" had to live by their own historiography, they'd shut down their presses for being "derivative of plantation ledgers." Do we dismantle the spreadsheet because some planters used columns? Do we abolish police in Boston because, in Charleston, patrols hunted human beings? Do we cancel the Declaration because its author sinned—or do we use it to indict the sin? The left's answers oscillate with political weather. Principle should not.

"De-centering" without disappearing

We are told to "decouple" American pride from its myths. Good. Myths are lazy. But do not decouple pride from the achievements themselves. The left's impulse to "de-center" often means subtracting the very universal claims that made outsiders insiders.

The Declaration spoke an audacious universal. Black Americans seized it. Women seized it. Immigrants seized it. Gay Americans seized it. If you replace that universal with a narrower math—only our group can pronounce judgment—you shrink the stage on which progress plays. You also hand future majorities a template for excluding you when the wheel turns.

What about the kids?

A classroom conversation worth having goes like this: "Here is the claim that America began in 1619. Here are the sources that argue 1776 is the founding. Here is why some scholars say 'multiple foundings.' Here's what the Revolution did and didn't do. Here's how slavery grew, how it was fought, and how it ended in law but not in hearts. Here's why some people today wish to reframe it. Now, let's read Douglass, Lincoln, Jacobs, Tubman, Walker, Truth, Garrison, Grimké, Calhoun, Fitzhugh, and let's argue."

What we get instead too often is a packaged catechism with QR codes to feelings. Feels are fine. Footnotes are better.

The charge sheet against the "reframing" project

• Overreach in causal claims: asserting the Revolution as a conspiracy to protect slavery [NYT Magazine, 2019] despite contradictory evidence and expert dissent [Wood, 2019; McPherson, 2019].

• Economic monoculture: insisting capitalism springs from whips and cotton ledgers, ignoring broader intellectual and institutional origins [Olmstead & Rhode; McCloskey; Hilt].

• Teleological moralizing: reading the past as a straight line toward present politics, erasing contingency and debate.

• Pedagogical instrumentalism: curriculums designed to produce conviction, not competence.

• Revision without confession: quiet edits to sweeping claims [NYT updates, 2020] instead of errata that teach students how knowledge corrects itself.

An invitation, not an excommunication

Here is the paradox: the left's better angels want students to see the wound. So do I. The disagreement is about what to do after seeing. Do we declare the body corrupt beyond cure, or do we practice surgery? Do we amputate memory, or rehabilitate it?

Conservatives argue for rehabilitation: keep the creed, expand its reach, teach the sin, honor the heroes, name the villains, and make citizenship harder, not easier.

Final questions, because they sharpen the mind

• If slavery is our "true founding," why does the nation's legal DNA—the Constitution—contain mechanisms that allowed slavery's abolition, civil rights expansion, and voting protections?

• If only whiteness explains power, how do you explain Black slaveholders, African slave traders, and the Barbary enslavement of Europeans and Americans?

• If capitalism is inherently slave-born, why do capitalist societies sustain the most robust abolitionist NGOs today, and why did market democracies lead in eliminating chattel slavery globally?

- If the press is the conscience, why did marquee outlets embellish, then soft-edit, rather than forthrightly revise?

- If "reframing" is honesty, why do reframers resist assigning critics like Wood and McPherson alongside their favored essays in class?

Respect where it's due

Respect means we can quote a progressive voice accurately and still disagree. "In order to understand the brutality of American capitalism, you have to start on the plantation" [NYT Magazine, 2019]. Noted. Considered. Disputed.

Respect also means we can quote Douglass calling the Constitution a liberty document [Douglass, 1852] and recognize that another abolitionist, Garrison, burned the Constitution in effigy. The argument is the tradition. We don't need a new catechism. We need better students of the old argument.

The closing note

America's memory is a contested commons. The left's recent "reframe" tried to fence it, hang new signs, and charge admission paid in guilt. The right answer is to take the fence down. Let everyone in with their sources and their scars. Let the dead speak in their own voices, even when those voices annoy our priors. And then let the living choose: republic of grown-ups, or seminar of scolds?

I WOULD NOW LIKE TO CLOSE THIS BOOK WITH A SIMPLE STATEMENT:

I choose the republic. I choose the promise that called enslaved people to run for Union lines, that taught schoolchildren to memorize a creed their grandparents could not fully enjoy, that pulled a quill through 1776 and a bayonet through 1863 and a pen through 1964. The year they tried to edit the past, they forgot who keeps the archive. We do. Citizens do. And citizens don't need a "true founding" in a headline. They need the whole, infuriating, magnificent ledger.

Inline citations

• "The American Revolution was fought in large part to preserve slavery," as characterized in the project's launch issue [NYT Magazine, 2019].

• Historian Gordon S. Wood disputing the claim as "wrong in so many ways" [Wood interview, 2019].

• James McPherson stating he saw "no evidence" for the Revolution-to-protect-slavery thesis [McPherson, 2019].

• Subsequent online edits and clarifications to project language about "true founding" [NYT updates, 2020].

• On indentured servitude's brutality and its relation to racial slavery [Morgan, 1975].

• On Barbary enslavement of Europeans and Americans [Davis, 2003; Lambert, 2005].

• On Native American slave trades [Gallay, 2002].

• On free Black slaveowners [Koger, 1985; Berlin, 1974].

- On economic claims linking plantation management to capitalism and rebuttals [Olmstead & Rhode, 2010; McCloskey, 2016; Hilt, 2017].

- On early northern emancipation and Massachusetts case law [Commonwealth v. Jennison, 1783].

- On Frederick Douglass's constitutional argument [Douglass, 1852].

- On Creole New Orleans' free people of color [Hirsch & Logsdon, 1992].

Footnotes

1. NYT Magazine, "The 1619 Project," August 2019, feature essays and introductory framing.

2. Gordon S. Wood, interviews and letters critiquing 1619 claims (2019).

3. James M. McPherson, comments on the Revolution's causes and lack of evidence for slavery-preservation motives (2019).

4. New York Times digital updates to 1619 framing language, 2020 redactions and clarifications.

5. Edmund S. Morgan, *American Slavery, American Freedom* (W. W. Norton, 1975).

6. Robert C. Davis, *Christian Slaves, Muslim Masters: White Slavery in the Mediterranean, the Barbary Coast, and Italy* (Palgrave Macmillan, 2003).

7. Andrew Lambert, *The Barbary Wars: American Independence in the Atlantic World* (FSG, 2005).

8. Alan Gallay, *The Indian Slave Trade: The Rise of the English Empire in the American South* (Yale University Press, 2002).

9. Larry Koger, *Black Slaveowners: Free Black Slave Masters in South Carolina, 1790–1860* (McFarland, 1985).

10. Ira Berlin, *Slaves Without Masters: The Free Negro in the Antebellum South* (The New Press, 1974).

11. Alan L. Olmstead and Paul W. Rhode, "Cotton, Slavery, and the New History of Capitalism," *Explorations in Economic History* (2010); plus subsequent critiques.

12. Deirdre N. McCloskey, *Bourgeois Equality* (University of Chicago Press, 2016).

13. Eric Hilt, "Economic History, Historical Analysis, and the 'New History of Capitalism'," *Journal of Economic History* (2017).

14. *Commonwealth v. Jennison* (Massachusetts, 1783), interpreting the 1780 Constitution's equality clause as incompatible with slavery.

15. Frederick Douglass, "What to the Slave Is the Fourth of July?" (1852), concluding defense of the Constitution as a liberty document.

16. Arnold R. Hirsch and Joseph Logsdon, *Creole New Orleans: Race and Americanization* (LSU Press, 1992).

Constitution of the United States

The Preamble

We the People of the United States, in order to form a more perfect Union, establish Justice, insure domestic Tranquility, provide for the common defense, promote the general Welfare, and secure the Blessings of Liberty to ourselves and our Posterity, do ordain and establish this Constitution for the United States of America.

Article I

Section 1

All legislative powers herein granted shall be vested in a Congress of the United States, which shall consist of a Senate and House of Representatives.

Section 2

The House of Representatives shall be composed of members chosen every second year by the people of the several states. The electors in each state shall have the qualifications requisite for electors of the most numerous branch of the state legislature.

No person shall be a representative who has not attained the age of twenty-five years, been seven years a citizen of the United States, and who shall not, when elected, be an inhabitant of the state in which they shall be chosen.

Representatives and direct taxes shall be apportioned among the several states within this Union according to their respective numbers. These shall be determined by adding to the whole number of free persons, including those bound to service for a term of years, and excluding Indians not taxed, three-fifths of all other persons.

The actual enumeration shall be made within three years after the first meeting of the Congress of the United States, and within every subsequent term of ten years, in such manner as they shall by law direct. The number of representatives shall not exceed one for every thirty thousand, but each state shall have at least one representative. Until such enumeration shall be made, the state of New Hampshire shall be entitled to choose three, Massachusetts eight, Rhode Island and Providence Plantations one, Connecticut five, New York six, New Jersey four, Pennsylvania eight, Delaware one, Maryland six, Virginia ten, North Carolina five, South Carolina five, and Georgia three.

When vacancies happen in the representation from any state, the executive authority thereof shall issue writs of election to fill such vacancies.

The House of Representatives shall choose their Speaker and other officers, and shall have the sole power of impeachment.

Section 3

The Senate of the United States shall be composed of two senators from each state, chosen by the legislature thereof for six years, and each senator shall have one vote.

Immediately after they shall be assembled in consequence of the first election, they shall be divided as equally as may be into three classes. The seats of the senators of the first class shall be vacated at the expiration of the second year, of the second class at the expiration of the fourth year, and of the third class at the expiration of the sixth year, so that one-third may be chosen every second year.

If vacancies happen by resignation or otherwise during the recess of the legislature of any state, the executive thereof may make temporary appointments until the next meeting of the legislature, which shall then fill such vacancies.

No person shall be a senator who has not attained the age of thirty years, been nine years a citizen of the United States, and who shall not, when elected, be an inhabitant of the state for which they shall be chosen.

The Vice President of the United States shall be President of the Senate but shall have no vote unless they be equally divided.

The Senate shall choose their other officers, and also a President pro tempore in the absence of the Vice President or when he shall exercise the office of President of the United States.

The Senate shall have the sole power to try all impeachments. When sitting for that purpose, they shall be on oath or affirmation. When the President of the United States is tried, the Chief Justice shall preside, and no person shall be convicted without the concurrence of two-thirds of the members present.

Judgment in cases of impeachment shall not extend further than to removal from office and disqualification to hold and enjoy any office of honor, trust, or profit under the United States; but the party convicted shall nevertheless be liable and subject to indictment, trial, judgment, and punishment according to law.

Section 4

The times, places, and manner of holding elections for senators and representatives shall be prescribed in each state by the legislature thereof. Congress may at any time by law make or alter such regulations, except as to the places of choosing senators.

Congress shall assemble at least once every year, and such meeting shall be on the first Monday in December, unless they shall by law appoint a different day.

Section 5

Each house shall be the judge of the elections, returns, and qualifications of its own members, and a majority of each shall constitute a quorum to do business. A smaller number may adjourn from day to day and may be authorized to compel the attendance of absent members, in such manner and under such penalties as each house may provide.

Each house may determine the rules of its proceedings, punish its members for disorderly behavior, and, with the concurrence of two-thirds, expel a member.

Each house shall keep a journal of its proceedings and from time to time publish the same, excepting such parts as may in their judgment require secrecy. The yeas and nays of the members of either house on any question shall, at the desire of one-fifth of those present, be entered on the journal.

Neither house, during the session of Congress, shall, without the consent of the other, adjourn for more than three days nor to any other place than that in which the two houses shall be sitting.

Section 6

The senators and representatives shall receive a compensation for their services, to be ascertained by law and paid out of the Treasury of the United States. They shall, in all cases except treason, felony, and breach of the peace, be privileged from arrest during their attendance at the session of their respective houses and in going to and returning from the same. For any speech or debate in either house, they shall not be questioned in any other place.

No senator or representative shall, during the time for which they were elected, be appointed to any civil office under the authority of the United States which shall have been created, or the emoluments of which shall have been increased during such time. No person holding any office under the United States shall be a member of either house during their continuance in office.

Section 7

All Bills for raising Revenue shall originate in the House of Representatives, but the Senate may propose or concur with amendments as on other bills.

Every bill that has passed the House of Representatives and the Senate shall, before it becomes a law, be presented to the President of the United States. If he approves, he shall sign it; but if not, he shall return it, with his objections, to the House in which it originated. That House shall enter the objections at large on its journal and proceed to reconsider it.

If, after such reconsideration, two-thirds of that House agree to pass the bill, it shall be sent, together with the objections, to the other House, which shall likewise reconsider it. If approved by two-thirds of that House, it shall become a law.

In all such cases, the votes of both Houses shall be determined by yeas and nays, and the names of the persons voting for and against the bill shall be entered on the journal of each House respectively. If any bill is not returned by the President within ten days (Sundays excepted) after it has been presented to him, it shall become a law in like manner as if he had signed it, unless Congress, by its adjournment, prevents its return, in which case it shall not become a law.

Every order, resolution, or vote requiring the concurrence of the Senate and House of Representatives (except on a question of adjournment) shall be presented to the President of the United States. Before it takes effect, it must be approved by him, or, if disapproved, be repassed by two-thirds of the Senate and House of Representatives, according to the rules and limitations prescribed in the case of a bill.

Section 8

The Congress shall have power:

To lay and collect taxes, duties, imposts, and excises to pay the debts and provide for the common defense and general welfare of the United States; but all duties, imposts, and excises shall be uniform throughout the United States.

To borrow money on the credit of the United States.

To regulate commerce with foreign nations, among the several states, and with the Indian tribes.

To establish a uniform rule of naturalization and uniform laws on the subject of bankruptcies throughout the United States.

To coin money, regulate the value thereof and of foreign coin, and fix the standard of weights and measures.

To provide for the punishment of counterfeiting the securities and current coin of the United States.

To establish post offices and post roads.

To promote the progress of science and useful arts by securing, for limited times, to authors and inventors the exclusive right to their respective writings and discoveries.

To constitute tribunals inferior to the Supreme Court.

To define and punish piracies and felonies committed on the high seas and offenses against the law of nations.

To declare war, grant letters of marque and reprisal, and make rules concerning captures on land and water.

To raise and support armies, but no appropriation of money for that use shall be for a longer term than two years.

To provide and maintain a navy.

To make rules for the government and regulation of the land and naval forces.

To provide for calling forth the militia to execute the laws of the Union, suppress insurrections, and repel invasions.

To provide for organizing, arming, and disciplining the militia, and for governing such part of them as may be employed in the service of the United States, reserving to the states respectively the appointment of the officers and the authority of training the militia according to the discipline prescribed by Congress.

To exercise exclusive legislation in all cases whatsoever over such district (not exceeding ten miles square) as may, by cession of particular states and the acceptance of Congress, become the seat of government of the United States, and to exercise like authority over all places purchased by the consent of the legislature of the state in which the same shall be, for the erection of forts, magazines, arsenals, dockyards, and other needful buildings.

To make all laws that shall be necessary and proper for carrying into execution the foregoing powers, and all other powers vested by this Constitution in the government of the United States, or in any department or officer thereof.

Section 9

The migration or importation of such persons as any of the states now existing shall think proper to admit shall not be prohibited by Congress prior to the year one thousand eight hundred and eight, but a tax or duty may be imposed on such importation, not exceeding ten dollars for each person.

The privilege of the writ of habeas corpus shall not be suspended, unless in cases of rebellion or invasion the public safety may require it.

No bill of attainder or ex post facto law shall be passed.

No capitation or other direct tax shall be laid unless in proportion to the census or enumeration herein before directed to be taken.

No tax or duty shall be laid on articles exported from any state.

No preference shall be given by any regulation of commerce or revenue to the ports of one state over those of another, nor shall vessels bound to or from one state be obliged to enter, clear, or pay duties in another.

No money shall be drawn from the treasury but in consequence of appropriations made by law, and a regular statement and account of the receipts and expenditures of all public money shall be published from time to time.

No title of nobility shall be granted by the United States. No person holding any office of profit or trust under them shall, without the consent of Congress, accept any present, emolument, office, or title of any kind whatever from any king, prince, or foreign state.

Section 10

No state shall enter into any treaty, alliance, or confederation; grant letters of marque and reprisal; coin money; emit bills of credit; make anything but gold and silver coin a tender in payment of debts; pass any bill of attainder, ex post facto law, or law impairing the obligation of contracts; or grant any title of nobility.

No state shall, without the consent of Congress, lay any imposts or duties on imports or exports except what may be absolutely necessary for executing its inspection laws. The net produce of all duties and imposts laid by any state on imports or exports shall be for the use of the treasury of the United States, and all such laws shall be subject to the revision and control of Congress.

No state shall, without the consent of Congress, lay any duty of tonnage, keep troops or ships of war in time of peace, enter into any agreement or compact with another state or with a foreign power, or engage in war unless actually invaded or in such imminent danger as will not admit of delay.

Article II

Section 1

The executive power shall be vested in a President of the United States of America. He shall hold his office during the term of four years and, together with the Vice President, chosen for the same term, be elected as follows:

Each State shall appoint, in such manner as the Legislature thereof may direct, a number of Electors equal to the whole number of Senators and Representatives to which the State may be entitled in the Congress; but no Senator or Representative, or person holding an office of trust or profit under the United States, shall be appointed an Elector.

The Electors shall meet in their respective States and vote by ballot for two persons, of whom one at least shall not be an inhabitant of the same State with themselves. They shall make a list of all the persons voted for, and of the number of votes for each, which list they shall sign and certify, and transmit sealed to the seat of the Government of the United States, directed to the President of the Senate.

The President of the Senate shall, in the presence of the Senate and House of Representatives, open all the certificates, and the votes shall then be counted. The person having the greatest number of votes shall be the President, if such number be a majority of the whole number of Electors appointed. If there be more than one who have such majority and have an equal number of votes, then the House of Representatives shall immediately choose by ballot one of them for President. If no person have a majority, then from the five highest on the list, the said House shall in like manner choose the President.

In choosing the President, the votes shall be taken by States, the representation from each State having one vote. A quorum for this purpose shall consist of a member or members from two-thirds of the States, and a majority of all the States shall be necessary to a choice. In every case, after the choice of the President, the person having the greatest number of votes of the Electors shall be the Vice President. If there should remain two or more who have equal votes, the Senate shall choose from them by ballot the Vice President.

The Congress may determine the time of choosing the Electors and the day on which they shall give their votes, which day shall be the same throughout the United States.

No person except a natural-born citizen, or a citizen of the United States at the time of the adoption of this Constitution, shall be eligible to the office of President. Neither shall any person be eligible to that office who shall not have attained the age of thirty-five years and been fourteen years a resident within the United States.

In case of the removal of the President from office, or of his death, resignation, or inability to discharge the powers and duties of the said office, the same shall devolve on the Vice President. The Congress may by law provide for the case of removal, death, resignation, or inability, both of the President and Vice President, declaring what officer shall then act as President. Such officer shall act accordingly until the disability be removed or a President shall be elected.

The President shall, at stated times, receive for his services a compensation which shall neither be increased nor diminished during the period for which he shall have been elected. He shall not receive within that period any other emolument from the United States or any of them.

Before he enters on the execution of his office, he shall take the following oath or affirmation:

I do solemnly swear (or affirm) that I will faithfully execute the Office of President of the United States, and will, to the best of my ability, preserve, protect, and defend the Constitution of the United States.

Section 2

The President shall be Commander in Chief of the Army and Navy of the United States, and of the militia of the several States when called into the actual service of the United States. He may require the opinion, in writing, of the principal officer in each of the executive departments upon any subject relating to the duties of their respective offices. He shall have power to grant reprieves and pardons for offenses against the United States, except in cases of impeachment.

He shall have power, by and with the advice and consent of the Senate, to make treaties, provided two-thirds of the Senators present concur. He shall nominate, and by and with the advice and consent of the Senate, shall appoint Ambassadors, other public Ministers and Consuls, Judges of the Supreme Court, and all other officers of the United States whose appointments are not otherwise provided for and which shall be established by law. The Congress may by law vest the appointment of such inferior officers, as they think proper, in the President alone, in the courts of law, or in the heads of departments.

The President shall have power to fill up all vacancies that may happen during the recess of the Senate, by granting commissions which shall expire at the end of their next session.

Section 3

He shall, from time to time, give to the Congress information of the state of the Union and recommend to their consideration such measures as he shall judge necessary and expedient. He may, on extraordinary occasions, convene both Houses, or either of them, and in case of disagreement between them with respect to the time of adjournment, he may adjourn them to such time as he shall think proper. He shall receive Ambassadors and other public Ministers, take care that the laws be faithfully executed, and commission all the officers of the United States.

Section 4

The President, Vice President, and all civil officers of the United States shall be removed from office on impeachment for, and conviction of, treason, bribery, or other high crimes and misdemeanors.

Article III

Section 1

The judicial power of the United States shall be vested in one Supreme Court and in such inferior courts as the Congress may from time to time ordain and establish. The Judges, both of the Supreme and inferior courts, shall hold their offices during good behavior and shall, at stated times, receive for their services a compensation which shall not be diminished during their continuance in office.

Section 2

The judicial power shall extend to all cases, in law and equity, arising under this Constitution, the laws of the United States, and treaties made or which shall be made under their authority; to all cases affecting Ambassadors, other public Ministers and Consuls; to all cases of admiralty and maritime jurisdiction; to controversies to which the United States shall be a party; to controversies between two or more States; between a State and citizens of another State; between citizens of different States; between citizens of the same

State claiming lands under grants of different States; and between a State, or the citizens thereof, and foreign States, citizens, or subjects.

In all cases affecting Ambassadors, other public Ministers and Consuls, and those in which a State shall be party, the Supreme Court shall have original jurisdiction. In all the other cases before mentioned, the Supreme Court shall have appellate jurisdiction, both as to law and fact, with such exceptions and under such regulations as the Congress shall make.

The trial of all crimes, except in cases of impeachment, shall be by jury, and such trial shall be held in the State where the said crimes shall have been committed. When not committed within any State, the trial shall be at such place or places as the Congress may by law have directed.

Section 3

Treason against the United States shall consist only in levying war against them, or in adhering to their enemies, giving them aid and comfort. No person shall be convicted of treason unless on the testimony of two witnesses to the same overt act, or on confession in open court.

The Congress shall have power to declare the punishment of treason, but no attainder of treason shall work corruption of blood, or forfeiture, except during the life of the person attainted.

Article IV

Section 1

Full faith and credit shall be given in each State to the public acts, records, and judicial proceedings of every other State. The Congress may by general laws prescribe the manner in which such acts, records, and proceedings shall be proved, and the effect thereof.

Section 2

The citizens of each State shall be entitled to all privileges and immunities of citizens in the several States.

A person charged in any State with treason, felony, or other crime, who shall flee from justice and be found in another State, shall, on demand of the executive authority of the State from which he fled, be delivered up to be removed to the State having jurisdiction of the crime.

No person held to service or labor in one State under the laws thereof, escaping into another, shall, in consequence of any law or regulation therein, be discharged from such service or labor, but shall be delivered up on claim of the party to whom such service or labor may be due.

Section 3

New States may be admitted by the Congress into this Union, but no new State shall be formed or erected within the jurisdiction of any other State, nor shall any State be formed by the junction of two or more States, or parts of States, without the consent of the legislatures of the States concerned as well as of the Congress.

The Congress shall have power to dispose of and make all needful rules and regulations respecting the territory or other property belonging to the United States. Nothing in this Constitution shall be so construed as to prejudice any claims of the United States or of any particular State.

Section 4

The United States shall guarantee to every State in this Union a republican form of government, and shall protect each of them against invasion, and, on application of the legislature, or of the executive (when the legislature cannot be convened), against domestic violence.

Article V

The Congress, whenever two-thirds of both Houses shall deem it necessary, shall propose amendments to this Constitution, or, on the application of the legislatures of two-thirds of the several States, shall call a convention for proposing amendments. In either case, such amendments shall be valid to all intents and purposes as part of this Constitution when ratified by the legislatures of three-fourths of the several States, or by conventions in three-fourths thereof, as the one or the other mode of ratification may be proposed by the Congress.

Provided that no amendment which may be made prior to the year one thousand eight hundred and eight shall in any manner affect the first and fourth clauses in the ninth section of the first article, and that no State, without its consent, shall be deprived of its equal suffrage in the Senate.

Article VI

All debts contracted and engagements entered into before the adoption of this Constitution shall be as valid against the United States under this Constitution as under the Confederation.

This Constitution, and the laws of the United States which shall be made in pursuance thereof, and all treaties made, or which shall be made, under the authority of the United States, shall be the supreme law of the land. The judges in every State shall be bound thereby, anything in the Constitution or laws of any State to the contrary notwithstanding.

The Senators and Representatives before mentioned, and the members of the several State legislatures, and all executive and judicial officers, both of the United States and of the several States, shall be bound by oath or affirmation to support this Constitution. No religious test shall ever be required as a qualification to any office or public trust under the United States.

Article VII

The ratification of the conventions of nine States shall be sufficient for the establishment of this Constitution between the States so ratifying the same.

First Amendment

Congress shall make no law respecting an establishment of religion or prohibiting the free exercise thereof, or abridging the freedom of speech or of the press, or the right of the people peaceably to assemble, and to petition the Government for a redress of grievances.

Second Amendment

A well-regulated militia, being necessary to the security of a free State, the right of the people to keep and bear arms, shall not be infringed.

Third Amendment

No soldier shall, in time of peace, be quartered in any house without the consent of the owner, nor in time of war, but in a manner to be prescribed by law.

Fourth Amendment

The right of the people to be secure in their persons, houses, papers, and effects against unreasonable searches and seizures shall not be violated, and no warrants shall issue but upon probable cause, supported by oath or affirmation, and particularly describing the place to be searched and the persons or things to be seized.

Fifth Amendment

No person shall be held to answer for a capital or otherwise infamous crime unless on a presentment or indictment of a Grand Jury, except in cases arising in the land or naval forces, or in the Militia, when in actual service in time of war or public danger. Nor shall any person be subject for the same offence to be twice put in jeopardy of life or limb. Nor shall he be compelled in any criminal case to be a witness against himself, nor be deprived of life, liberty, or property without due process of law, nor shall private property be taken for public use without just compensation.

Sixth Amendment

In all criminal prosecutions, the accused shall enjoy the right to a speedy and public trial by an impartial jury of the State and district wherein the crime shall have been committed, which district shall have been previously ascertained by law. He shall be informed of the nature and cause of the accusation, be confronted with the witnesses against him, have compulsory process for obtaining witnesses in his favor, and have the assistance of counsel for his defense.

Seventh Amendment

In suits at common law, where the value in controversy shall exceed twenty dollars, the right of trial by jury shall be preserved, and no fact tried by a jury shall be otherwise reexamined in any

Court of the United States than according to the rules of the common law.

Eighth Amendment

Excessive bail shall not be required, nor excessive fines imposed, nor cruel and unusual punishments inflicted.

Ninth Amendment

The enumeration in the Constitution of certain rights shall not be construed to deny or disparage others retained by the people.

Tenth Amendment

The powers not delegated to the United States by the Constitution, nor prohibited by it to the States, are reserved to the States respectively, or to the people.

Eleventh Amendment

The judicial power of the United States shall not be construed to extend to any suit in law or equity, commenced or prosecuted against one of the United States by citizens of another State, or by citizens or subjects of any foreign State.

Twelfth Amendment

The Electors shall meet in their respective States and vote by ballot for President and Vice President, one of whom, at least, shall not be an inhabitant of the same State with themselves. They shall name in their ballots the person voted for as President, and in distinct ballots the person voted for as Vice President. They shall make distinct lists of all persons voted for as President and of all persons voted for as Vice President, and of the number of votes for each, which lists they shall sign and certify, and transmit sealed to the seat of the government of the United States, directed to the President of the Senate.

The President of the Senate shall, in the presence of the Senate and House of Representatives, open all the certificates, and the votes shall then be counted. The person having the greatest number of votes for President shall be the President, if such number is a majority of the whole number of Electors appointed. If no person has such a majority, then from the persons having the highest numbers, not exceeding three on the list of those voted for as President, the House of Representatives shall choose immediately, by ballot, the President.

In choosing the President, the votes shall be taken by States, the representation from each State having one vote. A quorum for this purpose shall consist of a member or members from two-thirds of the States, and a majority of all the States shall be necessary to a choice.

[And if the House of Representatives shall not choose a President whenever the right of choice shall devolve upon them before the fourth day of March next following, then the Vice President shall act as President, as in case of the death or other constitutional disability of the President.]

The person having the greatest number of votes as Vice President shall be the Vice President, if such number is a majority of the whole number of Electors appointed. If no person has a majority, then from the two highest numbers on the list, the Senate shall choose the Vice President. A quorum for the purpose shall consist of two-thirds of the whole number of Senators, and a majority of the whole number shall be necessary to a choice. But no person constitutionally ineligible to the office of President shall be eligible to that of Vice President of the United States.

Thirteenth Amendment

Section 1

Neither slavery nor involuntary servitude, except as a punishment for crime whereof the party shall have been duly convicted, shall exist within the United States, or any place subject to their jurisdiction.

Section 2

ongress shall have power to enforce this article by appropriate legislation.

Fourteenth Amendment

Section 1

All persons born or naturalized in the United States, and subject to the jurisdiction thereof, are citizens of the United States and of the State wherein they reside. No State shall make or enforce any law which abridges the privileges or immunities of citizens of the United States, nor shall any State deprive any person of life, liberty, or property without due process of law, nor deny to any person within its jurisdiction the equal protection of the laws.

Section 2

Representatives shall be apportioned among the several States according to their respective numbers, counting the whole number of persons in each State, excluding Indians not taxed. But when the right to vote at any election for the choice of Electors for President and Vice President of the United States, Representatives in Congress, the Executive and Judicial officers of a State, or the members of the Legislature thereof, is denied to any of the male inhabitants of such State, being twenty-one years of age and citizens of the United States, or in any way abridged, except for participation in rebellion or other crime, the basis of representation therein shall be reduced in the proportion which the number of such male citizens shall bear to the whole number of male citizens twenty-one years of age in such State.

Section 3

No person shall be a Senator or Representative in Congress, or Elector of President and Vice President, or hold any office, civil or military, under the United States, or under any State, who, having previously taken an oath as a member of Congress, or as an officer of the United States, or as a member of any State legislature, or as an executive or judicial officer of any State, to support the Constitution of the United States, shall have engaged in insurrection or rebellion against the same, or given aid or comfort to the enemies thereof. But Congress may, by a vote of two-thirds of each House, remove such disability.

Section 4

The validity of the public debt of the United States, authorized by law, including debts incurred for payment of pensions and bounties for services in suppressing insurrection or rebellion, shall not be questioned. But neither the United States nor any State shall assume or pay any debt or obligation incurred in aid of insurrection or rebellion against the United States, or any claim for the loss or emancipation of any slave. All such debts, obligations, and claims shall be held illegal and void.

Section 5

The Congress shall have power to enforce, by appropriate legislation, the provisions of this article.

Fifteenth Amendment

Section 1

The right of citizens of the United States to vote shall not be denied or abridged by the United States or by any State on account of race, color, or previous condition of servitude.

Section 2

The Congress shall have power to enforce this article by appropriate legislation.

Sixteenth Amendment

The Congress shall have power to lay and collect taxes on incomes, from whatever source derived, without apportionment among the several States and without regard to any census or enumeration.

Seventeenth Amendment

The Senate of the United States shall be composed of two Senators from each State, elected by the people thereof for six years, and each Senator shall have one vote. The Electors in each State shall have the qualifications requisite for Electors of the most numerous branch of the State legislatures.

When vacancies happen in the representation of any State in the Senate, the executive authority of such State shall issue writs of election to fill such vacancies. Provided, that the legislature of any State may empower the executive thereof to make temporary appointments until the people fill the vacancies by election as the legislature may direct.

This amendment shall not be so construed as to affect the election or term of any Senator chosen before it becomes valid as part of the Constitution.

Eighteenth Amendment

After one year from the ratification of this article, the manufacture, sale, or transportation of intoxicating liquors within, the importation thereof into, or the exportation thereof from the

United States and all territory subject to the jurisdiction thereof for beverage purposes, is hereby prohibited.

The Congress and the several States shall have concurrent power to enforce this article by appropriate legislation.

This article shall be inoperative unless it shall have been ratified as an amendment to the Constitution by the legislatures of the several States, as provided in the Constitution, within seven years from the date of the submission hereof to the States by the Congress.

Nineteenth Amendment

The right of citizens of the United States to vote shall not be denied or abridged by the United States or by any State on account of sex.

Congress shall have power to enforce this article by appropriate legislation.

Twentieth Amendment

Section 1

The terms of the President and the Vice President shall end at noon on the 20th day of January, and the terms of Senators and Representatives at noon on the 3rd day of January, in the years in which such terms would have ended if this article had not been ratified. The terms of their successors shall then begin.

Section 2

The Congress shall assemble at least once every year, and such meeting shall begin at noon on the 3rd day of January, unless they shall by law appoint a different day.

Section 3

If, at the time fixed for the beginning of the term of the President, the President-elect shall have died, the Vice President-elect shall become President. If a President shall not have been chosen before the time fixed for the beginning of his term, or if the President-elect shall have failed to qualify, then the Vice President-elect shall act as President until a President shall have qualified. The Congress may by law provide for the case in which neither a President-elect nor a Vice President-elect shall have qualified, declaring who shall then act as President, or the manner in which one who is to act shall be selected, and such person shall act accordingly until a President or Vice President shall have qualified.

Section 4

The Congress may by law provide for the case of the death of any of the persons from whom the House of Representatives may choose a President whenever the right of choice shall have devolved upon them, and for the case of the death of any of the persons from whom the Senate may choose a Vice President whenever the right of choice shall have devolved upon them.

Section 5

Sections 1 and 2 shall take effect on the 15th day of October following the ratification of this article.

Section 6

This article shall be inoperative unless it shall have been ratified as an amendment to the Constitution by the legislatures of three-fourths of the several States within seven years from the date of its submission.

Twenty-First Amendment

Section 1

The eighteenth article of amendment to the Constitution of the United States is hereby repealed.

Section 2

The transportation or importation into any State, Territory, or possession of the United States for delivery or use therein of intoxicating liquors, in violation of the laws thereof, is hereby prohibited.

Section 3

This article shall be inoperative unless it shall have been ratified as an amendment to the Constitution by conventions in the several States, as provided in the Constitution, within seven years from the date of its submission to the States by the Congress.

Twenty-Second Amendment

Section 1

No person shall be elected to the office of the President more than twice, and no person who has held the office of President, or acted as President, for more than two years of a term to which some other person was elected President, shall be elected to the office of the President more than once. But this article shall not apply to any person holding the office of President when this article was proposed by the Congress, and shall not prevent any person who may be holding the office of President, or acting as President, during the term within which this article becomes operative, from holding the office of President or acting as President during the remainder of such term.

Section 2

This article shall be inoperative unless it shall have been ratified as an amendment to the Constitution by the legislatures of three-fourths of the several States within seven years from the date of its submission to the States by the Congress.

Twenty-Third Amendment

Section 1

The District constituting the seat of Government of the United States shall appoint, in such manner as the Congress may direct, a number of electors of President and Vice President equal to the whole number of Senators and Representatives in Congress to which the District would be entitled if it were a State, but in no event more than the least populous State. They shall be in addition to those appointed by the States, but they shall be considered, for the purposes of the election of President and Vice President, to be electors appointed by a State. They shall meet in the District and perform such duties as provided by the twelfth article of amendment.

Section 2

The Congress shall have power to enforce this article by appropriate legislation.

Twenty-Fourth Amendment

Section 1

The right of citizens of the United States to vote in any primary or other election for President or Vice President, for electors for President or Vice President, or for Senator or Representative in Congress, shall not be denied or abridged by the United States or by any State by reason of failure to pay any poll tax or other tax.

Section 2

The Congress shall have power to enforce this article by appropriate legislation.

Twenty-Fifth Amendment

Section 1

In case of the removal of the President from office or of his death or resignation, the Vice President shall become President.

Section 2

Whenever there is a vacancy in the office of the Vice President, the President shall nominate a Vice President who shall take office upon confirmation by a majority vote of both Houses of Congress.

Section 3

Whenever the President transmits to the President pro tempore of the Senate and the Speaker of the House of Representatives his written declaration that he is unable to discharge the powers and duties of his office, and until he transmits to them a written declaration to the contrary, such powers and duties shall be discharged by the Vice President as Acting President.

Section 4

Whenever the Vice President and a majority of either the principal officers of the executive departments or of such other body as Congress may by law provide transmit to the President pro tempore of the Senate and the Speaker of the House of Representatives their written declaration that the President is unable to discharge the powers and duties of his office, the Vice President shall immediately assume the powers and duties of the office as Acting President.

Thereafter, when the President transmits to the President pro tempore of the Senate and the Speaker of the House of Representatives his written declaration that no inability exists, he shall resume the powers and duties of his office unless the Vice

President and a majority of either the principal officers of the executive departments or of such other body as Congress may by law provide transmit within four days to the President pro tempore of the Senate and the Speaker of the House of Representatives their written declaration that the President is unable to discharge the powers and duties of his office.

Thereupon, Congress shall decide the issue, assembling within forty-eight hours for that purpose if not in session. If the Congress, within twenty-one days after receipt of the latter written declaration, or if Congress is not in session, within twenty-one days after Congress is required to assemble, determines by a two-thirds vote of both Houses that the President is unable to discharge the powers and duties of his office, the Vice President shall continue to discharge them as Acting President. Otherwise, the President shall resume the powers and duties of his office.

Twenty-Sixth Amendment Section 1

The right of citizens of the United States who are eighteen years of age or older to vote shall not be denied or abridged by the United States or by any State on account of age.

Section 2

The Congress shall have power to enforce this article by appropriate legislation.

Twenty-Seventh Amendment

No law varying the compensation for the services of the Senators and Representatives shall take effect until an election of Representatives shall have intervened.

GOD BLESS YOU ALL, AND GOD BLESS THE UNITED STATES OF AMERICA!

All My Best,

B.L. Horak

"Thank you for your attention to this matter."

Donald Trump on the bombing of Iran's nuclear facilities.

www.ingramcontent.com/pod-product-compliance
Lightning Source LLC
Chambersburg PA
CBHW052106030426
42335CB00025B/2867